400 Words

You Should

Know

Key Words to Improve and
Expand Your Vocabulary

FALL RIVER PRESS

This edition published by Fall River Press by arrangement with Houghton Mifflin Harcourt Publishing Company.

Previously published in a slightly different form as *100 Words Every High School Freshman Should Know* (© 2004), *100 Words Every High School Graduate Should Know* (© 2003), *100 Words Almost Everyone Confuses and Misuses* (© 2004), and *100 Words Every Word Lover Should Know* (© 2005) by Houghton Mifflin Harcourt Publishing Company.

Fall River Press
122 Fifth Avenue
New York, NY 10011

ISBN: 978-1-4351-2060-0

Manufactured in China

2 3 4 5 6 7 8 9 10-LEO-15 14 13 12

Table of Contents

Pronunciation Guide

Pronunciations appear in parentheses after boldface entry words. If a word has more than one pronunciation, the first pronunciation is usually more common than the other, but often they are equally common. Pronunciations are shown after inflections and related words where necessary.

Stress is the relative degree of emphasis that a word's syllables are spoken with. An unmarked syllable has the weakest stress in the word. The strongest, or primary, stress is indicated with a bold mark (**'**). A lighter mark (') indicates a secondary level of stress. The stress mark follows the syllable it applies to. Words of one syllable have no stress mark because there is no other stress level that the syllable can be compared to.

The key on page v shows the pronunciation symbols used in this book. To the right of the symbols are words that show how the symbols are pronounced. The letters whose sound corresponds to the symbols are shown in boldface.

The symbol (ə) is called *schwa*. It represents a vowel with the weakest level of stress in a word. The schwa sound varies slightly according to the vowel it represents or the sounds around it:

a·bun·dant (ə-bŭn**'**dənt)   **mo·ment** (mō**'**mənt)

civ·il (sĭv**'**əl)   **grate·ful** (grāt**'**fəl)

PRONUNCIATION KEY

Symbol	Examples	Symbol	Examples
ă	pat	oi	noise
ā	pay	ŏŏ	took
âr	care	ŏŏr	lure
ä	father	ōō	boot
b	bib	ou	out
ch	church	œ	*German* schön
d	deed, milled	p	pop
ĕ	pet	r	roar
ē	bee	s	sauce
f	fife, phase,	sh	ship, dish
	rough	t	tight, stopped
g	gag	th	thin
h	hat	*th*	this
hw	which	ŭ	cut
ĭ	pit	ûr	urge, term,
ī	pie, by		firm, word,
îr	deer, pier		heard
j	judge	v	valve
k	kick, cat, pique	w	with
l	lid, needle	y	yes
m	mum	z	zebra, xylem
n	no, sudden	zh	vision,
N	*French* bon		pleasure,
ng	thing		garage
ŏ	pot	ə	about, item,
ō	toe		edible, gallop,
ô	caught, paw		circus
ôr	core	ər	butter

100

words every
high school
freshman
should know

Guide to the Entries

ENTRY WORD The 100 words that constitute this section are listed alphabetically. The entry words, along with inflected and derived forms, are divided into syllables by centered dots. These dots show you where you would break the word at the end of a line. The pronunciation of the word follows the entry word. Please see the key on page v for an explanation of the pronunciation system.

PART OF SPEECH At least one part of speech follows each entry word. The part of speech tells you the grammatical category that the word belongs to. Parts of speech include *noun, adjective, adverb, transitive verb,* and *intransitive verb.* (A transitive verb is a verb that needs an object to complete its meaning. *Wash* is a transitive verb in the sentence *I washed the car.* The direct object of *wash* is *the car.* An intransitive verb is one that does not take an object, as *sleep* in the sentence *I slept for seven hours.* Many verbs are both transitive and intransitive.)

INFLECTIONS A word s inflected forms differ from the main entry form by the addition of a suffix or by a change in the base form to indicate grammatical features such as number, person, or tense. Inflected forms are set in boldface type, divided into syllables, and given pronunciations as necessary. The past tense, past participle, and the third person singular present tense inflections of all verbs are shown. The plurals of nouns are shown when they are spelled in a way other than by adding *s* to the base form.

ORDER OF SENSES Entries having more than one sense are arranged with the central and often the most commonly sought meanings first. In an entry with more than one part of speech, the senses are numbered in separate sequences after each part of speech, as at **flourish.**

EXAMPLES OF USAGE Examples often follow the definitions and are set in italic type. These examples show the entry words in typical contexts. Sometimes the examples are quotations from authors of books. These quotations are shown within quotation marks, and the quotation s author and source are shown.

RELATED WORDS At the end of many entries, additional boldface words appear without definitions. These words are related in basic meaning to the entry word and are usually formed from the entry word by the addition of a suffix.

NOTES Many entries include additional information about the entry words. Some notes explain a scientific concept in greater detail, as at **hologram** and **ozone**. Other notes provide information about the background or history of a word, as at **quarantine** and **yacht**.

EXERCISES At the end of this section, there are exercises designed to help you further strengthen your vocabulary.

"Hello," Danny Saunders said softly. "I'm sorry if I woke you. The nurse told me it was all right to wait here."

I looked at him in amazement. He was the last person in the world I had expected to visit me in the hospital. . . .

He smiled sadly, "Can I sit down? I've been standing here about fifteen minutes waiting for you to wake up."

I sort of nodded or did something with my head, and he took it as a sign of approval and sat down on the edge of the bed to my right. The sun streamed in from the windows behind him, and shadows lay over his face and **accentuated** the lines of his cheeks and jaw.

—Chaim Potok,
The Chosen

ac·cen·tu·ate (ăk-sĕnt′chōō-āt′)

transitive verb
    Past participle and past tense: **ac·cen·tu·at·ed**
    Present participle: **ac·cen·tu·at·ing**
    Third person singular present tense: **ac·cen·tu·ates**

1. To give prominence to; emphasize or intensify: *"The sun streamed in from the windows behind him, and shadows lay over his face and accentuated the lines of his cheeks and jaw"* (Chaim Potok, *The Chosen*). **2.** To pronounce with a stress or accent: *accentuate the second syllable in a word.* **3.** To mark with an accent mark: *accentuate a word in a line of poetry.*

RELATED WORD:
    noun —**ac·cen′tu·a′tion**

al·lit·er·a·tion (ə-lĭt′ə-rā′shən)

noun

The repetition of the same sounds, usually consonants or consonant clusters, especially at the beginning of words. Poets and writers often employ alliteration in their writing, such as *"I have __stood still__ and __stopped__ the sound of feet"* in Robert Frost's "Acquainted with the Night."

RELATED WORD:
　　　adjective — **al·lit′er·a·tive**

a·nal·o·gy (ə-năl′ə-jē)

noun
　　Plural: **a·nal·o·gies**

1. Similarity in some respects between things that are otherwise unlike. **2.** An explanation of something by comparing it with something similar: *The author uses the analogy of a beehive when describing the bustling city.*

RELATED WORDS:
　　　adjective — **a·nal′o·gous** (ə-năl′ə-gəs)
　　　adverb — **a·nal′o·gous·ly**

4

an·ti·bod·y (ăn′tĭ-bŏd′ē)

noun

Plural: **an·ti·bod·ies**

A protein produced in the blood or tissues in response to the presence of a specific toxin, foreign blood cell, or other antigen. Antibodies provide immunity against certain microorganisms and toxins by binding with them and often by deactivating them.

NOTE: Antibodies are complex, Y-shaped protein molecules that guard our bodies against diseases. The immune system's B lymphocytes, or B cells, develop into plasma cells, which can produce a huge variety of antibodies, each one capable of grabbing an invading molecule at the top ends of the Y. The molecules that antibodies recognize can be quite specific — they might exist only on a particular bacterium or virus. When that bacterium or virus enters the body, the antibodies quickly recognize its molecules, as if a sentry recognized an enemy soldier from his uniform. Once the invader is caught, the antibodies may make it inactive or lead it to cells that can destroy it. High numbers of a particular antibody may persist for months after an infection. The numbers may then get quite small, but the experienced B cells can quickly make more of that specific antibody if necessary. Vaccines work by training B cells to do just that.

5

as·pire (ə-spīr′)

transitive verb

> Past participle and past tense: **as·pired**
> Present participle: **as·pir·ing**
> Third person singular present tense: **as·pires**

To have a great ambition; desire strongly: *aspire to become a good soccer player; aspire to great knowledge.*

RELATED WORDS:

> *noun* — **as′pi·ra′tion**
> *noun* — **as·pir′er**

6

bam·boo·zle (băm-boō′zəl)

transitive verb

> Past participle and past tense: **bam·boo·zled**
> Present participle: **bam·boo·zling**
> Third person singular present tense: **bam·boo·zles**

Informal
To deceive by elaborate trickery; hoodwink: *In The Music Man, the con man bamboozles the citizens of River City into believing that he can teach their children to play in a marching band.*

bi·zarre (bĭ-zär**′**)

adjective

Very strange or odd: *a bizarre hat; a bizarre idea.*

RELATED WORD:
   adverb — **bi·zarre′ly**

bois·ter·ous (boi**′**stər-əs *or* boi**′**strəs)

adjective

1. Rough and stormy; violent: *boisterous winds.* **2.** Noisy and lacking restraint or discipline: *the boisterous cheers of an excited crowd.*

RELATED WORDS:
   adverb — **bois′ter·ous·ly**
   noun — **bois′ter·ous·ness**

boy·cott (boi′kŏt′)

transitive verb

Past participle and past tense: **boy·cott·ed**
Present participle: **boy·cott·ing**
Third person singular present tense: **boy·cotts**

To act together in refusing to use, buy from, or deal with, especially as an expression of protest: *boycott a store; boycott foreign-made goods.*

noun

1. A refusal to buy from or deal with a person, business, or nation, especially as a form of protest. **2.** A refusal to buy or use a product or service.

NOTE: Even though his name is now a word in English as well as many other languages around the world, Charles C. Boycott probably did not enjoy becoming so famous. He was an English rent-collector in 19th-century Ireland who refused to lower the high rents that Irish farmers paid to English landowners, and he evicted families who could not pay. In 1880, as part of the struggle for Irish independence from the British Empire, people decided to ignore Boycott and his family completely. The servants stopped showing up for work, the mailman would not deliver the mail, and no one would sell the Boycotts anything in the stores. After the success of the *boycott* of Mr. Boycott in Ireland, his name quickly became the usual word for this way of raising protest without resorting to violence.

10

cam·ou·flage (kăm′ə-fläzh′ *or* kăm′ə-fläj′)

noun

1. A method of concealing military troops or equipment by making them appear to be part of the natural surroundings. **2.** Protective coloring or a disguise that conceals: *An alligator's camouflage makes it look like a log floating in the water.* **3.** Cloth or other material used for camouflage.

transitive verb
> Past participle and past tense: **cam·ou·flaged**
> Present participle: **cam·ou·flag·ing**
> Third person singular present tense: **cam·ou·flag·es**

To conceal or hide by camouflage.

11

chro·nol·o·gy (krə-nŏl′ə-jē)

noun
> Plural: **chro·nol·o·gies**

1. The order or sequence of events: *The lawyer disputed the chronology of events preceding the murder.* **2.** A list or table of events analyzed in order of time of occurrence: *a detailed chronology of modern history.*

RELATED WORDS:
> *adjective*— **chron′o·log′i·cal**
> (krŏn′ə-lŏj′ĭ-kəl)
> *adverb*— **chron′o·log′i·cal·ly**

com·mem·o·rate (kə-měm′ə-rāt′)

transitive verb

>Past participle and past tense: **com·mem·o·rat·ed**
>Present participle: **com·mem·o·rat·ing**
>Third person singular present tense:
>**com·mem·o·rates**

1. To honor the memory of (someone or something), especially with a ceremony: *The crowd gathered in the park to commemorate the firefighters' sacrifice.* **2.** To be a memorial to, as a holiday, ceremony, or statue: *Independence Day commemorates the adoption of the Declaration of Independence.*

RELATED WORDS:
>*noun* — **com·mem′o·ra′tion**
>*adjective* — **com·mem′o·ra·tive**
>*adverb* — **com·mem′o·ra·tive·ly**

cow·er (kou′ər)

intransitive verb

>Past participle and past tense: **cow·ered**
>Present participle: **cow·er·ing**
>Third person singular present tense: **cow·ers**

To crouch or draw back, as from fear or pain; cringe: *"Then the dwarves forgot their joy and their confident boasts of a moment before and cowered down in fright"* (J.R.R. Tolkien, *The Hobbit*).

The dwarves were still passing the cup from hand to hand and talking delightedly of the recovery of their treasure, when suddenly a vast rumbling woke in the mountain underneath as if it was an old volcano that had made up its mind to start eruptions once again. The door behind them was pulled nearly to, and blocked from closing with a stone, but up the long tunnel came the dreadful echoes, from far down in the depths, of a bellowing and a trampling that made the ground beneath them tremble.

Then the dwarves forgot their joy and their confident boasts of a moment before and **cowered** down in fright. Smaug was still to be reckoned with. It does not do to leave a live dragon out of your calculations.

— J.R.R. Tolkien,
The Hobbit

14

de·cor·um (dĭ-kôr′əm)

noun

Proper behavior or conduct; propriety: *"She had pull with the police department, so the men in their flashy suits and fleshy scars sat with churchlike decorum and waited to ask favors from her"* (Maya Angelou, *I Know Why the Caged Bird Sings*).

15

de·duc·tion (dĭ-dŭk′shən)

noun

1. The act of subtracting; subtraction: *The sales clerk's deduction of the cost of installation persuaded us to buy the dishwasher.* **2.** An amount that is or may be subtracted: *She claimed a deduction from her taxable income for medical expenses.* **3.** The process of reaching a conclusion by reasoning, especially from general principles. **4.** A conclusion reached by this process: *The article discusses the judge's deduction that the law violated the Fourteenth Amendment.*

deign (dān)

verb

> Past participle and past tense: **deigned**
> Present participle: **deign·ing**
> Third person singular present tense: **deigns**

intransitive verb

To be willing to do something that one considers beneath one's dignity; condescend: *"'We better hurry or we'll be late for dinner,' I said . . . [H]is right foot flashed into the middle of my fast walk and I went pitching forward into the grass. 'Get those one hundred and fifty pounds off me!' I shouted, because he was sitting on my back. Finny got up, patted my head genially, and moved on across the field, not deigning to glance around for my counterattack . . ."* (John Knowles, *A Separate Peace*).

transitive verb

To condescend to give: *The movie star didn't deign so much as a nod in our direction.*

de·spon·dent (dĭ-spŏn′dənt)

adjective

Feeling depression of spirits from loss of hope, confidence, or courage; dejected: *"It rained. The procession of weary soldiers became a bedraggled train, despondent and muttering, marching with churning effort in a trough of liquid brown mud under a low, wretched sky"* (Stephen Crane, *The Red Badge of Courage*).

RELATED WORDS:
> *noun* — **de·spon′dence, de·spon′den·cy**
> *adverb* — **de·spon′dent·ly**

di·a·logue (*also spelled* **di·a·log**) (dī′ə-lôg′)

noun

1. A conversation between two or more people: *a friendly dialogue between neighbors.* **2.** The words spoken by the characters of a play or story: *The dialogue of the comedy was very witty.* **3.** A literary work written in the form of a conversation: *Many students of philosophy have read the dialogues of Plato.* **4.** An exchange of ideas or opinions: *a lively dialogue among members of the committee.*

19

di·vulge (dĭ-vŭlj**′**)

transitive verb

> Past participle and past tense: **di·vulged**
> Present participle: **di·vulg·ing**
> Third person singular present tense: **di·vulg·es**

To make known; reveal; tell: *divulge a secret.*

RELATED WORD:
> *noun* — **di·vulg′er**

20

e·clec·tic (ĭ-klĕk**′**tĭk)

adjective

Choosing or taking what appears to be the best from various sources: *an eclectic musician blending elements of classical music, jazz, and punk rock.*

RELATED WORD:
> *adverb* — **e·clec′ti·cal·ly**

el·lipse (ĭ-lĭps′)

noun

A figure that forms a closed curve shaped like an oval with both ends alike. An ellipse can be formed by intersecting a cone with a plane that is not parallel or perpendicular to the cone's base. (See top illustration.) The sum of the distances of any point on an ellipse from two fixed points (called the *foci*) remains constant no matter where the point is on the curve. (See bottom illustration.)

THREE-
DIMENSIONAL
ELLIPSE

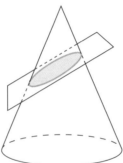

TWO-
DIMENSIONAL
ELLIPSE

The line running through the foci (*F* and *F₁*) of an ellipse is the major axis. The vertices (*V* and *V₁*) mark where the major axis intersects the ellipse.

em·bar·go (ĕm-bär′gō)

noun
    Plural: **em·bar·goes**

1. An order by a government prohibiting merchant ships from entering or leaving its ports. **2.** A prohibition by a government on certain or all trade with a foreign nation.

transitive verb
    Past participle and past tense: **em·bar·goed**
    Present participle: **em·bar·go·ing**
    Third person singular present tense: **em·bar·goes**

To place an embargo on: *The Union government embargoed Confederate ports during the Civil War.*

en·thu·si·as·tic (ĕn-tho͞o′zē-ăs′tĭk)

adjective

Having or showing great interest or excitement: *The principal gave an enthusiastic welcome to the new teachers.*

RELATED WORD:
    adverb — **en·thu′si·as′ti·cal·ly**

ex·po·nent (ĭk-spō′nənt *or* ĕk′spō′nənt)

noun

1. A number or symbol, placed to the right of and above the expression to which it applies, that indicates the number of times a mathematical expression is used as a factor. For example, the exponent 3 in 5^3 indicates $5 \times 5 \times 5$; the exponent 2 in $(x + y)^2$ indicates $(x + y) \times (x + y)$. **2.** A person who speaks for, represents, or advocates something: *exponents of mass transit as a way of reducing pollution.*

RELATED WORDS:
adjective — **ex′po·nen′tial**
adverb — **ex′po·nen′tial·ly**

ex·ult (ĭg-zŭlt′)

intransitive verb
Past participle and past tense: **ex·ult·ed**
Present participle: **ex·ult·ing**
Third person singular present tense: **ex·ults**

To rejoice greatly; be jubilant or triumphant: "*Laurie threw up his hat, then remembered that it wouldn't do to exult over the defeat of his guests, and stopped in the middle of the cheer to whisper to his friend, 'Good for you, Jo! He did cheat, I saw him'*" (Louisa May Alcott, *Little Women*).

"Yankees have a trick of being generous to their enemies," said Jo, with a look that made the lad redden, "especially when they beat them," she added, as, leaving Kate's ball untouched, she won the game by a clever stroke.

Laurie threw up his hat, then remembered that it wouldn't do to **exult** over the defeat of his guests, and stopped in the middle of the cheer to whisper to his friend, "Good for you, Jo! He did cheat, I saw him. We can't tell him so, but he won't do it again, take my word for it."

—Louisa May Alcott,
Little Women

fal·la·cy (făl′ə-sē)

noun
    Plural: **fal·la·cies**

A false notion or mistaken belief: *It is a fallacy that being popular always means being happy.*

RELATED WORDS:
    adjective—**fal·la′cious** (fə-lā′shəs)
    adverb—**fal·la′cious·ly**

flour·ish (flûr′ĭsh)

verb

Past participle and past tense: **flour·ished**
Present participle: **flour·ish·ing**
Third person singular present tense: **flour·ish·es**

intransitive verb

1. To grow or develop well or luxuriantly; thrive: *Most flowers flourish in full sunlight.* **2.** To do well; prosper: *The lawyer's practice flourished.* **3.** To be actively working, especially in a period of great accomplishment: *a writer who flourished in the later 1600s.*

transitive verb

To wave (something) vigorously or dramatically: *The athletes on the winning team flourished their medals in front of the cameras.*

noun

1. A dramatic action or gesture: *The teacher waved the report with a flourish.* **2.** An added decorative touch; an embellishment: *handwriting with many graceful flourishes.* **3.** In music, a showy passage or a fanfare: *Trumpets played a flourish before the king entered.*

for·mi·da·ble (fôr′mĭ-də-bəl *or* fôr-mĭd′ə-bəl)

adjective

1. Arousing fear, dread, alarm, or great concern: *"The men wish to purchase straw field hats to protect themselves from your formidable Arkansas sun"* (Bette Greene, *The Summer of My German Soldier*). **2.** Admirable; awe-inspiring: *a formidable musical talent.* **3.** Difficult to surmount, defeat, or undertake: *The new assignment was a formidable challenge for the young reporter.*

RELATED WORDS:
> *noun* — **for′mid·a·bil′i·ty**
> *adverb* — **for′mi·da·bly**

When the nine prisoners were gathered around the counter the corporal shouted, "Reiker!"

Reiker didn't look quite so tall or strong as the others. His eyes, specked with green, sought communication with my father.

"The men wish to purchase straw field hats to protect themselves from your **formidable** Arkansas sun."

— Bette Greene,
The Summer of My German Soldier

29

gar·goyle (gär′goil′)

noun

A waterspout or ornamental figure in the form of a grotesque animal or person projecting from the gutter of a building.

30

guer·ril·la (*also spelled* **gue·ril·la**) (gə-rĭl′ə)

noun

A member of a military force that is not part of a regular army and operates in small bands in occupied territory to harass the enemy, as by surprise raids.

31

gu·ru (go͝or′o͞o)

noun
    Plural: **gu·rus**

1. A Hindu spiritual teacher. **2.** A person who is followed as a leader or teacher.

32

her·i·tage (hĕr′ĭ-tĭj)

noun

1. Something other than property passed down from preceding generations; a tradition: *"We will win our freedom because the sacred heritage of our nation and the eternal will of God are embodied in our echoing demands"* (Martin Luther King, Jr., *Letter from Birmingham Jail*). **2.** Property that is or can be inherited.

hi·er·o·glyph·ic (hī′ər-ə-glĭf′ĭk *or* hī′rə-glĭf′ĭk)

adjective

Of or related to a system of writing, such as that of ancient Egypt, in which pictures or symbols are used to represent words or sounds: *The ancient tombs of the Pharaohs are marked with hieroglyphic writing.*

noun

1. A picture or symbol used in hieroglyphic writing; a hieroglyph. **2.** *often* **hieroglyphics** Hieroglyphic writing, especially that of the ancient Egyptians.

RELATED WORDS:
>   *noun* — **hi′er·o·glyph′**
>   *adverb* — **hi′er·o·glyph′i·cal·ly**

✍ **NOTE:** *Hieroglyphic* comes from a Greek word meaning "sacred carvings." *Hieros* meant "sacred" in Greek, and *glyphein* meant "to carve." Although the Egyptians wrote hieroglyphs on papyrus and painted them on walls, the Greeks who visited Egypt must have been more impressed by the stately carvings on the stones of immense temples and tombs. The Egyptians' own word for their writing system was *mdw ntr,* "words of the god." You could pronounce this (mĕd′ōō nĕch′ĕr). The Egyptians thought the gods themselves used these symbols, which possessed great power. When they wrote hieroglyphs showing dangerous animals, such as snakes, on the walls of their tombs, they would sometimes leave the symbols unfinished — or even damage them intentionally. This would prevent the hieroglyphs from coming alive and harming the person entombed there.

The Egyptians enclosed the names of royalty in an oval shape called a *cartouche*. This oval represented the circular path of the sun around the world, and so indicated that the pharaoh was ruler of "all that the sun encircles."

Below is the full name of one of the greatest pharaohs, Ramses II, written in its original Egyptian form.

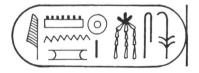

hol·o·gram (hŏl′ə-grăm′ *or* hō′lə-grăm′)

noun

The photographic record of a three-dimensional image
produced by recording on a photographic plate or film
the pattern of interference formed by a split laser beam.
The plate or film is then illuminated with a laser or
with ordinary light to form the image.

> ✍ **NOTE:** If you tear an ordinary photograph in two, each piece
> shows only a part of the original image. If you break a *hologram*
> in two, each piece shows the entire original scene, although
> from slightly different points of view. That's because each spot
> on a hologram contains enough information to show how the
> entire scene would look if it were viewed from a particular
> point of view. Imagine looking at a room through a peephole set
> in a solid door. What you see depends on where in the door the
> peephole is placed. Each piece of the hologram is a "peephole"
> view, and that's what makes the image look three-dimensional:
> as you move the hologram around or look at different parts of
> it, you see the original object from different angles, just as if you
> were walking around it. For this reason, holograms are much
> harder to copy than simple two-dimensional images, because to
> forge one you'd have to know what the original object looked
> like from many angles. And that's why credit cards and other
> important items include stickers bearing holograms as indica-
> tors of authenticity.

hy·poc·ri·sy (hĭ-pŏk′rĭ-sē)

noun

The practice of showing or expressing feelings, beliefs, or virtues that one does not actually hold or possess.

RELATED WORD:
    noun — **hyp′o·crite′** (hĭp′ə-krĭt′)

im·mune (ĭ-myo͞on′)

adjective

1. Protected from disease naturally or by vaccination or inoculation: *I'm immune to chickenpox because I had it when I was young.* **2.** Not subject to an obligation imposed on others; exempt: *As a diplomat, he is immune from criminal prosecution.* **3.** Not affected by a given influence; unresponsive: *"I am immune to emotion. I have been ever since I can remember. Which is helpful when people appeal to my sympathy. I don't seem to have any"* (Ellen Wittlinger, *Hard Love*).

RELATED WORD:
    verb — **im′mu·nize′** (ĭm′yə-nīz′)

im·per·ti·nent (ĭm-pûr**ʹ**tn-ənt)

adjective

1. Offensively bold; rude: *"'I don't like the look of it at all,' said the King: 'however, it may kiss my hand if it likes.' 'I'd rather not,' the Cat remarked. 'Don't be impertinent,' said the King, 'and don't look at me like that!'"* (Lewis Carroll, *Alice's Adventures in Wonderland*). **2.** Not pertinent; irrelevant: *The discussion went on for hours because of the many impertinent questions and remarks.*

RELATED WORD:

adverb—**im·per***ʹ***ti·nent·ly**

"Who *are* you talking to?" said the King, coming up to Alice, and looking at the Cat's head with great curiosity.

"It's a friend of mine — a Cheshire Cat," said Alice: "allow me to introduce it."

"I don't like the look of it at all," said the King: "however, it may kiss my hand if it likes."

"I'd rather not," the Cat remarked.

"Don't be **impertinent**," said the King, "and don't look at me like that!" He got behind Alice as he spoke.

"A cat may look at a king," said Alice. "I've read that in some book, but I don't remember where."

— Lewis Carroll,
Alice's Adventures in Wonderland

in·fer·ence (ĭn′fər-əns)

noun

1. The act or process of deciding or concluding by reasoning from evidence: *arrive at a logical conclusion by inference.* **2.** Something that is decided or concluded by reasoning from evidence; a conclusion: *The evidence is too scanty to draw any inferences from it.*

> ✎ **NOTE:** When we say that a speaker or sentence makes an **implication** or **implies** something, we mean that it is indicated or suggested without being stated outright: *Even though you say you like sports, your lack of enthusiasm implies that you don't.* To make an **inference** about something or **infer** something, on the other hand, is to draw conclusions that are not stated openly in what is said: *I infer from your lack of enthusiasm that you don't like sports.*

RELATED WORD:
  verb — **in·fer′**

in·tro·spec·tion (ĭn′trə-spĕk′shən)

noun

The examination of one's own thoughts and feelings.

RELATED WORDS:
  adjective — **in′tro·spec′tive**
  adverb — **in′tro·spec′tive·ly**

jaun·ty (jônt′tē *or* jänt′tē)

adjective
>Comparative: **jaun·ti·er**
>Superlative: **jaun·ti·est**

1. Having or showing a carefree self-confident air: *"A figure was approaching us over the moor, and I saw the dull red glow of a cigar. The moon shone upon him, and I could distinguish the dapper shape and jaunty walk of the naturalist"* (Arthur Conan Doyle, *The Hound of the Baskervilles*). **2.** Stylish or smart in appearance: *a jaunty hat.*

RELATED WORDS:
>*adverb* — **jaun′ti·ly**
>*noun* — **jaun′ti·ness**

jo·vi·al (jō′vē-əl)

adjective

Full of fun and good cheer; jolly: *a jovial host.*

RELATED WORDS:
>*noun* — **jo′vi·al′i·ty** (jō′vē-ăl′ĭ-tē)
>*adverb* — **jo′vi·al·ly**

kil·o·me·ter (kǐ-lǒm′ǐ-tər *or* kǐl′ə-mē′tər)

noun

A unit of length equal to 1,000 meters or 0.62 of a mile.

☙ **NOTE:** The metric system is a system of measurement that is based on the number 10. Because 12 inches make a foot, and 3 feet make a yard, calculating the number of inches in a given number of yards or miles can often be cumbersome. In the metric system, multiplication is easy. *Kilo-* is a prefix meaning "a thousand," so one kilometer is equal to a thousand meters, and one kilogram is equal to a thousand grams. Likewise, if you know something is 18 kilometers away, you can easily calculate that it's 18,000 meters away.

Some common prefixes in the metric system are:

milli-	"one thousandth"	kilo-	"one thousand"
centi-	"one hundredth"	cento-	"one hundred"
deci-	"one tenth"	deca-	"ten"

The basic units of measurement in the metric system are the *gram*, for weight; the *liter*, for volume; and the *meter*, for distance. The prefixes can be combined with these units to form different measurements: a *centigram* is a hundredth (1/100) of a gram; a *milliliter* is a thousandth (1/1000) of a liter.

But the metric system isn't limited to these units: a *kilowatt* is a thousand watts, and a *millisecond* is a thousandth of second.

There are even more prefixes for larger and smaller units!

micro-	"one millionth"	mega-	"one million"
nano-	"one billionth"	giga-	"one billion"
pico-	"one trillionth"	tera-	"one trillion"

lab·y·rinth (lăb′ə-rĭnth′)

noun

1. A complex structure of connected passages through which it is difficult to find one's way; a maze. **2. Labyrinth** In Greek mythology, the maze built by Daedalus in Crete to confine the Minotaur. **3.** Something complicated or confusing in design or construction. **4.** The system of tubes and spaces that make up the inner ear of many vertebrate animals.

la·con·ic (lə-kŏn′ĭk)

adjective

Using few words; terse; concise: *a laconic reply.*

RELATED WORD:
     adverb — **la·con′i·cal·ly**

li·chen (lī′kən)

noun

An organism that consists of a fungus and an alga growing in close association with each other. Lichens often live on rocks and tree bark and can also be found in extremely cold environments.

light-year (līt′yîr′)

noun

The distance that light travels in one year, about 5.88 trillion miles (9.47 trillion kilometers).

ma·neu·ver (mə-nōō′vər)

noun

1. A planned movement of troops or warships: *By a series of brilliant maneuvers, the general outwitted the enemy.* **2.** *often* **maneuvers** A large-scale military exercise in which battle movements are practiced. **3.** A controlled change in movement or direction of a vehicle or vessel, especially an aircraft. **4.** A movement or procedure that involves skill or cunning: *The gymnast made an acrobatic maneuver and landed squarely on the mat.*

verb

> Past participle and past tense: **ma·neu·vered**
> Present participle: **ma·neu·ver·ing**
> Third person singular present tense: **ma·neu·vers**

intransitive verb

1. To change tactics or approach; plan skillfully: *Our lawyer maneuvered in order to get the trial postponed.* **2.** To carry out a military maneuver. **3.** To make controlled changes in movement or direction: *The ship had to maneuver carefully to avoid the icebergs.*

transitive verb

1. To cause (troops or warships) to carry out a military maneuver. **2.** To direct skillfully by changes in course or in position: *"He let me maneuver the skiff through the wreckage of the flood without even peeking over his shoulder to see what I might be about to hit"* (Katherine Paterson, *Jacob Have I Loved*). **3.** To manage or direct, especially by trickery: *She maneuvered her opponent into taking a position that lost him the election.*

RELATED WORDS:

noun — **ma·neu′ver·a·bil′i·ty**
adjective — **ma·neu′ver·a·ble**

48

mar·su·pi·al (mär-sōō′pē-əl)

noun

Any of various mammals, such as the kangaroo, opossum, or wombat, whose young continue to develop after birth in a pouch on the outside of the female's body.

met·a·phor (mĕt′ə-fôr′)

noun

A figure of speech in which a word or phrase that is ordinarily associated with one thing is applied to something else, thus making a comparison between the two. For example, when Shakespeare wrote, "All the world's a stage," and "Life's but a walking shadow," he was using metaphors.

mo·sa·ic (mō-zā′ĭk)

noun

1. A picture or design made on a surface by fitting and cementing together small colored pieces, as of tile, glass, or stone. **2.** The art or process of making such pictures or designs. **3.** Something that resembles a mosaic: *I tried to understand the mosaic of impressions the author had after visiting Mexico.* **4.** A viral disease of certain plants, such as tobacco or tomatoes, that causes the leaves to become spotted or wrinkled.

51

mu·ta·tion (myōo-tā′shən)

noun

1. A change in a gene or chromosome of an organism that can be inherited by its offspring. **2.** The process by which such a change occurs. **3.** An organism or individual that has undergone such a change. **4.** A change, as in form.

RELATED WORD:
verb — **mu′tate**

52

neb·u·la (nĕb′yə-lə)

noun
Plural: **neb·u·lae** (nĕb′yə-lē′) *or* **neb·u·las**

A thinly spread cloud of interstellar gas and dust. It will appear as a bright patch in the night sky if it reflects light from nearby stars, emits its own light, or re-emits ultraviolet radiation from nearby stars as visible light. If it absorbs light, the nebula appears as a dark patch. In dark nebulae, stars form from clumps of hydrogen gas.

RELATED WORD:
adjective — **neb′u·lar**

There were three circumstances in particular which made me think that its [The Morlocks'] rare emergence above ground was the outcome of a long-continued underground look common in most animals that live largely in the dark —the white fish of the Kentucky caves, for instance. Then, those large eyes, with that capacity for reflecting light, are common features of **nocturnal** things—witness the owl and the cat. And last of all, that evident confusion in the sunshine, that hasty yet fumbling awkward flight towards dark shadow, and that peculiar carriage of the head while in the light — all reinforced the theory of an extreme sensitiveness of the retina.

—H.G. Wells,
The Time Machine

53

noc·tur·nal (nŏk-tûr′nəl)

adjective

1. Of, relating to, or occurring at night: *a nocturnal breeze.* **2.** Active at night: *"[T]hose large eyes, with that capacity for reflecting light, are common features of nocturnal things—witness the owl and the cat"* (H.G. Wells, *The Time Machine*).

RELATED WORD:
  adverb—**noc·tur′nal·ly**

54

nui·sance (nōō′səns)

noun

A source of inconvenience or annoyance; a bother.

om·ni·vore (ŏm′nə-vôr′)

noun

An organism that eats both plants and animals.

🐾 **NOTE:** Our word *omnivore* comes from Latin *omnivorus,* "eating everything." Like many scientific words that English has borrowed from Latin, *omnivore* is a compound — a single word made by putting two other words together. The first part of the Latin word, *omni-,* means "all" or "every." The second part, *-vorus,* means "eating, swallowing." We can find this same root *-vor-* at the end of several other English words. For example, *carnivore* means literally "meat-eating." Here we see *-vor-* added to the same *carn-* as in *chili con carne,* "chili with meat." *Herbivore,* meaning "plant eater," has the same *herb-* as in *herbal tea.* The English verb *devour* comes from Latin *dēvorāre,* which also contains the root *-vor-.* The same root is found at the beginning of yet another word in this book, *voracious,* from Latin *vorāx,* "ravenous."

out·ra·geous (out-rā′jəs)

adjective

Exceeding all bounds of what is right or proper; immoral or offensive: *an outrageous crime; outrageous prices.*

RELATED WORD:
> *adverb* — **out·ra′geous·ly**
> *noun* — **out·ra′geous·ness**

o·zone (ō′zōn′)

noun

A poisonous, unstable form of oxygen that has three atoms per molecule rather than the usual two. It is produced by electricity and is present in the air, especially after a thunderstorm. Commercially, it is produced for use in water purification, air conditioning, and as a bleaching agent.

NOTE: For the earth's organisms, including people, *ozone* can be a lifesaver or a threat to health, depending on how high it is found in the atmosphere. The ozone that lingers in the lower atmosphere is a pollutant and contributes to respiratory diseases like asthma. But in the upper atmosphere, ozone protects us from the more severe forms of the sun's radiation. The region of the atmosphere in which ozone is most concentrated is known as the *ozone layer,* which lies from about 10 to 20 miles (16 to 32 kilometers) above the earth. Because ozone absorbs certain wavelengths of harmful ultraviolet radiation, this layer acts as an important protection for life on the earth. In recent years the ozone has thinned or disappeared in parts of the ozone layer, especially over the polar regions, creating ozone "holes" that let in dangerous amounts of ultraviolet radiation. Ozone holes are created in part by the presence of certain industrial or commercial chemicals released into the atmosphere.

58

par·a·site (păr′ə-sīt′)

noun

1. An organism that lives in or on a different kind of organism from which it gets nourishment and to which it is sometimes harmful. Lice and tapeworms are parasites. **2.** A person who takes advantage of the generosity of others without making any useful return.

59

par·ti·ci·ple (pär′tĭ-sĭp′əl)

noun

A verb form that is used with auxiliary verbs to indicate certain tenses and that can also function as an adjective. The present participle is indicated by *–ing*, as in *running* and *sleeping*. The past participle is usually indicated by *–ed*, as in *walked* and *nailed*, but many English verbs have irregular past participles, such as *fought, sung,* and *known.* Past participles are also used to make the passive voice: *The board was nailed to the wall.*

> 🖋 **NOTE:** You should always avoid the "dangling" participle, as in the sentence *Turning the corner, the view was quite different.* This sentence is constructed so that it seems that the present participle *turning* modifies the noun *view.* As you read the sentence, you might at first think that the view is turning the corner. You should rewrite such sentences: *The view was quite different when we turned the corner,* or *Turning the corner, we saw a different view.*

60

phlo·em (flō′ĕm′)

noun

A plant tissue that conducts food from the leaves to the other plant parts. Phloem consists primarily of tube-like cells that have porous openings. In mature woody plants it forms a sheathlike layer of tissue in the stem, just inside the bark.

61

pla·teau (plă-tō′)

noun

Plural: **pla·teaus** *or* **pla·teaux** (plă-tōz′)

1. An elevated, comparatively level expanse of land. **2.** A relatively stable level or stage of growth or development: *The economy has reached a new plateau.*

pol·y·gon (pŏl'ē-gŏn')

noun

A flat, closed geometric figure bounded by three or more line segments. Triangles, rectangles, and octagons are all examples of polygons.

RELATED WORD:
    adjective—**po·lyg'o·nal** (pə-lĭg'ə-nəl)

EXAMPLES OF POLYGONS

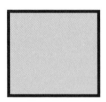

SQUARE

RECTANGLE

PARALLELOGRAM

RHOMBUS

 TRIANGLE

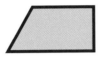 TRAPEZOID

 PENTAGON

 HEXAGON

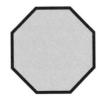 OCTAGON

63

pro·tag·o·nist (prō-tăg′ə-nĭst)

noun

The main character in a drama or literary work.

64

pul·ver·ize (pŭl′və-rīz′)

verb

Past participle and past tense: **pul·ver·ized**
Present participle: **pul·ver·iz·ing**
Third person singular present tense: **pul·ver·iz·es**

transitive verb
To pound, crush, or grind to powder or dust: *"He felt that the stars had been pulverized by the sound of the black jets and that in the morning the earth would be covered with their dust like a strange snow"* (Ray Bradbury, *Fahrenheit 451*).

intransitive verb
To be ground or reduced to powder or dust.

RELATED WORD:
noun—**pul′ver·i·za′tion** (pŭl′vər-ĭ-zā′shən)

He felt that the stars had been **pulverized** by the sound of the black jets and that in the morning the earth would be covered with their dust like a strange snow. That was his idiot thought as he stood shivering in the dark, and let his lips go on moving and moving.

—Ray Bradbury,
Fahrenheit 451

quan·da·ry (kwŏn′də-rē *or* kwŏn′drē)

noun
    Plural: **quan·da·ries**

A condition of uncertainty or doubt; a dilemma: *I'm in a quandary over what to do next.*

quar·an·tine (kwŏr′ən-tēn′)

noun

A condition, period of time, or place in which a person or animal is confined or kept in isolation in an effort to prevent a disease from spreading.

transitive verb
    Past participle and past tense: **quar·an·tined**
    Present participle: **quar·an·tin·ing**
    Third person singular present tense: **quar·an·tines**

To keep (someone or something) confined or isolated, especially as a way to keep a disease from spreading; place (someone or something) in quarantine.

NOTE: The word *quarantine* comes from Italian *quarantina*, "a group of forty"—in this case, a group of forty days. The word originally described the number of days in which a newly arrived ship was kept in isolation, a practice begun in Venice and other port cities as a defense against the plague. The Italian word for "forty," *quaranta*, may remind you of words in other languages you may know, such as French *quarante* or Spanish *cuarenta*. They all descend from Latin *quadrāgintā*, "forty." The first part of this word, *quadr-*, means "four," and we can find it in many other English words. A *quadrangle* has four angles. A *squadron* was originally a group of soldiers in *square* (that is, four-sided) formation. A *quarry* was a place where stone was cut into blocks with square sides.

quo·ta (kwō**'**tə)

noun

1. An amount of something assigned, as to be done, made, or sold: *a machine shop's production quota.* **2.** A number or percentage, especially of people, that represents an upper limit: *strict immigration quotas.* **3.** A number or percentage, especially of people, that represents a required or targeted minimum: *a system of quotas for hiring minority applicants.*

68

rain·for·est (*also spelled* **rain forest**) (rān′fôr′ĭst)

noun

A dense evergreen forest with an annual rainfall of at least 160 inches (406 centimeters).

🖋 **NOTE:** Rainforests are, not surprisingly, forests where it rains a lot—between 160 and 400 inches (406 and 1,016 centimeters) a year. Most of the world's rainforests lie near the equator and have tropical climates. However, there are also cooler rainforests, such as the one in the northwest United States and southwestern Canada along the Pacific Ocean. The largest rainforest, covering as much territory as the rest of the world's rainforests combined, is in the Amazon River basin in South America. Rainforests are extremely important because they help regulate the world's climate and because they contain a wider variety of plants and animals than any other environment on the earth. Among the many benefits of this biodiversity is its support of important biological research. For example, many of the natural chemicals used in prescription drugs are found in plants that grow only in rainforests.

69

ran·dom (răn′dəm)

adjective

Having no specific pattern, purpose, or objective: *the random movements of leaves falling from the trees.*

idiom

at random

Without a method or purpose; unsystematically: *Choose a card at random from the deck.*

RELATED WORDS:
　　　adverb — **ran′dom·ly**
　　　noun — **ran′dom·ness**

70

re·cede (rĭ-sēd′)

intransitive verb
　　　Past participle and past tense: **re·ced·ed**
　　　Present participle: **re·ced·ing**
　　　Third person singular present tense: **re·cedes**

1. To move back or away from a limit, degree, point, or mark: *The floodwaters receded from the streets.* **2.** To grow less or diminish, as in intensity: *"[H]e stood and held his abdomen until the hunger cramps receded"* (Gary Paulsen, *Hatchet*). **3.** To slope backward: *a man with a chin that recedes.* **4.** To become fainter or more distant: *Over the years his memory of that summer receded.*

He stood, went back to the water, and took small drinks. As soon as the cold water hit his stomach, he felt the hunger sharpen, as it had before, and he stood and held his abdomen until the hunger cramps **receded**.

He had to eat. He was weak with it again, down with the hunger, and he had to eat.

—Gary Paulsen,
Hatchet

ren·ais·sance (rĕn′ĭ-säns′ *or* rĕn′ĭ-säns′)

noun

1. A rebirth or revival: *a renaissance of downtown business.* **2. Renaissance** The revival of classical art, literature, architecture, and learning in Europe that occurred from the 14th through the 16th century.

adjective

Renaissance Of or relating to the Renaissance or its artistic works or styles.

NOTE: When the Roman Empire crumbled in the middle of the fifth century, literate people in western Europe took refuge in monasteries, where they contemplated the nature of God and prepared for the next world. The art and literature of the ancient Greeks and Romans, and the values that they expressed, were largely forgotten or ignored because of their pagan origins. During the centuries just after the collapse of the empire, it was difficult to pass on knowledge from the past because of the great decline in living conditions. Then in the fourteenth and fifteenth centuries, a new interest was kindled in the achievements of Greece and Rome—first in Italy and then spreading to the rest of western Europe. A thousand years after the fall of Rome, the fall of another empire helped bring about a revival of classical civilization in the West. The Greeks of the Byzantine Empire had preserved manuscripts of classical literature and the knowledge of how to read them. As the Byzantine Empire crumbled and finally fell to the Turks in 1453, Greek scholars fled as refugees to Italy, and manuscripts were brought to western Europe for preservation. When Western scholars and artists examined the great achievements of Greece and Rome, they found new inspiration to create art and literature for their own age. In its vibrancy and vitality, this age was like a new birth for European culture, and so we now call it the Renaissance.

ren·e·gade (rĕn′ĭ-gād′)

noun

1. A person who rejects a cause, allegiance, religion, or group for another. **2.** An outlaw.

adjective

Of, relating to, or resembling a renegade; traitorous.

re·pose (rĭ-pōz′)

noun

1. The act of resting or the state of being at rest. **2.** Peace of mind; freedom from anxiety: *seeking security and repose.* **3.** Calmness; tranquility: "*It was the cool gray dawn, and there was a delicious sense of repose and peace in the deep pervading calm and silence of the woods*" (Mark Twain, *The Adventures of Tom Sawyer*).

verb
>Past participle and past tense: **re·posed**
>Present participle: **re·pos·ing**
>Third person singular present tense: **re·pos·es**

transitive verb
To lay (oneself) down to rest.

intransitive verb
1. To lie at rest; relax or sleep. **2.** To lie supported by something: *a dish reposing on the table.*

When Tom awoke in the morning, he wondered where he was. He sat up and rubbed his eyes and looked around. Then he comprehended. It was the cool gray dawn, and there was a delicious sense of **repose** and peace in the deep pervading calm and silence of the woods. Not a leaf stirred; not a sound obtruded upon great Nature's meditation. Beaded dewdrops stood upon the leaves and grasses. A white layer of ashes covered the fire, and a thin blue breath of smoke rose straight into the air. Joe and Huck still slept.

— Mark Twain,
The Adventures of Tom Sawyer

sac·ri·fice (săk′rə-fīs′)

noun

1. The act of giving up something highly valued for the sake of something else considered to be of greater value: *He was willing to make sacrifices in order to become a musician.* **2.** The act of offering something, such as an animal's life, to a deity in worship or to win favor or forgiveness. **3.** A victim offered this way. **4.** In baseball: **a.** A bunt that allows a runner to advance a base while the batter is retired. **b.** A fly ball enabling a runner to score after it is caught by a fielder.

verb

    Past participle and past tense: **sac·ri·ficed**
    Present participle: **sac·ri·fic·ing**
    Third person singular present tense: **sac·ri·fic·es**

transitive verb

1. To offer (something or someone) as a sacrifice to a deity. **2.** To give up (one thing) for another thing considered to be of greater value.

intransitive verb

1. To make or offer a sacrifice. **2.** In baseball, to hit a sacrifice bunt or sacrifice fly.

RELATED WORD:
    adjective — **sac′ri·fi′cial** (săk′rə-fĭsh′əl)

sil·hou·ette (sĭl′o͞o-ĕt′)

noun

1. A drawing consisting of the outline of something, especially a human profile, filled in with a solid color. **2.** An outline of something that appears dark against a light background: *"A storm was coming up from the south, moving slowly. It looked something like a huge blue-gray shower curtain being drawn along by the hand of God. You could just barely see through it, enough to make out the silhouette of the mountains on the other side"* (Barbara Kingsolver, *The Bean Trees*).

transitive verb
> Past participle and past tense: **sil·hou·et·ted**
> Present participle: **sil·hou·et·ting**
> Third person singular present tense: **sil·hou·ettes**

To cause to be seen as a silhouette: *The lamp silhouetted his profile against the window shade.*

sol·stice (sŏl′stĭs *or* sōl′stĭs)

noun

Either of the times of year when the sun is farthest north or south of the equator. In the Northern Hemisphere, the summer solstice occurs on June 20 or 21 and the winter solstice occurs on December 21 or 22.

spec·trum (spĕk′trəm)

noun

Plural: **spec·tra** (spĕk′trə) *or* **spec·trums**

1. A band of colors seen when white light is broken up according to wavelengths, as when passing through a prism or striking drops of water. **2.** The entire range of electromagnetic radiation, from gamma rays, which have the shortest wavelengths and highest frequencies, to radio waves, which have the longest wavelengths and lowest frequencies. Visible light, with intermediate wavelengths and frequencies, is near the center of the electromagnetic spectrum. **3.** A broad range of related qualities, ideas, or activities: *This class will cover a wide spectrum of ideas.*

78

ster·e·o·type (stĕr′ē-ə-tīp′)

noun

A conventional or oversimplified idea or image: *the stereotype of the meek librarian.*

transitive verb
> Past participle and past tense: **ster·e·o·typed**
> Present participle: **ster·e·o·typ·ing**
> Third person singular present tense: **ster·e·o·types**

To make a stereotype of: *a movie that stereotypes farmers as unsophisticated.*

RELATED WORD:
> *noun* — **ster′e·o·typ′er**

79

strat·e·gy (străt′ə-jē)

noun
> Plural: **strat·e·gies**

1. The science of using all the forces of a nation as effectively as possible during peace or war. **2.** A plan of action arrived at by means of this science or intended to accomplish a specific goal.

RELATED WORD:
> *adjective* — **stra·te′gic** (strə-tē′jĭk)

suf·frage (sŭf′rĭj)

noun

The right to vote in political elections: *Susan B. Anthony campaigned for women's suffrage.*

sym·bi·o·sis (sĭm′bē-ō′sĭs *or* sĭm′bī-ō′sĭs)

noun

Plural: **sym·bi·o·ses** (sĭm′bē-ō′sēz′ *or* sĭm′bī-ō′sēz′)

The close association between two or more different organisms of different species, often but not necessarily benefiting each member.

> **NOTE:** Two organisms that live together in **symbiosis** may have one of three kinds of relationships: *mutualism, commensalism,* or *parasitism.* The *mutualism* shown by the rhinoceros and the tickbird benefits both. Riding on the rhino's back, the tickbird eats its fill of the ticks that bother the rhino while the rhino gets warning calls from the bird when it senses danger. In *commensalism,* one member benefits and the other is unaffected. The ocean fish known as the remora attaches to a shark by a suction disk on its head and gets to eat the scraps left after the shark feeds. But the shark is unaffected by the remora's presence. In *parasitism,* though, one species generally gets hurt, as when fleas infest a dog's coat and feed on its blood.

tar·iff (tăr′ĭf)

noun

1. A tax or duty imposed by a government on a category of imported or exported goods, such as automobiles or steel. **2.** A list or system of these taxes or duties. **3.** A list or table of prices or fees.

tech·nique (těk-nēk′)

noun

1. A procedure or method for accomplishing a complicated task, as in a science or an art: *a new technique for making computer chips.* **2.** Skill in handling such procedures or methods: *As a pianist, she has nearly perfect technique.*

tem·po (těm′pō)

noun
  Plural: **tem·pos** *or* **tem·pi** (těm′pē)

1. The speed at which music is or ought to be played. **2.** A characteristic rate or rhythm of something; a pace: *the rapid tempo of life in a city.*

tox·in (tŏk′sĭn)

noun

A poisonous substance produced by a living organism. Toxins can be products of ordinary metabolism (such as those found in urine), can be produced to kill or immobilize prey (such as the toxins in snake venom), or can be produced for self-defense (such as the cyanide produced by several plants). Toxins produced by bacteria cause disease.

RELATED WORD:
   adjective — **tox′ic**

tran·quil·i·ty (*also spelled* **tran·quil·li·ty**)
(trăng-kwĭl′ĭ-tē *or* trăn-kwĭl′ĭ-tē)

noun

The quality or condition of being free from disturbance; calmness; serenity: *"We the people of the United States, in order to form a more perfect union, establish justice, insure domestic tranquility . . . do ordain and establish this Constitution for the United States of America"* (Preamble to the Constitution of the United States of America).

We the people of the United States, in order to form a more perfect union, establish justice, insure domestic **tranquility**, provide for the common defense, promote the general welfare, and secure the blessings of liberty to ourselves and our posterity, do ordain and establish this Constitution for the United States of America.

— Preamble to the
Constitution of the
United States of America

tu·mult (tōo′mŭlt′)

noun

1. Noisy and disorderly activity; a commotion or disturbance; an uproar. **2.** Emotional or mental commotion or agitation.

RELATED WORD:
    adjective—**tu·mul′tu·ous** (tōo-mŭl′chōo-əs)

tun·dra (tŭn′drə)

noun

A cold, treeless, usually lowland area of far northern regions. The subsoil of tundras is permanently frozen,
but in summer the top layer of soil thaws and can support low-growing mosses, lichens, grasses, and small
shrubs: *"As I looked about me at the stark and cloud-
topped hills, the waste of pressure-rippled ice, and, beyond
the valley, to the desolate and treeless roll of tundra, I had
no doubt that this was excellent wolf country"* (Farley
Mowatt, *Never Cry Wolf*).

As I looked about me at the stark and cloud-topped hills, the waste of pressure-rippled ice, and, beyond the valley, to the desolate and treeless roll of **tundra**, I had no doubt that this was excellent wolf country. Indeed, I suspected that many pairs of lupine eyes were already watching me with speculative interest. I burrowed into my mountain of gear, found the revolver, and then took stock of the situation.

— Farley Mowatt,
Never Cry Wolf

ul·tra·vi·o·let (ŭl′trə-vī′ə-lĭt)

adjective

Of or relating to electromagnetic radiation having wavelengths shorter than those of visible light but longer than those of x-rays.

u·nan·i·mous (yōō-năn′ə-məs)

adjective

1. Sharing the same opinion; being fully in agreement: *"[N]eighborhood opinion was unanimous that Mrs. Dubose was the meanest old woman who ever lived"* (Harper Lee, *To Kill a Mockingbird*). **2.** Based on or characterized by complete agreement: *a unanimous vote.*

RELATED WORD:
  adverb — **u·nan′i·mous·ly**

Cecil Jacobs, who lived at the far end of our street next door to the post office, walked a total of one mile per school day to avoid the Radley Place and old Mrs. Henry Lafayette Dubose. Mrs. Dubose lived two doors up the street from us; neighborhood opinion was **unanimous** that Mrs. Dubose was the meanest old woman who ever lived.

—Harper Lee,
To Kill a Mockingbird

91
un·du·late (ŭn′jə-lāt′)

intransitive verb
>Past participle and past tense: **un·du·lat·ed**
>Present participle: **un·du·lat·ing**
>Third person singular present tense: **un·du·lates**

1. To move in waves or with a smooth wavy motion: *wheat undulating in the breeze.* **2.** To have a wavy appearance or form: *A line undulated across the chalkboard.*

RELATED WORD:
>*noun* — **un′du·la′tion**

vac·cine (văk-sēn′)

noun

A substance that stimulates cells in the immune system to recognize and attack disease-causing agents, especially through the production of antibodies. Most vaccines are given by injection or are swallowed as liquids. Vaccines may contain a weaker form of the disease-causing virus or bacterium or even a DNA fragment or some other component of the agent.

RELATED WORD:

noun — **vac′ci·na′tion**

🐄 **NOTE:** The word *vaccine* ultimately comes from Latin *vacca*, "cow," a word that may be familiar to you as French *vache* or Spanish *vaca*. Before the days of vaccination, the dread disease smallpox had long been a leading cause of death all over the world. In 1796, however, the English doctor Edward Jenner noticed that people who had caught cowpox, a mild disease contracted from dairy cows, did not get smallpox afterwards. Jenner took liquid from the cowpox sores of a milkmaid and injected a boy with it. Later, Jenner exposed the boy to smallpox, but the boy did not get sick. In this way, Jenner had discovered a safe way to prevent smallpox. From the Latin name for cowpox, *variolae vaccīnae* (literally, "smallpox of cows"), Jenner's technique became known as *vaccination*, and the liquid he injected as *vaccine*.

vac·il·late (văs′ə-lāt′)

intransitive verb
> Past participle and past tense: **vac·il·lat·ed**
> Present participle: **vac·il·lat·ing**
> Third person singular present tense: **vac·il·lates**

To be unable to decide between one opinion or course of action and another; waver: *I vacillated between going on vacation with my family or going to summer camp.*

RELATED WORD:
> *noun*— **vac′il·la′tion**

ver·te·brate (vûr′tə-brĭt *or* vûr′tə-brāt′)

noun

Any of a large group of animals having a backbone, including the fishes, amphibians, reptiles, birds, and mammals.

adjective

1. Having a backbone: *vertebrate animals.* **2.** Of or characteristic of a vertebrate or vertebrates: *the vertebrate brain.*

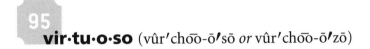

95

vir·tu·o·so (vûr′chōō-ō′sō *or* vûr′chōō-ō′zō)

noun

Plural: **vir·tu·o·sos** *or* **vir·tu·o·si** (vûr′chōō-ō′sē)

1. A musical performer of great excellence, technique, or ability. **2.** A person of great skill or technique: *a chef who was a virtuoso in the kitchen.*

adjective

Exhibiting the ability, technique, or personal style of a virtuoso: *a virtuoso performance.*

vo·ra·cious (və-rāʹshəs)

adjective

1. Eating or eager to eat great amounts of food; ravenous: *"Oliver Twist and his companions suffered the tortures of slow starvation for three months: at last they got so voracious and wild with hunger, that one boy . . . hinted darkly to his companions, that unless he had another basin of gruel per diem, he was afraid he might some night happen to eat the boy who slept next him. . . ."* (Charles Dickens, *Oliver Twist*). **2.** Having or marked by an insatiable appetite for an activity or occupation: *a voracious reader.*

RELATED WORDS:
> *adverb* — **vo·raʹcious·ly**
> *noun* — **vo·raʹcious·ness**

Boys have generally excellent appetites. Oliver Twist and his companions suffered the tortures of slow starvation for three months: at last they got so **voracious** and wild with hunger, that one boy, who was tall for his age, and hadn't been used to that sort of thing (for his father had kept a small cook-shop), hinted darkly to his companions, that unless he had another basin of gruel *per diem*, he was afraid he might some night happen to eat the boy who slept next him, who happened to be a weakly youth of tender age. He had a wild, hungry eye; and they implicitly believed him. A council was held; lots were cast who should walk up to the master after supper that evening, and ask for more; and it fell to Oliver Twist.

—Charles Dickens,
Oliver Twist

wretch·ed (rĕch′ĭd)

adjective

    Comparative: **wretch·ed·er** *or* **more wretched**
    Superlative: **wretch·ed·est** *or* **most wretched**

1. Very unhappy or unfortunate; miserable: *a wretched prisoner.* **2.** Characterized by or causing distress or unhappiness: *"But my night was wretched, my rest broken: the ground was damp, the air cold: besides, intruders passed near me more than once, and I had again and again to change my quarters: no sense of safety or tranquillity befriended me"* (Charlotte Brontë, *Jane Eyre*). **3.** Hateful or contemptible: *a bigot with a wretched personality.* **4.** Inferior in quality: *The movie was wretched.*

RELATED WORDS:

    adverb — **wretch′ed·ly**
    noun — **wretch′ed·ness**

I could not hope to get a lodging under a roof, and sought it in the wood I have before alluded to. But my night was **wretched**, my rest broken: the ground was damp, the air cold: besides, intruders passed near me more than once, and I had again and again to change my quarters: no sense of safety or tranquillity befriended me. Towards morning it rained; the whole of the following day was wet. Do not ask me, reader, to give a minute account of that day; as before, I sought work; as before, I was repulsed; as before, I starved; but once did food pass my lips. At the door of a cottage I saw a little girl about to throw a mess of cold porridge into a pig trough. "Will you give me that?" I asked.

—Charlotte Brontë,
Jane Eyre

98
xy·lem (zī′ləm)

noun

A plant tissue that carries water and dissolved minerals up from the roots through the stem to the leaves and provides support for the softer tissues. Xylem consists of various elongated cells that function as tubes. In a tree trunk, the innermost part of the wood is dead but structurally strong xylem.

99
yacht (yät)

noun

Any of various relatively small sailing or motor-driven vessels used for pleasure trips or racing.

NOTE: Many English words related to the sea or seafaring are borrowed from Dutch, including *brackish, corvette, deck, dock, freebooter, harpoon, hoist, maelstrom, mesh* (of a net), *reef, school* (of fish), *skipper, sloop, tackle, trawl,* and *walrus.* The word *yacht,* the only common English word in which *ch* is silent, was probably borrowed from Dutch *jaght,* now spelled *jacht.* Norwegian also has the word *jakt,* related to Dutch *jacht,* and possibly both languages contributed to the development of English *yacht.* These words ultimately come from Middle Low German *jachtschip,* or "hunting ship." The original Dutch *jacht,* a fast, light boat, actually served the practical purposes of pursuing smugglers. In 1660, the Dutch East India Company gave Charles II of England a *jacht* of this type. However, he used it for pleasure *cruises*—another word from Dutch!

In Dutch, the *ch* is actually pronounced as a separate sound, like the one you make when you clear your throat—it is like the *ch* at the end of the German pronunciation of the composer *Bach.* English used to have this sound, too. Everyone is familiar with silent *gh* from words such as *bought* and *thought.* This silent *gh* once spelled the same throat-clearing sound, which disappeared in English in the sixteenth century. By the time the English borrowed the Dutch word *jacht,* they could no longer say the *ch* very well, so it was left out of the pronunciation. But the spelling of the word stayed the same.

zo·ol·o·gy (zō-ŏl′ə-jē *or* zōō-ŏl′ə-jē)

noun

 Plural: **zo·ol·o·gies**

1. The branch of biology that deals with animals. **2.** The animals of a particular area or period: *The zoology of Australia is very different from the zoology of North America.*

Exercises
to Improve and
Enrich Your Vocabulary

Knowing and being able to use the *100 Words Every High School Freshman Should Know* is just one step that you can take to expand your vocabulary. Along with a good dictionary, such as the *American Heritage® Student Dictionary* or the *American Heritage® High School Dictionary*, you can use these 100 words as a starting point to discover new words. The exercises shown below are among the many ways you can become more familiar with your dictionary and improve your vocabulary.

Building your vocabulary is an ongoing process that you can continue throughout your life. If you feel discouraged because you can't retain the definitions of all the words that you encounter, approach the task of expanding your vocabulary more slowly. If learning ten words a week is too difficult, aim for three, or five.

What is important is not the quantity of words you're learning. Rather, what is important is your process behind learning the words and the commitment you make to yourself to strengthen your vocabulary over time.

Choose ten words from the list of *100 Words Every High School Freshman Should Know*. Look these ten words up in your dictionary.

On each page that these ten words are listed, choose a new word whose meaning you do not know. Create a document on your computer and type in that word along with its definition, or write the word down on paper with its definition.

For example, other words appearing on the same page as **bamboozle** in the *American Heritage Student Dictionary* that you might choose to learn include **balsam, balustrade,** or **banal**.

Keep a record of the new words that you learn. Every so often, go back and refresh your memory by rereading the definitions to these words. Create sentences that use these words so that you can become comfortable using them.

EXERCISE II

Choose a magazine or newspaper that you like to read at least once a week. Create a document on your computer or start a journal in a notebook. Every time you read a word whose meaning you're unsure of, add that word to your computer file or journal entry.

Look up the word in your dictionary, and write or type out the definition. Does knowing the precise definition of the word help you understand the article?

After you have acquired a list of ten words, memorize them until they are part of your active vocabulary.

EXERCISE III

Many of the words in the list of *100 Words Every High School Freshman Should Know* include terms from specific areas of study. For example, **ellipse** and **polygon** are both from the field of geometry. **Antibody** and **mutation** are from biology.

What fields of learning interest you? Create a list of ten words that you think people should know if they were to learn more about that topic. Think about how you would define those words, and compare your definitions with the definitions you find in your dictionary.

100

words every high school graduate should **know**

Guide to the Entries

ENTRY WORD The 100 words that constitute this section are listed alphabetically. The entry words, along with inflected and derived forms, are divided into syllables by centered dots. These dots show you where you would break the word at the end of a line. The pronunciation of the word follows the entry word. Please see the pronunciation guide and key on pages iv–v for an explanation of the pronunciation system.

PART OF SPEECH At least one part of speech follows each entry word. The part of speech tells you the grammatical category that the word belongs to. Parts of speech include *noun, adjective, adverb, transitive verb,* and *intransitive verb.* (A transitive verb is a verb that needs an object to complete its meaning. *Wash* is transitive in the sentence *I washed the car.* The direct object of *wash* is *the car.* An intransitive verb is one that does not take an object, as *sleep* in the sentence *I slept for seven hours.* Many verbs are both transitive and intransitive.)

INFLECTIONS A word's inflected form differs from the main entry form by the addition of a suffix or by a change in its base form to indicate grammatical features such as number, person, or tense. They are set in boldface type, divided into syllables, and given pronunciations as necessary. The past tense, past participle, and the third person singular present tense inflections of all verbs are shown. The plurals of nouns are shown when they are spelled in a way other than by adding *s* to the base form.

LABELS A subject label identifies the special area of knowledge a definition applies to, as at **metamorphosis.** Information applicable only to a particular sense is shown after the number or letter of that sense; at **metamorphosis,** the biology sense is applicable to sense 2.

The *Usage Problem* label warns of possible difficulties involving grammar, diction, and writing style. A word or definition with this label is discussed in a Usage Note, as at **paradigm.**

Certain nouns are spelled as plurals but sometimes take a singular verb. This information is indicated in italic type, as at **thermodynamics.**

ORDER OF SENSES Entries having more than one sense are arranged with the central and often the most commonly sought meaning first. Senses and subsenses are grouped to show their relationships with each other. Boldface letters before senses indicate that two or more subsenses are closely related, as at **parameter.**

In an entry with more than one part of speech, the senses are numbered in separate sequences after each part of speech, as at **kowtow.**

EXAMPLES OF USAGE Examples often follow the definitions and are set in italic type. These examples show the entry words in typical contexts. Sometimes the examples are quotations from authors of books or newspaper articles. These quotations are shown within quotation marks and are followed by the quotation's author and source.

ETYMOLOGIES Etymologies appear in square brackets following the last definition. An etymology traces the history of a word as far back in time as can be determined with reasonable certainty. The stage most closely preceding Modern English is given first, with each earlier stage following in sequence. A language name, linguistic form (in italics), and brief definition of the form are given for each stage of the derivation. To avoid redundancy, a language, form, or definition is not repeated if it is identical to the corresponding item in the immediately preceding stage. Occasionally, a form will be given that is not actually preserved in written documents but which scholars are confident did exist—such a form will be marked by an asterisk (*). The word *from* is used to indicate origin of any kind: by inheritance, borrowing, or derivation. When an etymology splits a compound word into parts, a colon introduces the parts and each element is then traced back to its origin, with those elements enclosed in parentheses.

RELATED WORDS At the end of many entries, additional boldface words appear without definitions. These words are related in basic meaning to the entry word and are usually formed from the entry word by the addition of suffixes.

NOTES Some entries include Usage Notes or Word Histories. Usage Notes present important information and guidance on matters of grammar, diction, pronunciation, and nuances. Some refer to responses from our Usage Panel, a group of more than 200 respected writers, scholars, and critics. The editors of the *American Heritage Dictionaries* regularly survey these people on a broad range of usage questions. Word Histories are found at words whose etymologies are of particular interest. The bare facts of the etymology are explained to give a fuller understanding of how important linguistic processes operate, how words move from one language to another, and how the history of an individual word can be related to historical and cultural developments.

At the end of this section, there are exercises that are designed to help you further strengthen your vocabulary.

The strong-bas'd promontory
Have I made shake, and by the spurs pluck'd up
The pine and cedar; graves at my command
Have wak'd their sleepers, op'd, and let 'em forth,
By my so potent art. But this rough magic
I here **abjure**.

—William Shakespeare,
The Tempest

ab·jure (ăb-jŏor′)

transitive verb
> Past participle and past tense: **ab·jured**
> Present participle: **ab·jur·ing**
> Third person singular present tense: **ab·jures**

1. To recant solemnly; renounce or repudiate: *"But this rough magic I here abjure"* (William Shakespeare, *The Tempest*). **2.** To renounce under oath; forswear: *The defendant abjured his previous testimony.*

[Middle English *abjuren*, from Old French *abjurer*, from Latin *abiūrāre* : *ab-*, away + *iūrāre*, to swear.]

RELATED WORDS:
> *noun* — **ab′ju·ra′tion** (ăb′jə-rā′shən)
> *noun* — **ab·jur′er**

ab·ro·gate (ăb′rə-gāt′)

transitive verb

> Past participle and past tense: **ab·ro·gat·ed**
> Present participle: **ab·ro·gat·ing**
> Third person singular present tense: **ab·ro·gates**

To abolish, do away with, or annul, especially by authority: *"In 1982, we were told that this amendment meant that our existing Aboriginal and treaty rights were now part of the supreme law of the land, and could not be abrogated or denied by any government"* (Matthew Coon-Come, *Native Americas*).

[Latin *abrogāre, abrogāt-* : *ab-*, away + *rogāre*, to ask.]

RELATED WORD:
> *noun*—**ab′ro·ga′tion** (ăb′rə-gā′shən)

ab·ste·mi·ous (ăb-stē′mē-əs *or* əb-stē′mē-əs)

adjective

1. Eating and drinking in moderation: *"Mr. Brooke was an abstemious man, and to drink a second glass of sherry quickly at no great interval from the first was a surprise to his system"* (George Eliot, *Middlemarch*). **2.** Characterized by abstinence or moderation: *The hermit led an abstemious way of life.*

[From Latin *abstēmius* : *abs-, ab-*, away + **tēmum*, liquor, variant of *tēmētum*.]

RELATED WORDS:
> *adverb*—**ab·ste′mi·ous·ly**
> *noun*—**ab·ste′mi·ous·ness**

4

ac·u·men (ăk′yə-mən *or* ə-kyoo′mən)

noun

Quickness and keenness of judgment or insight: *"'No, no, my dear Watson! With all respect for your natural acumen, I do not think that you are quite a match for the worthy doctor'"* (Arthur Conan Doyle, *The Adventure of the Missing Three-Quarter*).

[Latin *acūmen*, from *acuere*, to sharpen, from *acus*, needle.]

USAGE NOTE: The pronunciation (ə-kyoo′mən), with stress on the second syllable, is an older, traditional pronunciation reflecting the word's Latin origin. In recent years it has been supplanted as the most common pronunciation of the word by a variant with stress on the first syllable, (ăk′yə-mən). In our 1997 Usage Panel survey, 68 percent of the Panelists chose this as their pronunciation, while 29 percent preferred the pronunciation with stress on the second syllable. The remaining 3 percent said they use both pronunciations.

5

an·te·bel·lum (ăn′tē-bĕl′əm)

adjective

Belonging to the period before a war, especially the American Civil War: *While vacationing in Georgia, we took a tour of stately antebellum houses.*

[From Latin *ante bellum*, before the war : *ante*, before + *bellum*, war.]

6

aus·pi·cious (ô-spĭsh′əs)

adjective

1. Attended by favorable circumstances; propitious: *My boss was in a good mood, so I thought it was an auspicious time to ask for a raise.* **2.** Marked by success; prosperous: *The auspicious fundraiser allowed the charity to donate hundreds of toys to the orphanage.*

[From Latin *auspicium*, bird divination, from *auspex, auspic-*, one who foretold the future by watching the flights of birds.]

RELATED WORDS:
> *adverb*— **aus·pic′ious·ly**
> *noun*— **aus·pic′ious·ness**

7

be·lie (bē-lī′, bĭ-lī′)

transitive verb
> Past participle and past tense: **be·lied**
> Present participle: **be·ly·ing**
> Third person singular present tense: **be·lies**

1. To give a false representation to; misrepresent: *"He spoke roughly in order to belie his air of gentility"* (James Joyce, *Dubliners*). **2.** To show to be false; contradict: *Their laughter belied their outward anger.*

[Middle English *bilien*, from Old English *belēogan*, to deceive with lies.]

RELATED WORD:
> *noun*— **be·li′er**

He spoke roughly in order to **belie** his air of gentility, for his entry had been followed by a pause of talk. His face was heated. To appear natural he pushed his cap back on his head and planted his elbows on the table.

— James Joyce,
Dubliners

·8

bel·li·cose (bĕl′ĭ-kōs′)

adjective

Warlike or hostile in manner or temperament: *The nations exchanged bellicose rhetoric over the border dispute.*

[Middle English, from Latin *bellicōsus,* from *bellicus,* of war, from *bellum,* war.]

RELATED WORDS:
> *adverb* — **bel′li·cose′ly**
> *noun* — **bel′li·cos′i·ty** (bĕl′ĭ-kŏs′ĭ-tē)
> *noun* — **bel′li·cose′ness**

9

bowd·ler·ize (bōd′lə-rīz′ *or* boud′lə-rīz′)

transitive verb
> Past participle and past tense: **bowd·ler·ized**
> Present participle: **bowd·ler·iz·ing**
> Third person singular present tense: **bowd·ler·iz·es**

To remove material that is considered objectionable or offensive from (a book, for example); expurgate: *The publisher bowdlerized the bawdy 18th-century play for family audiences.*

[After Thomas *Bowdler* (1754–1825), who published an expurgated edition of Shakespeare in 1818.]

RELATED WORDS:
> *noun* — **bowd′ler·ism**
> *noun* — **bowd′ler·i·za′tion**
>> (bōd′lər-ĭ-zā′shən
>> *or* boud′lər-ĭ-zā′shən)
> *noun* — **bowd′ler·iz′er**

10

chi·can·er·y (shĭ-kāʹnə-rē *or* chĭ-kāʹnə-rē)

noun

Deception by trickery or sophistry: *"The successful man . . . who has risen by conscienceless swindling of his neighbors, by deceit and chicanery, by unscrupulous boldness and unscrupulous cunning, stands toward society as a dangerous wild beast"* (Theodore Roosevelt, *The Strenuous Life*).

[From *chicane,* to deceive, from French *chicaner,* from Old French, to quibble.]

11

chro·mo·some (krōʹmə-sōmʹ)

noun

1. A threadlike linear strand of DNA and associated proteins in the nucleus of eukaryotic cells that carries the genes and functions in the transmission of hereditary information: *Chromosomes occur in pairs in all of the cells of eukaryotes except the reproductive cells.* **2.** A circular strand of DNA in bacteria that contains the hereditary information of the cell.

[*chromo-,* colored (from Greek *khrōma,* color) + *-some,* body (from Greek *sōma*).]

RELATED WORDS:

> *adjective*— **chroʹmo·somʹal** (krōʹmə-sōʹməl)
> *adjective*— **chroʹmo·somʹic** (krōʹmə-sōʹmĭk)

12

churl·ish (chûr′lĭsh)

adjective

1. Of, like, or befitting a churl; boorish or vulgar. **2.** Having a bad disposition; surly: *"He is as valiant as the lion, churlish as the bear"* (William Shakespeare, *Troilus and Cressida*).

[From *churl*, rude person, from Middle English, from Old English *ceorl*, peasant.]

RELATED WORDS:
    adverb—**chur′lish·ly**
    noun—**chur′lish·ness**

13

cir·cum·lo·cu·tion (sûr′kəm-lō-kyōō′shən)

noun

1. The use of unnecessarily wordy and indirect language: *"There lives no man who at some period has not been tormented, for example, by an earnest desire to tantalize a listener by circumlocution"* (Edgar Allan Poe, *The Imp of the Perverse*). **2.** Evasiveness in speech or writing. **3.** A roundabout expression: *"At such time as"* is a circumlocution for the word *"when."*

[Middle English *circumlocucioun*, from Latin *circumlocūtiō*, *circumlocūtiōn-*, from *circumlocūtus*, past participle of *circumloquī* : *circum-*, around + *loquī*, to speak.]

RELATED WORD:
    adjective—**cir′cum·loc′u·to′ry**
        (sûr′kəm-lŏk′yə-tôr′ē)

There lives no man who at some period has not been tormented, for example, by an earnest desire to tantalize a listener by **circumlocution**.

— Edgar Allan Poe,
The Imp of the Perverse

14

cir·cum·nav·i·gate (sûr′kəm-năv′ĭ-gāt′)

transitive verb

> Past participle and past tense: **cir·cum·nav·i·gat·ed**
> Present participle: **cir·cum·nav·i·gat·ing**
> Third person singular present tense: **cir·cum·nav·i·**
> **gates**

1. To proceed completely around: *"The whale he had struck must also have been on its travels; no doubt it had thrice circumnavigated the globe"* (Herman Melville, *Moby-Dick*). **2.** To go around; circumvent: *I circumnavigated the downtown traffic by taking side streets on the west side of town.*

[*circum-*, around (from Latin) + *navigate*, to sail (from Latin *nāvigāre, nāvigāt-* : *nāvis*, ship + *agere*, to drive, lead).]

RELATED WORDS:

> *noun* — **cir′cum·nav·i·ga′tion**
> (sûr′kəm-năv′ĭ-gā′shən)
> *noun* — **cir′cum·nav′i·ga′tor**

15

de·cid·u·ous (dĭ-sĭj′ōō-əs)

adjective

1. Shedding or losing foliage at the end of the growing season: *"Orange-picking begins in December and overlaps the pruning of the deciduous orchards"* (Mary Austin, *Art Influence in the West*). **2.** Falling off or shed at a specific season or stage of growth: *Male deer have deciduous antlers.* **3.** Not lasting; ephemeral.

[From Latin *dēciduus,* from *dēcidere,* to fall off : *dē-,* down from + *cadere,* to fall.]

RELATED WORDS:
> *adverb* — **de·cid′u·ous·ly**
> *noun* — **de·cid′u·ous·ness**

16

del·e·te·ri·ous (dĕl′ĭ-tîr′ē-əs)

adjective

Having a harmful effect; injurious: *"I will follow that system of regimen which, according to my ability and judgment, I consider for the benefit of my patients, and abstain from whatever is deleterious and mischievous"* (Hippocratic Oath).

[From Greek *dēlētērios,* from *dēlētēr,* destroyer, from *dēleisthai,* to harm.]

RELATED WORDS:
> *adverb* — **del′e·te′ri·ous·ly**
> *noun* — **del′e·te′ri·ous·ness**

17

dif·fi·dent (dĭf′ĭ-dənt *or* dĭf′ĭ-dĕnt′)

adjective

Lacking or marked by a lack of self-confidence; shy and timid: *"He was too diffident to do justice to himself; but when his natural shyness was overcome, his behaviour gave every indication of an open affectionate heart"* (Jane Austen, *Sense and Sensibility*).

[Middle English, from Latin *diffīdēns, diffīdent-*, present participle of *diffīdere*, to mistrust : *dis-*, not, do the opposite of + *fīdere*, to trust.]

RELATED WORD:
adverb — **dif′fi·dent·ly**

18

en·er·vate (ĕn′ər-vāt′)

transitive verb
> Past participle and past tense: **en·er·vat·ed**
> Present participle: **en·er·vat·ing**
> Third person singular present tense: **en·er·vates**

To weaken or destroy the strength or vitality of: *"What is the nature of the luxury which enervates and destroys nations?"* (Henry David Thoreau, *Walden*).

[Latin *ēnervāre, ēnervāt-* : *ē-, ex-*, out of, from + *nervus*, sinew.]

RELATED WORDS:
> *noun* — **en′er·va′tion** (ĕn′ər-vā′shən)
> *adjective* — **en′er·va′tive**
> *noun* — **en′er·va′tor**

✍ **USAGE NOTE:** Sometimes people mistakenly use *enervate* to mean "to invigorate" or "to excite" by assuming that this word is

---

diffident / enfranchise   **108**

a close cousin of *energize*. In fact, *enervate* means essentially the opposite. *Enervate* comes from Latin *nervus*, "sinew," and thus means "to cause to become 'out of muscle'," that is, "to weaken or deplete of strength." *Enervate* has no historical connection with *energize*.

19 en·fran·chise (ĕn-frăn′chīz′)

transitive verb
> Past participle and past tense: **en·fran·chised**
> Present participle: **en·fran·chis·ing**
> Third person singular present tense: **en·fran·chis·es**

1. To endow with the rights of citizenship, especially the right to vote: *Many people who were enfranchised were nonetheless unable to vote because of onerous poll taxes.*
2. To free, as from slavery or bondage.

[Middle English *enfraunchisen*, from Old French *enfranchir, en-franchiss-*, to set free : *en-*, intensive prefix + *franchir*, to free (from *franc*, free).]

RELATED WORD:
> *noun* — **en·fran′chise′ment**

e·piph·a·ny (ĭ-pĭf′ə-nē)

noun

Plural: **e·piph·a·nies**

1. Epiphany a. A Christian feast celebrating the man-ifestation of the divine nature of Jesus to the Gentiles as represented by the Magi. **b.** January 6, on which date this feast is traditionally observed. **2.** A revelatory manifestation of a divine being. **3.** A sudden manifes-tation of the essence or meaning of something; a revela-tion: *"I experienced an epiphany, a spiritual flash that would change the way I viewed myself"* (Frank Maier, *Newsweek*).

[Middle English *epiphanie,* from Old French, from Late Latin *epiphania,* from Greek *epiphaneia,* manifestation, from *epiphainesthai,* to appear : *epi-,* forth + *phainein, phan-,* to show.]

RELATED WORD:

adjective — **ep′i·phan′ic** (ĕp′ə-făn′ĭk)

e·qui·nox (ē′kwə-nŏks′ *or* ĕk′wə-nŏks′)

noun
    Plural: **e·qui·nox·es**

1. Either of the two times during a year when the sun crosses the celestial equator and when the length of day and night are approximately equal: *The vernal equinox occurs on March 20 or 21, and the autumnal equinox occurs on September 22 or 23.* **2.** Either of two points on the celestial sphere at which the ecliptic intersects the celestial equator.

[Middle English, from Old French *equinoxe*, from Medieval Latin *aequinoxium*, from Latin *aequinoctium* : *aequi-*, equal + *nox, noct-*, night.]

RELATED WORD:
    adjective—**e′qui·noc′tial** (ē′kwə-nŏk′shəl *or* ĕk′wə-nŏk′shəl)

eu·ro or Eu·ro (yŏor′ō)

noun
    Plural: **eu·ros or Eu·ros**

The basic unit of currency among members of the European Monetary Union: *Italy and France are two countries that have adopted the euro.*

[After *Europe*.]

23

ev·a·nes·cent (ĕv′ə-nĕs′ənt)

adjective

Vanishing or likely to vanish like vapor: *"Most certainly I shall find this thought a horrible vision—a maddening, but evanescent dream"* (Mary Wollstonecraft Shelley, *The Last Man*).

[From Latin *ēvānēscere*, to vanish : *ē-*, *ex-*, away + *vānēscere*, to disappear (from *vānus*, empty).]

RELATED WORDS:
> *verb* — **ev′a·nesce′** (ĕv′ə-nĕs′)
> *adverb* — **ev′a·nes′cent·ly**

24

ex·pur·gate (ĕk′spər-gāt′)

transitive verb
> Past participle and past tense: **ex·pur·gat·ed**
> Present participle: **ex·pur·gat·ing**
> Third person singular present tense: **ex·pur·gates**

To remove erroneous, vulgar, obscene, or otherwise objectionable material from (a book, for example) before publication: *The R-rated movie was expurgated before it was shown on network television.*

[Latin *expūrgāre*, *expūrgāt-*, to purify : *ex-*, intensive prefix + *pūrgāre*, to cleanse (from *pūrus*, pure).]

RELATED WORDS:
> *noun* — **ex′pur·ga′tion** (ĕk′spər-gā′shən)
> *noun* — **ex′pur·ga′tor**

fa·ce·tious (fə-sē′shəs)

adjective

Playfully jocular; humorous: *The employee's facetious remarks were not appreciated during the meeting.*

[French *facétieux*, from *facétie*, jest, from Latin *facētia*, from *facētus*, witty.]

RELATED WORDS:
    adverb — **fa·ce′tious·ly**
    noun — **fa·ce′tious·ness**

fat·u·ous (făch′ōō-əs)

adjective

Foolish or silly, especially in a smug or self-satisfied way: *"Don't you like the poor lonely bachelor?' he yammered in a fatuous way"* (Sinclair Lewis, *Main Street*).

[From Latin *fatuus*.]

RELATED WORDS:
    adverb — **fat′u·ous·ly**
    noun — **fat′u·ous·ness**

feck·less (fĕk′lĭs)

adjective

1. Lacking purpose or vitality; feeble or ineffective: *"She glowered at the rows of feckless bodies that lay sprawled in the chairs"* (Willa Cather, *The Song of the Lark*). **2.** Careless and irresponsible: *The feckless student turned in yet another late paper.*

[Scots *feck*, effect + *-less*.]

RELATED WORDS:
    adverb—**feck′less·ly**
    noun—**feck′less·ness**

fi·du·ci·ar·y (fĭ-dōō′shē-ĕr′ē *or* fĭ-dōō′shə-rē *or* fī-dōō′shē-ĕr′ē *or* fī-dōō′shə-rē)

adjective

1a. Of or relating to a holding of something in trust for another. **b.** Of or being a trustee or trusteeship. **c.** Held in trust. **2.** Of or consisting of legal tender, especially paper currency, authorized by a government but not based on or convertible into gold or silver.

noun
    Plural: **fi·du·ci·ar·ies**

One, such as a company director, that has a special relation of trust, confidence, or responsibility in certain obligations to others.

[Latin *fīdūciārius*, from *fīdūcia*, trust, from *fīdere*, to trust.]

She was going to have a few things before she died. She realized that there were a great many trains dashing east and west on the face of the continent that night, and that they all carried young people who meant to have things. But the difference was that *she was going to get them!* That was all. Let people try to stop her! She glowered at the rows of **feckless** bodies that lay sprawled in the chairs. Let them try it once!

—Willa Cather,
The Song of the Lark

fil·i·bus·ter (fĭl′ə-bŭs′tər)

noun

1a. The use of obstructionist tactics, especially pro-longed speechmaking, for the purpose of delaying legislative action. **b.** An instance of the use of such tactics: *The senator's filibuster lasted over 24 hours.* **2.** An adventurer who engages in a private military action in a foreign country.

verb

Past participle and past tense: **fil·i·bus·tered**
Present participle: **fil·i·bus·ter·ing**
Third person singular present tense: **fil·i·bus·ters**

intransitive: **1.** To use obstructionist tactics in a legislative body. **2.** To take part in a private military action in a foreign country.

transitive: To use a filibuster against (a legislative measure, for example).

[From Spanish *filibustero*, freebooter, from French *flibustier*, from Dutch *vrijbuiter*, pirate, freebooter, from *vrijbuit*, plunder : *vrij*, free + *buit*, booty (from Middle Dutch *būte*, of Middle Low German origin).]

RELATED WORD:
noun — **fil′i·bus′ter·er**

30

gam·ete (găm′ēt′ *or* gə-mēt′)

noun

A reproductive cell having the haploid number of chromosomes, especially a mature sperm or egg capable of fusing with a gamete of the opposite sex to produce the fertilized egg.

[New Latin *gameta*, from Greek *gametē*, wife, and *gametēs*, husband, from *gamein*, to marry, from *gamos*, marriage.]

RELATED WORD:
    adjective — **ga·met′ic** (gə-mĕt′ĭk)

31

gauche (gōsh)

adjective

Lacking grace or social polish; awkward or tactless: "*A good man often appears gauche simply because he does not take advantage of the myriad mean little chances of making himself look stylish*" (Iris Murdoch, *The Black Prince*).

[French, awkward, lefthanded, from Old French, from *gauchir*, to turn aside, walk clumsily, of Germanic origin.]

RELATED WORDS:
    adverb — **gauche′ly**
    noun — **gauche′ness**

ger·ry·man·der (jĕr′ē-măn′dər *or* gĕr′ē-măn′dər)

transitive verb

> Past participle and past tense: **ger·ry·man·dered**
> Present participle: **ger·ry·man·der·ing**
> Third person singular present tense: **ger·ry·man·ders**

To divide (a geographic area) into voting districts so as to give unfair advantage to one party in elections.

noun

1. The act, process, or an instance of gerrymandering.
2. A district or configuration of districts differing widely in size or population because of gerrymandering.

[After Elbridge *Gerry* + *(sala)mander* (from the shape of an election district created while Gerry was governor of Massachusetts).]

🐉 **WORD HISTORY:** *"An official statement of the returns of voters for senators give[s] twenty nine friends of peace, and eleven gerrymanders."* So reported the May 12, 1813, edition of the *Massachusetts Spy.* A gerrymander sounds like a strange political beast, which it is, considered from a historical perspective. This beast was named by combining the word *salamander,* "a small lizardlike amphibian," with the last name of Elbridge Gerry, a former governor of Massachusetts. Gerry was immortalized in this word because an election district created by members of his party in 1812 looked like a salamander. The word is first recorded in April 1812 in reference to the creature or its caricature, but it soon came to mean not only "the action of shaping a district to gain political advantage" but also "any representative elected from such a district by that method." Within the same year, *gerrymander* was also recorded as a verb.

33

he·gem·o·ny (hĭ-jĕm**′**ə**′**nē *or* hĕj**′**ə-mō**′**nē)

noun
Plural: **he·gem·o·nies**

The predominant influence of a state, region, or group, over others: *The hegemony of communism in Eastern Europe crumbled in the late 1980s.*

[Greek *hēgemoniā,* from *hēgemōn,* leader, from *hēgeisthai,* to lead.]

RELATED WORDS:
adjective—**heg′e·mon′ic** (hĕj**′**ə-mŏn**′**ĭk)
noun & adjective—**he·gem′o·nist** (hə-jĕm**′**ə-nĭst)

🖎 **USAGE NOTE:** *Hegemony* may be stressed on either the first or second syllable. In a 1988 survey of the Usage Panel, 72 percent of the Panelists preferred the latter pronunciation.

34

he·mo·glob·in (hē**′**mə-glō**′**bĭn)

noun

The iron-containing pigment in red blood cells of vertebrates, consisting of about 6 percent heme and 94 percent globin. In vertebrates, hemoglobin carries oxygen from the lungs to the tissues of the body and carries carbon dioxide from the tissues to the lungs.

[Ultimately short for *hematinoglobulin* : *hematin,* a compound formed from hemoglobin (*hemato-,* blood, from Greek *haima,* blood + -*in,* chemical suffix) + *globulin,* a kind of protein (*globule,* from French, from Latin *globulus,* diminutive of *globus,* sphere + -*in,* chemical suffix).]

There is no safety in unlimited technological **hubris**, none in simple-minded trust of the Kremlin, and none in a confident affection for expanding thermonuclear arsenals.

—McGeorge Bundy,
New York Times Magazine

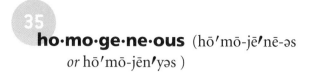

ho·mo·ge·ne·ous (hō′mō-jē′nē-əs
or hō′mō-jēn′yəs)

adjective

1. Uniform in structure or composition: *"Although the Vietnamese in America were at first a homogenous group, in the course of five separate waves of immigration they have encompassed a diverse cross-section of Vietnamese society"* (Lowell Weiss, *Atlantic Monthly*). **2.** Of the same or similar nature or kind. **3.** *Mathematics* Consisting of terms of the same degree or elements of the same dimension.

[From Medieval Latin *homogeneus,* from Greek *homogenēs* : *homo-,* same + *genos,* kind.]

RELATED WORDS:
　　adverb—**ho′mo·ge′ne·ous·ly**
　　noun—**ho′mo·ge′ne·ous·ness**

hu·bris (hyōō′brĭs)

noun

Overbearing pride or presumption; arrogance: *"There is no safety in unlimited technological hubris"* (McGeorge Bundy, *New York Times Magazine*).

[Greek, excessive pride, wanton violence.]

RELATED WORDS:
　　adjective—**hu·bris′tic** (hyōō-brĭs′tĭk)
　　adverb—**hu·bris′tic·al·ly**

hy·pot·e·nuse (hī-pŏt′n-ōōs)

noun

The side of a right triangle opposite the right angle: "*You cannot write a textbook of geometry without reference to a hypotenuse and triangles and a rectangular parallelepiped. You simply have to learn what those words mean or do without mathematics*" (Hendrick Van Loon, *The Story of Mankind*).

[Latin *hypotēnūsa,* from Greek *hupoteinousa,* from feminine present participle of *hupoteinein,* to stretch or extend under : *hupo-,* under + *teinein,* to stretch.]

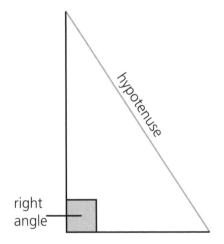

THE HYPOTENUSE
OF A RIGHT TRIANGLE

38

im·peach (ĭm-pēch′)

transitive verb
    Past participle and past tense: **im·peached**
    Present participle: **im·peach·ing**
    Third person singular present tense: **im·peach·es**

1a. To make an accusation against (a person). **b.** To charge (a public official) with improper conduct in office before a proper tribunal: *The House of Representatives impeached Andrew Johnson in 1868 and Bill Clinton in 1998; neither was convicted.* **2.** To challenge the validity of; try to discredit: *The lawyer impeached the witness's credibility with a string of damaging questions.*

[Middle English *empechen*, to impede, accuse, from Anglo-Norman *empecher*, from Late Latin *impedicāre*, to entangle : Latin *in-*, in + Latin *pedica*, fetter.]

RELATED WORDS:
    adjective—**im·peach′a·ble**
    noun—**im·peach′ment**

🖋 **USAGE NOTE:** When an irate citizen demands that a disfavored public official be impeached, the citizen clearly intends for the official to be removed from office. This popular use of *impeach* as a synonym of "throw out" (even if by due process) does not accord with the legal meaning of the word. As recent history has shown, when a public official is impeached, that is, formally accused of wrongdoing, this is only the start of what can be a lengthy process that may or may not lead to the official's removal from office. In strict usage, an official is impeached (accused), tried, and then convicted or acquitted. The vaguer use of *impeach* reflects disgruntled citizens' indifference to whether the official is forced from office by legal means or chooses to resign to avoid further disgrace.

in·cog·ni·to (ĭn'kŏg-nē'tō)

adjective & adverb

With one's identity disguised or concealed: *The spy traveled incognito into enemy territory.*

noun
Plural: in·cog·ni·tos

The identity assumed by a person whose actual identity is disguised or concealed.

[Italian, from Latin *incognitus*, unknown : *in-*, not + *cognitus*, past participle of *cognōscere*, to learn, recognize.]

in·con·tro·vert·i·ble (ĭn-kŏn'trə-vûr'tə-bəl *or* ĭn'kŏn-trə-vûr'tə-bəl)

adjective

Impossible to dispute; unquestionable: *The lawyer presented incontrovertible proof of her client's innocence.*

[*in-*, not + *controvertible*, able to be opposed by argument, from *controvert*, to oppose by argument, back-formation from *controversy* (on the model of such pairs as *inverse, invert*), from Middle English *controversie*, from Latin *contrōversia*, from *contrōversus*, disputed: *contrō-*, variant of *contrā-*, against + *versus*, past participle of *vertere*, to turn.]

RELATED WORDS:
> *noun* — **in·con'tro·vert'i·bil'i·ty**
> *adverb* — **in·con'tro·vert'i·bly**

41

in·cul·cate (ĭn-kŭl′kāt′ *or* ĭn′kŭl-kāt′)

transitive verb
> Past participle and past tense: **in·cul·ca·ted**
> Present participle: **in·cul·ca·ting**
> Third person singular present tense: **in·cul·cates**

1. To impress (something) upon the mind of another by frequent instruction or repetition; instill: "*In the jungle might is right, nor does it take long to inculcate this axiom in the mind of a jungle dweller, regardless of what his past training may have been*" (Edgar Rice Burroughs, *The Son of Tarzan*). **2.** To teach (others) by frequent instruction or repetition; indoctrinate: *inculcate the young with a sense of duty.*

[Latin *inculcāre, inculcāt-*, to force upon : *in-*, on + *calcāre*, to trample (from *calx, calc-*, heel).]

RELATED WORDS:
> *noun* — **in′cul·ca′tion** (ĭn′kŭl-kā′shən)
> *noun* — **in·cul′ca′tor**

42

in·fra·struc·ture (ĭn′frə-strŭk′chər)

noun

1. The basic facilities, services, and installations needed for the functioning of a community or society, such as transportation and communications systems, water and power lines, and public institutions including schools, post offices, and prisons: *"To be fair, none of us really knows how much the country's infrastructure—services to the desperate underclass—had improved during the ten years from when we left until the Revolution"* (Terence Ward, *Searching for Hassan*). **2.** The basic system or underlying structure of an organization.

[*infra-*, below (from Latin *īnfrā*) + *structure* (from Middle English, the process of building, from Latin *strūctūra*, from *strūctus*, past participle of *struere*, to construct).]

Never in my life had I seen conditions as grim. To be fair, none of us really knows how much the country's **infrastructure** — services to the desperate underclass — had improved during the ten years from when we left until the Revolution. But one thing's certain. Whatever changes took place, it was too little, too late. Those forlorn dust heaps of villages, cut off from the world, with no medical facilities, no school, no decent roads to get goods to market. There seemed to be no hope at all.

— Terence Ward,
Searching for Hassan

43

in·ter·po·late (ĭn-tûr′pə-lāt′)

verb
> Past participle and past tense: **in·ter·po·la·ted**
> Present participle: **in·ter·po·la·ting**
> Third person singular present tense: **in·ter·po·lates**

transitive: **1.** To insert or introduce between other elements or parts. **2a.** To insert (material) into a text. **b.** To insert into a conversation. **3.** To change or falsify (a text) with new or incorrect material. **4.** *Mathematics* To estimate a value of (a function or series) between two known values: *The researchers had actual statistics for the years 1998, 2000, and 2002, and they interpolated the values for 1999 and 2001.*

intransitive: To make insertions or additions.

[Latin *interpolāre, interpolāt-*, to touch up, refurbish, from *interpolis*, refurbished; akin to *polīre*, to polish.]

RELATED WORDS:
> *noun* — **in·ter′po·la′tion** (ĭn-tûr′pə-lā′shən)
> *adjective* — **in·ter′po·la′tive**
> *noun* — **in·ter′po·la′tor**

44

i·ro·ny (ī′rə-nē *or* ī′ər-nē)

noun
> Plural: **i·ro·nies**

1a. The use of words to express something different from and often opposite to their literal meaning. **b.** An expression or utterance marked by a deliberate contrast between apparent and intended meaning. **c.** A literary

---

style employing such contrasts for humorous or rhetorical effect. **2a.** Incongruity between what might be expected and what actually occurs. **b.** An occurrence, result, or circumstance notable for such incongruity. **3.** The dramatic effect achieved by leading an audience to understand an incongruity between a situation and the accompanying speeches, while the characters in the play remain unaware of the incongruity; dramatic irony.

[French *ironie*, from Old French, from Latin *īrōnīa*, from Greek *eirōneia*, feigned ignorance, from *eirōn*, dissembler, probably from *eirein*, to say.]

RELATED WORDS:
> *adjective* — **i·ron′ic**
> *adverb* — **i·ron′i·cal·ly**

🙣 **USAGE NOTE:** The words *ironic, irony,* and *ironically* are sometimes used of events and circumstances that might better be described as simply "coincidental" or "improbable," in that they suggest no particular lessons about human vanity or folly. The Usage Panel dislikes the looser use of these words; 78 percent reject the use of *ironically* in the sentence *In 1969 Susie moved from Ithaca to California where she met her husband-to-be, who, ironically, also came from upstate New York.* Some Panelists noted that this particular usage might be acceptable if Susie had in fact moved to California in order to find a husband, in which case the story could be taken as exemplifying the folly of supposing that we can know what fate has in store for us. By contrast, 73 percent accepted the sentence *Ironically, even as the government was fulminating against American policy, American jeans and videocassettes were the hottest items in the stalls of the market,* where the incongruity can be seen as an example of human inconsistency.

je·june (jə-jo͞on′)

adjective

1. Not interesting; dull: *"Let a professor of law or physic find his place in a lecture room, and there pour forth jejune words and useless empty phrases, and he will pour them forth to empty benches"* (Anthony Trollope, *Barchester Towers*). **2.** Lacking maturity; childish: *The coach was dismayed at the players' jejune behavior after they won the game.* **3.** Lacking in nutrition: *The sickly child suffered from a jejune diet.*

[From Latin *iēiūnus*, meager, dry, fasting.]

RELATED WORDS:
> *adverb* — **je·june′ly**
> *noun* — **je·june′ness**

ki·net·ic (kə-nĕt′ĭk *or* kī-nĕt′ĭk)

adjective

1. Of, relating to, or produced by motion: *Any object that is moving has kinetic energy.* **2.** Relating to or exhibiting kinesis (movement or activity of an organism in response to a stimulus such as light).

[Greek *kīnētikos*, from *kīnētos*, moving, from *kīnein*, to move.]

RELATED WORD:
> *adverb* — **ki·net′i·cal·ly**

kow·tow (kou-tou′ *or* kou′tou′)

intransitive verb
>Past participle and past tense: **kow·towed**
>Present participle: **kow·tow·ing**
>Third person singular present tense: **kow·tows**

1. To kneel and touch the forehead to the ground in expression of deep respect, worship, or submission, as formerly done in China. **2.** To show servile deference: *Because everyone on staff was afraid of being laid off, they all kowtowed to their strict boss.*

noun

1. The act of kneeling and touching the forehead to the ground: *"We were always greeted in a grassy area near the headmen's fortresses, where tents were pitched especially for me to receive kowtows, enjoy good food, and watch singing and dancing"* (Alai, *Red Poppies*). **2.** An obsequious act.

[From Chinese (Mandarin) *kòu tóu* : *kòu*, to knock + *tóu*, head.]

lais·sez faire also lais·ser faire
(lĕs'ā fâr' *or* lā'zā fâr')

noun

1. An economic doctrine that opposes governmental regulation of or interference in commerce beyond the minimum necessary for a free-enterprise system to operate according to its own economic laws. **2.** Noninterference in the affairs of others.

[French : *laissez*, second person plural imperative of *laisser*, to let, allow (from Latin *laxāre*, to loosen, from *laxus*, loose) + *faire*, to do (from Latin *facere*).]

lex·i·con (lĕk'sĭ-kŏn')

noun
Plural: **lex·i·cons** or **lex·i·ca** (lĕk'sĭ-kə')

1. A dictionary. **2.** A stock of terms used in a particular profession, subject, or style; a vocabulary: *The lexicon of anatomy includes terms such as "aorta" and "duodenum."*

[Medieval Latin, from Greek *lexikon (biblion)*, word (book), neuter of *lexikos*, of words, from *lexis*, word, from *legein*, to speak.]

RELATED WORDS:
adjective— **lex'i·cal**
adverb— **lex'i·cal·ly**

50

lo·qua·cious (lō-kwāʹshəs)

adjective

Very talkative; garrulous: *The loquacious barber always told stories while cutting the customers' hair.*

[From Latin *loquāx, loquāc-*, from *loquī*, to speak.]

RELATED WORDS:
> *adverb*—**lo·quaʹcious·ly**
> *noun*—**lo·quaʹcious·ness**
> *noun*—**lo·quacʹi·ty** (lō-kwăsʹĭ-tē)

51

lu·gu·bri·ous (lŏŏ-gōōʹbrē-əs)

adjective

Mournful, dismal, or gloomy, especially to an exaggerated or ludicrous degree: *"This croak was as lugubrious as a coffin"* (Stephen Crane, *The Sergeant's Private Madhouse*).

[From Latin *lūgubris*, from *lūgēre*, to mourn.]

RELATED WORDS:
> *adverb*—**lu·guʹbri·ous·ly**
> *noun*—**lu·guʹbri·ous·ness**

met·a·mor·pho·sis (mĕt′ə-môr′fə-sĭs)

noun

Plural: **met·a·mor·pho·ses** (mĕt′ə-môr′fə-sēz′)

1. A marked change in appearance, character, condition, or function; a transformation: *"I sought out the myths of metamorphosis, tales of the weaver Arachne, who hanged herself and was changed by Athena into a spider"* (Jennifer Ackerman, *Chance in the House of Fate*). **2.** *Biology* Change in the form and often habits of an animal during normal development after the embryonic stage. Metamorphosis includes, in insects, the transformation of a maggot into an adult fly and a caterpillar into a butterfly, and, in amphibians, the changing of a tadpole into a frog.

[Latin *metamorphōsis*, from Greek, from *metamorphoun*, to transform : *meta-*, meta- + *morphē*, form.]

RELATED WORDS:

　　　adjective—**met′a·mor′phic** (mĕt′ə-môr′fĭk)
　　　verb—**met′a·mor′phose** (mĕt′ə-môr′fōz′ *or* mĕt′ə-môr′fōs′)
　　　adjective—**met′a·mor′phous** (mĕt′ə-môr′fəs)

53

mi·to·sis (mī-tō′sĭs)

noun
　　Plural: **mi·to·ses** (mī-tō′sēz)

The process in cell division by which the nucleus divides, typically consisting of four stages, prophase, metaphase, anaphase, and telophase, and normally resulting in two new nuclei, each of which contains a complete copy of the parental chromosomes. Division of the cytoplasm follows the division of the nucleus, resulting in the formation of two distinct cells.

[Greek *mitos*, warp thread + -*ōsis*, condition.]

RELATED WORDS:
　　adjective— **mi·tot′ic** (mī-tŏt′ĭk)
　　adverb— **mi·tot′i·cal·ly**

54

moi·e·ty (moi′ĭ-tē)

noun
　　Plural: **moi·e·ties**

1. A half: "*Tom divided the cake and Becky ate with good appetite, while Tom nibbled at his moiety*" (Mark Twain, *The Adventures of Tom Sawyer*). **2.** A part, portion, or share. **3.** Either of two kinship groups based on unilateral descent that together make up a tribe or society.

[Middle English *moite*, from Old French *meitiet, moitie*, from Late Latin *medietās*, from Latin, the middle, from *medius*, middle.]

nan·o·tech·nol·o·gy (năn′ə-tĕk-nŏl′ə-jē)

noun

The science and technology of building devices, such as electronic circuits, from individual atoms and molecules.

[*nano-*, at the molecular level (from Greek *nānos, nannos,* little old man, dwarf, from *nannās,* uncle) + *technology* (Greek *tekhnē,* art, skill + Greek *-logiā,* study, from *logos,* word).]

RELATED WORD:
 noun— **nan′o·tech·nol′o·gist**

ni·hil·ism (nī′ə-lĭz′əm *or* nē′ə-lĭz′əm)

noun

1. *Philosophy* **a.** An extreme form of skepticism that denies that existence is real: *"Nihilism is not only despair and negation, but above all the desire to despair and to negate"* (Albert Camus, *The Rebel*). **b.** The belief that all values are baseless and that nothing can be known or communicated. **2.** The rejection of all distinctions in moral or religious value and a willingness to repudiate all previous theories of morality or religious belief. **3.** The belief that destruction of existing political or social institutions is necessary for future improvement. **4.** also **Nihilism** A movement of mid-19th-century Russia that scorned authority and believed in reason, materialism, and radical change in society through terrorism and assassination. **5.** *Psychology* A delusion that the world or one's mind, body, or self does not exist.

[Latin *nihil*, nothing + *-ism.*]

RELATED WORDS:
        noun—**ni′hi·list**
        adjective—**ni′hi·lis′tic**
        adverb—**ni′hi·lis′ti·cal·ly**

57

no·men·cla·ture (nō′mən-klā′chər
or nō-mĕn′klə-chər)

noun

1. A system of names used in an art or science: *The nomenclature of mineralogy is a classification of types of rock.* **2.** The procedure of assigning names to organisms listed in a taxonomic classification: *Our biology teacher explained the rules of nomenclature for plants and animals.*

[Latin *nōmenclātūra*, from *nōmenclātor*, nomenclator, a slave who accompanied his master to tell him the names of people he met, variant of *nōmenculātor* : *nōmen*, name + *calātor*, servant, crier (from *calāre*, to call).]

58

non·sec·tar·i·an (nŏn′sĕk-târ′ē-ən)

adjective

Not limited to or associated with a particular religious denomination: *The airport chapel conducts nonsectarian services daily.*

[*non-*, not (from Middle English, from Old French, from Latin *nōn*) + *sectarian*, partisan (*sect*, sect, ultimately from Latin *sequī*, to follow + *-arian*, belonging to).]

RELATED WORD:
  noun—**non′sec·tar′i·an·ism**

59

no·ta·rize (nō′tə-rīz′)

transitive verb

    Past participle and past tense: **no·ta·rized**
    Present participle: **no·ta·riz·ing**
    Third person singular present tense: **no·ta·riz·es**

To certify or attest to (the validity of a signature on a document, for example) as a notary public: *Before I submitted the sales agreement at the real estate office, it had to be notarized.*

[*notar(y)* (from Middle English *notarie*, from Old French, from Latin *notārius*, relating to shorthand, shorthand writer, from *nota*, mark) + *-ize.*]

RELATED WORD:
    noun—**no′ta·ri·za′tion** (nō′tə-rĭ-zā′shən)

60

ob·se·qui·ous
    (ŏb-sē′kwē-əs *or* əb-sē′kwē-əs)

adjective

Full of or exhibiting servile compliance; fawning: *The movie star was surrounded by a large group of obsequious assistants.*

[Middle English, from Latin *obsequiōsus*, from *obsequium*, compliance, from *obsequī*, to comply : *ob-*, to; + *sequī*, to follow.]

RELATED WORDS:
    adverb—**ob·se′qui·ous·ly**
    noun—**ob·se′qui·ous·ness**

For they that are discontented under monarchy call it tyranny; and they that are displeased with aristocracy call it **oligarchy**: so also, they which find themselves grieved under a democracy call it anarchy.

— Thomas Hobbes,
Leviathan

ol·i·gar·chy (ŏl′ĭ-gär′kē *or* ō′lĭ-gär′kē)

noun
   Plural: **ol·i·gar·chies**

1a. Government by a few, especially by a small faction of persons or families: *"They that are displeased with aristocracy call it oligarchy"* (Thomas Hobbes, *Leviathan*). **b.** Those making up such a government. **2.** A state governed by a few persons.

[*olig(o)-*, few (from Greek *oligos*, little) + *-archy*, rule (from Greek *-arkhiā*, from *arkhein*, to rule).]

RELATED WORDS:
   adjective — **ol′i·gar′chic** (ŏl′ĭ-gär′kĭk
      or ō′lĭ-gär′kĭk)
   adjective — **ol′i·gar′chic·al**

62

om·nip·o·tent (ŏm-nĭp′ə-tənt)

adjective

Having unlimited or universal power, authority, or force; all-powerful: *"I began to instruct him in the knowledge of the true God . . . that He was omnipotent, and could do everything for us, give everything to us, take everything from us"* (Daniel Defoe, *Robinson Crusoe*).

noun

the Omnipotent God.

[Middle English, from Old French, from Latin *omnipotēns*, *omnipotent-* : *omni-*, all + *potēns*, present participle of *posse*, to be able.]

RELATED WORDS:
  noun — **om·nip′o·tence**
  noun — **om·nip′o·ten·cy**
  adverb — **om·nip′o·tent·ly**

---

63 **or·thog·ra·phy** (ôr-thŏg′rə-fē)

noun
   Plural: **or·thog·ra·phies**

1. The art or study of correct spelling according to established usage. **2.** The aspect of language study concerned with letters and their sequences in words. **3.** A
method of representing a language or the sounds of
language by written symbols; spelling: *The orthography
of Spanish includes the letters í and ñ.*

[*ortho-*, straight, correct (from Greek *orthos*) + *-graphy*,
writing (from Greek *-graphiā*, from *graphein*, to write).]

RELATED WORDS:
   noun — **or·thog′ra·pher**
   noun — **or·thog′ra·phist**
   adjective — **or′tho·graph′ic** (ôr′thə-grăf′ĭk)
   adverb — **or′tho·graph′i·cal·ly**

64

ox·i·dize (ŏk′sĭ-dīz′)

verb

   Past participle and past tense: **ox·i·dized**
   Present participle: **ox·i·diz·ing**
   Third person singular present tense: **ox·i·diz·es**

transitive **1.** To combine with oxygen; make into an oxide: *The metal fender had begun to oxidize, as evidenced by the large rust stains.* **2.** To increase the positive charge or valence of (an element) by removing electrons. **3.** To coat with oxide.

intransitive To become oxidized.

[*oxid(e)*, compound containing oxygen (from French : *ox(ygène)*, oxygen + *(ac)ide*, acid) + *-ize.*]

RELATED WORDS:
   adjective—**ox′i·di′za·ble**
   noun—**ox′i·di·za′tion** (ŏk′sĭ-dĭ-zā′shən)

pa·rab·o·la (pə-răb′ə-lə)

noun

A plane curve formed by the intersection of a right circular cone and a plane parallel to an element of the cone or by the locus of points equidistant from a fixed line and a fixed point not on the line.

[New Latin, from Greek *parabolē*, comparison, application, parabola (from the relationship between the line joining the vertices of a conic and the line through its focus and parallel to its directrix), from *paraballein*, to compare : *para-*, beside + *ballein*, to throw.]

RELATED WORD:

  adjective— **par′a·bol′ic** (păr′ə-bŏl′ĭk)

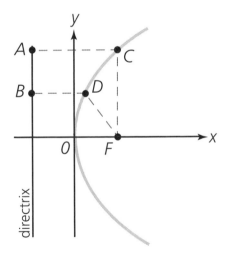

PARABOLA

Any point on a parabola is the same distance from the directrix as it is from the focus. *AC* = *CF* and *BD* = *DF*.

par·a·digm (păr′ə-dīm′ *or* păr′ə-dĭm′)

noun

1. One that serves as pattern or model. **2.** A set or list of all the inflectional forms of a word or of one of its grammatical categories: *The Latin textbook outlined the paradigms of the different sets of regular verbs.* **3.** A set of assumptions, concepts, values, and practices that constitutes a way of viewing reality for the community that shares them, especially in an intellectual discipline.

[Middle English, example, from Late Latin *paradīgma*, from Greek *paradeigma*, from *paradeiknunai*, to compare : *para-*, alongside + *deiknunai*, to show.]

RELATED WORD:

adjective—**par′a·dig·mat′ic** (păr′ə-dĭg-măt′ĭk)

🖉 **USAGE NOTE:** *Paradigm* first appeared in English in the 15th century, meaning "an example or pattern," and it still bears this meaning today: *Their company is a paradigm of small high-tech firms.* For nearly 400 years *paradigm* has also been applied to the patterns of inflections that are used to sort the verbs, nouns, and other parts of speech of a language into groups that are more easily studied. Since the 1960s, *paradigm* has been used in science to refer to a theoretical framework, as when Nobel Laureate David Baltimore cited colleagues' work that "*really established a new paradigm for our understanding of the causation of cancer.*" Thereafter, researchers in many different fields, including sociology and literary criticism, often saw themselves as working in or trying to break out of paradigms. Applications of the term in other contexts show that it can sometimes be used more loosely to mean "the prevailing view of things." In a 1994 Usage Panel survey, the Panelists split down the middle on these nonscientific uses of *paradigm.* Fifty-two percent disapproved of the sentence *The paradigm governing international competition and competitiveness has shifted dramatically in the last three decades.*

---

paradigm

Paradigm of present tense Spanish verbs with infinitives ending in -AR

-o	-amos
-as	-áis
-a	-an

hablar — to speak

First person singular: *habl<u>o</u>*

Second person singular: *habl<u>as</u>*

Third person singular: *habl<u>a</u>*

First person plural: *habl<u>amos</u>*

Second person plural: *habl<u>áis</u>*

Third person plural: *habl<u>an</u>*

pa·ram·e·ter (pə-răm**′**ĭ-tər)

noun

1. *Mathematics* **a.** A constant in an equation that varies in other equations of the same general form, especially such a constant in the equation of a curve or surface that can be varied to represent a family of curves or surfaces. **b.** One of a set of independent variables that express the coordinates of a point. **2a.** One of a set of measurable factors, such as temperature and pressure, that define a system and determine its behavior and are varied in an experiment. **b.** *(Usage Problem)* A factor that restricts what is possible or what results. **c.** A factor that determines a range of variations; a boundary: *The principal of the experimental school made sure that the parameters of its curriculum continued to expand.* **3.** *Statistics* A quantity, such as a mean, that is calculated from data and describes a population. **4.** *(Usage Problem)* A distinguishing characteristic or feature.

[New Latin *parametrum*, a line through the focus and parallel to the directrix of a conic : Greek *para-*, beside + Greek *metron*, measure.]

RELATED WORDS:

> *verb*—**pa·ram′e·ter·ize′** (pə-răm**′**ə-tə-rīz**′**)
> *adjective*—**par′a·met′ric** (păr**′**ə-mĕt**′**rĭk)
> *adjective*—**par′a·met′ri·cal**
> *adverb*—**par′a·met′ri·cal·ly**

✍ **USAGE NOTE:** The term *parameter,* which originates in mathematics, has a number of specific meanings in fields such as astronomy, electricity, crystallography, and statistics. Perhaps because of its ring of technical authority, it has been used more generally in recent years to refer to any factor that determines a range of variations and especially to a factor that restricts what can result from a process or policy. In this use it often comes close to meaning "a limit or boundary." Some of these new uses have a clear connection to the technical senses of the word. For example, the provisions of a zoning ordinance that limit the height or density of new construction can be reasonably likened to mathematical parameters that establish the limits of other variables. Therefore one can say *The zoning commission announced new planning parameters for the historic district of the city.* But other uses go one step further and treat *parameter* as a high-toned synonym for *characteristic.* In the 1988 Usage Panel Survey, 80 percent of Panelists rejected this use of *parameter* in the example *The Judeo-Christian ethic is one of the important parameters of Western culture.*

Some of the difficulties with the nontechnical use of *parameter* appear to arise from its resemblance to the word *perimeter,* with which it shares the sense "limit," though the precise meanings of the two words differ. This confusion probably explains the use of *parameter* in a sentence such as *US forces report that the parameters of the mine area in the Gulf are fairly well established,* where the word *perimeter* would have expressed the intended sense more exactly. This example of a use of *parameter* was unacceptable to 61 percent of the Usage Panel.

There had come an improvement in their **pecuniary** position, which earlier in their experience would have made them cheerful. Jude had quite unexpectedly found good employment at his old trade almost directly he arrived, the summer weather suiting his fragile constitution; and outwardly his days went on with that monotonous uniformity which is in itself so grateful after vicissitude.

— Thomas Hardy,
Jude the Obscure

68

pe·cu·ni·ar·y (pǐ-kyōō′nē-ěr′ē)

adjective

1. Of or relating to money: *"There had come an improvement in their pecuniary position, which earlier in their experience would have made them cheerful"* (Thomas Hardy, *Jude the Obscure*). **2.** Requiring payment of money: *A speeding ticket is generally a pecuniary offense.*

[Latin *pecūniārius*, from *pecūnia*, property, wealth, money.]

RELATED WORD:
  adverb— **pe·cu′ni·ar′i·ly**

69

pho·to·syn·the·sis (fō′tō-sǐn′thǐ-sǐs)

noun

The process by which green plants and certain other organisms synthesize carbohydrates from carbon dioxide and water using light as an energy source. Most forms of photosynthesis release oxygen as a byproduct.

[*photo-*, light (from Greek *phōto-*, from *phōs, phōt-*) + *synthesis*, the building of chemical compounds (from Latin, collection, from Greek *sunthesis*, from *suntithenai*, to put together : *sun-*, with, together + *tithenai*, *the-*, to put).]

RELATED WORDS:
  verb— **pho′to·syn′the·size′**
      (fō′tō-sǐn′thǐ-sīz′)
  adjective— **pho′to·syn·thet′ic**
      (fō′tō-sǐn-thět′ǐk)
  adverb— **pho′to·syn·thet′i·cal·ly**

---

pla·gia·rize (plā′jə-rīz′)

verb

> Past participle and past tense: **pla·gia·rized**
> Present participle: **pla·gia·riz·ing**
> Third person singular present tense: **pla·gia·riz·es**

transitive **1.** To use and pass off (the ideas or writings of another) as one's own: *Gina plagiarized a science website by cutting and pasting large portions of its text into her paper.* **2.** To appropriate for use as one's own passages or ideas from (another): *Because Darren plagiarized Charles Dickens, the teacher could easily determine that he had cheated.*

intransitive To put forth as original to oneself the ideas or words of another: *Our teacher's policy is to fail any student who plagiarizes.*

[From Latin *plagiārius*, kidnapper, one who plagiarizes, from *plagium*, kidnapping, from *plaga*, net.]

RELATED WORD:

> *noun* — **pla′gia·riz′er**

plas·ma (plăz′mə) also **plasm** (plăz′əm)

noun

1. The clear yellowish fluid portion of blood or lymph in which cells are suspended. It differs from serum in that it contains fibrin and other soluble clotting elements. **2.** Blood plasma that has been sterilized and from which all cells have been removed, used in transfusions. **3.** The protoplasm or cytoplasm of a cell. **4.** The fluid portion of milk from which the curd has been separated by coagulation; whey. **5.** An electrically neutral state of matter similar to a gas but consisting of positively charged ions with most or all of their detached electrons moving freely about. Plasmas are produced by very high temperatures, as in the sun, and also by the ionization resulting from exposure to an electric current, as in a neon sign. Plasmas are distinct from solids, liquids, and normal gases.

[New Latin, from Late Latin, image, figure, from Greek, from *plassein*, to mold.]

RELATED WORDS:
    adjective—**plas·mat′ic** (plăz-măt′ĭk)
    adjective—**plas′mic** (plăz′mĭk)

pol·y·mer (pŏl′ə-mər)

noun

Any of numerous natural or synthetic compounds of usually high molecular weight consisting of repeated linked units, each a relatively light and simple molecule: *Some polymers, like cellulose, occur naturally, while others, like nylon, are artificial.*

[Greek *polumerēs*, consisting of many parts : *polu-*, many- + *meros*, part.]

pre·cip·i·tous (prĭ-sĭp′ĭ-təs)

adjective

1. Resembling a precipice; extremely steep. **2.** Having several precipices: *The hikers avoided the trail through the precipitous areas of the park.* **3.** *(Usage Problem)* Extremely rapid or abrupt; precipitate.

[Probably from obsolete *precipitious*, from Latin *praecipitium*, precipice, from *praeceps, praecipit-*, headlong : *prae-*, before, in front + *caput, capit-*, head.]

RELATED WORDS:

> *adverb* — **pre·cip′i·tous·ly**
> *noun* — **pre·cip′i·tous·ness**

✍ **USAGE NOTE:** The adjective *precipitate* and the adverb *precipitately* were once applied to physical steepness but are now used primarily of rash, headlong actions: *Their precipitate entry into the foreign markets led to disaster. He withdrew precipitately from the race.* Precipitous currently means "steep" in both literal and figurative senses: *the precipitous rapids of the upper river; a precipitous drop in commodity prices.* But *precipitous* and *precipi-*

tously are also frequently used to mean "abrupt, hasty," which takes them into territory that would ordinarily belong to *precipitate* and *precipitately*: *their precipitous decision to leave.* This usage is a natural extension of the use of *precipitous* to describe a rise or fall in a quantity over time: *a precipitous increase in reports of measles* is also an abrupt or sudden event. Though this extended use of *precipitous* is well attested in the work of reputable writers, it is still widely regarded as an error.

qua·sar (kwā′sär′)

noun

An extremely distant, and thus old, celestial object whose power output is several thousand times that of the entire Milky Way galaxy. Some quasars are more than ten billion light years away from earth.

[*quas(i-stellar) + (st)ar.*]

75

quo·tid·i·an (kwō-tĭd′ē-ən)

adjective

Commonplace or ordinary, as from everyday experi-ence: *"There's nothing quite like a real ... train conductor to add color to a quotidian commute"* (Anita Diamant, *Boston Magazine*).

[Middle English *cotidien*, from Old French, from Latin *quōtīdiānus*, from *quōtīdiē*, each day : *quot*, how many, as many as + *diē*, ablative of *diēs*, day.]

re·ca·pit·u·late (rē′kə-pĭch′ə-lāt′)

verb

> Past participle and past tense: **re·ca·pit·u·lat·ed**
> Present participle: **re·ca·pit·u·lat·ing**
> Third person singular present tense: **re·ca·pit·u·lates**

transitive **1.** To repeat in concise form: "*Uninitiated readers can approach this bewitching new rogue's tale as if nothing had happened. Whatever took place previously is recapitulated, now bathed in the warm light of memory*" (Janet Maslin, *New York Times*). **2.** *Biology* To appear to repeat (the evolutionary stages of the species) during the embryonic development of the individual organism.

intransitive To make a summary: *At the end of my presentation about the solar system, the teacher asked me to recapitulate.*

[Latin *recapitulāre, recapitulāt-* : *re-*, again + *capitulum*, main point, heading, diminutive of *caput, capit-*, head.]

RELATED WORDS:

> *noun*—**re′ca·pit′u·la′tion**
> (rē′kə-pĭch′ə-lā′shən)
> *adjective*—**re′ca·pit′u·la′tive**
> *adjective*—**re′ca·pit′u·la·to′ry**

re·cip·ro·cal (rĭ-sĭp′rə-kəl)

adjective

1. Existing, done, or experienced on both sides: *The two chess players showed reciprocal respect throughout the match.* **2.** Done, given, felt, or owed in return: *After hearing the emcee's kind remark, the guest of honor felt obliged to make a reciprocal compliment.* **3.** Interchangeable; complementary: *The hardware store stocks reciprocal electric outlets.* **4.** *Grammar* Expressing mutual action or relationship. Used of some verbs and compound pronouns. **5.** *Mathematics* Of or relating to the reciprocal of a quantity. **6.** *Physiology* Of or relating to a neuromuscular phenomenon in which the inhibition of one group of muscles accompanies the excitation of another. **7.** *Genetics* Of or being a pair of crosses in which the male or female parent in one cross is of the same genotype or phenotype as the complementary female or male parent in the other cross.

noun

1. Something that is reciprocal to something else. **2.** *Mathematics* A number related to another in such a way that when multiplied together their product is 1. For example, the reciprocal of 7 is 1/7; the reciprocal of 2/3 is 3/2.

[From Latin *reciprocus*, alternating.]

RELATED WORDS:

    noun — **re·cip′ro·cal′i·ty**
    adverb — **re·cip′ro·cal·ly**
    noun — **rec′i·proc′i·ty** (rĕs′ə-prŏs′ĭ-tē)

78

rep·a·ra·tion (rĕp′ə-rā′shən)

noun

1. The act or process of making amends for a wrong.
2. Something done or money paid to compensate or make amends for a wrong. **3. reparations** Compensation or remuneration required from a defeated nation as indemnity for damage or injury during a war.
4. The act or process of repairing or the condition of being repaired.

[Middle English *reparacion*, from Old French, from Late Latin *reparātiō, reparātiōn-*, restoration, from Latin *reparātus*, past participle of *reparāre*, to repair : *re-*, again + *parāre*, to prepare.]

res·pi·ra·tion (rĕs′pə-rā′shən)

noun

1a. The act or process of inhaling and exhaling; breathing: *"Every sudden emotion, including astonishment, quickens the action of the heart, and with it the respiration"* (Charles Darwin, *The Expression of the Emotions in Man and Animal*). **b.** The act or process by which an organism without lungs, such as a fish or a plant, exchanges gases with its environment. **2a.** The oxidative process in living cells by which the chemical energy of organic molecules is released in metabolic steps involving the consumption of oxygen and the liberation of carbon dioxide and water. **b.** Any of various analogous metabolic processes by which certain organisms, such as fungi and anaerobic bacteria, obtain energy from organic molecules.

[Latin *respīrātiō, respīrātiōn-*, from *respīrātus*, past participle of *respīrāre*, to breathe again : *re-*, again + *spīrāre*, to breathe.]

RELATED WORDS:
 adjective—**re′spi·ra′tion·al**
 adverb—**re′spi·ra′tion·al·ly**
 verb—**re·spire′** (rĭ-spīr′)

---

respiration

Every sudden emotion, including astonishment, quickens the action of the heart, and with it the **respiration**.

— Charles Darwin,
The Expression of the Emotions in Man and Animal

san·guine (săng′gwĭn)

adjective

1. Cheerfully confident; optimistic: *"Haggard and red-eyed, his hopes plainly had deserted him, his sanguine mood was gone, and all his worst misgivings had come back"* (Charles Dickens, *The Mystery of Edwin Drood*). **2a.** In medieval physiology, having blood as the dominant humor. **b.** Having the temperament and ruddy complexion once thought to be characteristic of this humor; passionate. **3a.** Of the color of blood; red: *"This fellow here, with envious carping tongue / Up-braided me about the rose I wear / Saying the sanguine colour of the leaves / Did represent my master's blushing cheeks"* (William Shakespeare, *Henry VI, Part I*). **b.** Of a healthy reddish color; ruddy: *Because he worked outdoors, the farmer had a sanguine complexion.*

[Middle English, from Old French *sanguin*, from Latin *sanguineus*, from *sanguis, sanguin-*, blood.]

RELATED WORDS:
> *adverb* — **san′guine·ly**
> *noun* — **san′guine·ness**
> *noun* — **san·guin′i·ty**

WORD HISTORY: The similarity in form between *sanguine*, "cheerfully optimistic," and *sanguinary*, "bloodthirsty," may prompt one to wonder how they have come to have such different meanings. The explanation lies in medieval physiology with its notion of the four humors or bodily fluids (blood, bile, phlegm, and black bile). The relative proportions of these fluids was thought to determine a person's temperament. If blood was the predominant humor, one had a ruddy face and a disposition marked by courage, hope, and a readiness to fall in love. Such a temperament was called *sanguine,* the Middle English ancestor of our word *sanguine.* The source of the Middle English word was Old French *sanguin,* itself from Latin *sanguineus.* Both the Old French and Latin words meant "bloody," "blood-colored," Old French *sanguin* having the sense "sanguine in temperament" as well. Latin *sanguineus* was in turn derived from *sanguis,* "blood," just as English *sanguinary* is. The English adjective *sanguine,* first recorded in Middle English before 1350, continues to refer to the cheerfulness and optimism that accompanied a sanguine temperament but no longer has any direct reference to medieval physiology.

so·lil·o·quy (sə-lĭl′ə-kwē)

noun

Plural: **so·lil·o·quies**

1. A dramatic or literary form of discourse in which a character talks to himself or herself or reveals his or her thoughts when alone or unaware of the presence of other characters: *Shakespeare employs soliloquy in most of his plays.* **2.** A specific speech or piece of writing in this form of discourse: *"To be or not to be" is the beginning of a famous soliloquy in* Hamlet.

[Late Latin *sōliloquium* : Latin *sōlus*, alone + Latin *loquī*, to speak.]

RELATED WORDS:

noun — **so·lil′o·quist** (sə-lĭl′ə-kwĭst)
verb — **so·lil′o·quize** (sə-lĭl′ə-kwīz′)
noun — **so·lil′o·quiz′er** (sə-lĭl′ə-kwī′zər)

82

sub·ju·gate (sŭb′jə-gāt′)

transitive verb
    Past participle and past tense: **sub·ju·gat·ed**
    Present participle: **sub·ju·gat·ing**
    Third person singular present tense: **sub·ju·gates**

1. To bring under control; conquer: *The intention of the conquistadors was to subjugate the peoples of the New World.* **2.** To make subservient or submissive; subdue: *The new owners subjugated the defiant workers by threatening layoffs.*

[Middle English *subjugaten*, from Latin *subiugāre, subiugāt-* : *sub-*, under + *iugum*, yoke.]

RELATED WORDS:
    noun— **sub′ju·ga′tion** (sŭb′jə-gā′shən)
    noun— **sub′ju·ga′tor** (sŭb′jə-gā′tər)

83

suf·fra·gist (sŭf′rə-jĭst)

noun

An advocate of the extension of political voting rights, especially to women: *Tireless suffragists worked to ensure the passage of the Nineteenth Amendment in 1920.*

[*suffrag(e)* (ultimately from Latin *suffrāgium*, the right to vote, from *suffrāgārī*, to express support : *sub-*, under, in support of + *frāgārī*, to vote) + *-ist.*]

RELATED WORD:
    noun— **suf′fra·gism** (sŭf′rə-jĭz′əm)

su·per·cil·i·ous (soo′pər-sĭl′ē-əs)

adjective

Feeling or showing haughty disdain: *"Assuming his most supercilious air of distant superiority, he planted himself, immovable as a noble statue, upon the hearth, as if a stranger to the whole set"* (Fanny Burney, *Dr. Johnson and Fanny Burney*).

[Latin *superciliōsus,* from *supercilium,* eyebrow, pride : *super,* above + *cilium,* lower eyelid.]

RELATED WORDS:
> *adverb* — su′per·cil′i·ous·ly
> *noun* — su′per·cil′i·ous·ness

tau·tol·o·gy (tô-tŏl′ə-jē)

noun
> Plural: **tau·tol·o·gies**

1a. Needless repetition of the same sense in different words; redundancy. **b.** An instance of such repetition. **2.** *Logic* An empty or vacuous statement composed of simpler statements in a fashion that makes it logically true whether the simpler statements are factually true or false; for example, *Either it will rain tomorrow or it will not rain tomorrow.*

[Late Latin *tautologia,* from Greek *tautologiā,* from *tautologos,* redundant : *tauto-,* the same + *legein,* to say.]

RELATED WORDS:
> *adjective* — tau′to·log′i·cal (tôt′l-ŏj′ĭ-kəl)
> *adverb* — tau′to·log′i·cal·ly

tax·on·o·my (tăk-sŏn′ə-mē)

noun
  Plural: **tax·on·o·mies**

1. The classification of organisms in an ordered system that indicates natural relationships. **2.** The science, laws, or principles of classification; systematics. **3.** Division into ordered groups or categories.

[French *taxonomie* : Greek *taxis*, arrangement + *-nomie*, method (from Greek *-nomiā*, from *nomos*, law).]

RELATED WORDS:
  adjective—**tax′o·nom′ic** (tăk′sə-nŏm′ĭk)
  adverb—**tax′o·nom′i·cal·ly**
  noun—**tax·on′o·mist** (tăk-sŏn′ə-mĭst)

tec·ton·ic (těk-tŏn′ĭk)

adjective

1. Of or relating to the forces involved in forming the geological features, such as mountains, continents, and oceans, of the earth's lithosphere. The processes of plate tectonics, such as mountain building, are tectonic events. **2a.** Relating to construction or building. **2b.** Architectural.

[Late Latin *tectonicus*, from Greek *tektonikos*, from *tektōn*, builder.]

RELATED WORD:
  adverb—**tec·ton′i·cal·ly**

tem·pes·tu·ous (tĕm-pĕsʹchoo-əs)

adjective

1. Of, relating to, or resembling a tempest: *"The 31st of January was a wild, tempestuous day: there was a strong north wind, with a continual storm of snow drifting on the ground and whirling through the air"* (Anne Brontë, *Agnes Grey*). **2.** Characterized by violent emotions or actions; tumultuous; stormy: *"For perhaps the first time in her life she thought of him as a man, young, unhappy, tempestuous, full of desires and faults"* (Virginia Woolf, *Night and Day*).

[Middle English, from Late Latin *tempestuōsus*, from *tempestūs*, tempest, variant of *tempestās*.]

RELATED WORDS:
    adverb — **tem·pesʹtu·ous·ly**
    noun — **tem·pesʹtu·ous·ness**

ther·mo·dy·nam·ics (thûrʹmō-dī-nămʹĭks)

noun

1. *(used with a singular verb)* The branch of physics that deals with the relationships and conversions between heat and other forms of energy. **2.** *(used with a plural verb)* Thermodynamic phenomena and processes.

[*thermo-*, heat (from Greek *thermē*, heat, from *thermos*, warm) + *dynamics*, study of motion (from Greek *dunamikos*, powerful, from *dunamis*, power, from *dunasthai*, to be able).]

RELATED WORD:
    adjective — **therʹmo·dy·namʹic**

She wondered what he was looking for; were there waves beating upon a shore for him, too, she wondered, and heroes riding through the leaf-hung forests? For perhaps the first time in her life she thought of him as a man, young, unhappy, **tempestuous**, full of desires and faults.

—Virginia Woolf,
Night and Day

to·tal·i·tar·i·an (tō-tăl′ĭ-târ′ē-ən)

adjective

Of, relating to, being, or imposing a form of govern-ment in which the political authority exercises absolute and centralized control over all aspects of life, the indi-vidual is subordinated to the state, and opposing politi-cal and cultural expression is suppressed: *"A totalitarian regime crushes all autonomous institutions in its drive to seize the human soul"* (Arthur M. Schlesinger, Jr., *Cycles of American History*).

noun

A practitioner or supporter of such a government.

[*total + (author)itarian*]

RELATED WORD:
   noun— **to·tal′i·tar′i·an·ism**
              (tō-tăl′ĭ-târ′ē-ə-nĭz′əm)

unc·tu·ous (ŭngk′chōō-əs)

adjective

1. Characterized by affected, exaggerated, or insincere earnestness: *I didn't believe a word that the unctuous spokesperson said.* **2.** Having the quality or characteris-tics of oil or ointment; slippery: *"They had march'd seven or eight miles already through the slipping unctuous mud"* (Walt Whitman, *Specimen Days*). **3.** Containing or composed of oil or fat.

[Middle English, from Old French *unctueus*, from Medieval Latin *ūnctuōsus*, from Latin *ūnctum*, ointment, from neuter past participle of *unguere*, to anoint.]

RELATED WORDS:

noun — **unc′tu·os′i·ty** (ŭngk′chōō-ŏs′ĭ-tē)
adverb — **unc′tu·ous·ly**
noun — **unc′tu·ous·ness**

92

u·surp (yōō-sûrp′ *or* yōō-zûrp′)

verb

Past participle and past tense: **u·surped**
Present participle: **u·surp·ing**
Third person singular present tense: **u·surps**

transitive **1.** To seize and hold (the power or rights of another, for example) by force and without legal authority: *"The principle that one class may usurp the power to legislate for another is unjust"* (Susan B. Anthony, quoted in Ida Husted Harper's *The Life and Work of Susan B. Anthony*). **2.** To take over or occupy without right: *The squatters illegally usurped the farmer's land.*

intransitive To seize another's place, authority, or possession wrongfully.

[Middle English *usurpen*, from Old French *usurper*, from Latin *ūsūrpāre*, to take into use, usurp.]

RELATED WORDS:

noun — **u′sur·pa′tion** (yōō′sər-pā′shən
        or yōō′zər-pā′shən)
noun — **u·surp′er**

vac·u·ous (văk′yoo-əs)

adjective

1a. Lacking intelligence; stupid. **b.** Devoid of substance or meaning; inane: *The interview with the celebrity produced a series of vacuous comments.* **c.** Devoid of expression; vacant: *"The narrow, swinelike eyes were open, no more vacuous in death than they had been in life"* (Nicholas Proffitt, *The Embassy House*). **2.** Devoid of matter; empty.

[From Latin *vacuus*, empty.]

RELATED WORDS:
> *adverb* — **vac′u·ous·ly**
> *noun* — **vac′u·ous·ness**

ve·he·ment (vē′ə-mənt)

adjective

Forceful or intense in expression, emotion, or conviction; fervid: *The senator issued a vehement denial regarding the report linking him to a scandal.*

[Middle English, from Old French, from Latin *vehemēns, vehement-*, perhaps from *vehere*, to carry.]

RELATED WORDS:
> *noun* — **ve′he·mence**
> *noun* — **ve′he·men·cy**
> *adverb* — **ve′he·ment·ly**

vor·tex (vôr′tĕks′)

noun
    Plural: **vor·tex·es** *or* **vor·ti·ces** (vôr′tĭ-sēz′)

1. A spiral motion of fluid, especially a whirling mass of water or air that sucks everything near it toward its center. Eddies and whirlpools are examples of vortexes.
2. A place or situation regarded as drawing into its center all that surrounds it: *"Madam, is it not better that he showed repentance than that he never showed it at all? Better to atone for one minute than live in a vortex of despair?"* (Edna O'Brien, *In The Forest*).

[Latin *vortex, vortic-*, variant of *vertex*, from *vertere*, to turn.]

win·now (wĭn′ō)

verb

> Past participle and past tense: **win·nowed**
> Present participle: **win·now·ing**
> Third person singular present tense: **win·nows**

transitive **1.** To separate the chaff from (grain) by means of a current of air. **2.** To blow (chaff) off or away. **3.** To examine closely in order to separate the good from the bad; sift: *The judges winnowed a thousand essays down to six finalists.* **4a.** To separate or get rid of (an undesirable part); eliminate: *The accountant was adept at winnowing out errors in the spreadsheet.* **b.** To sort or select (a desirable part); extract: *The investigators winnowed the facts from the testimony.* **5.** To blow on; fan: *A breeze winnowed the grass.*

intransitive **1.** To separate grain from chaff. **2.** To separate the good from the bad.

noun

1. A device for winnowing grain. **2.** An act of winnowing.

[Middle English *winnewen*, alteration of *windwen*, from Old English *windwian*, from *wind*, wind.]

RELATED WORD:
> *noun* — **win′now·er**

Such is thy pow'r, nor are thine orders vain,

O thou the leader of the mental train:

In full perfection all thy works are **wrought**

And thine the sceptre o'er the realms of thought.

— Phillis Wheatley,
"On Imagination"

97

wrought (rôt)

verb

A past tense and a past participle of **work**: *"In full perfection all thy works are wrought/And thine the sceptre o'er the realms of thought"* (Phillis Wheatley, "On Imagination").

adjective

1. Put together; created: *The jewel thieves concocted a carefully wrought plan.* **2.** Shaped by hammering with tools. Used chiefly of metals or metalwork: *The horseshoe was made of wrought iron.*

[Middle English *wroght*, from Old English *geworht*, past participle of *wyrcan*, to work.]

98

xen·o·phobe (zĕn′ə-fōb′ *or* zē′nə-fōb′)

noun

A person unduly fearful or contemptuous of that which is foreign, especially of strangers or foreign peoples.

[*xeno-*, a stranger (from Greek *xenos*) + *-phobe*, one who fears (from French, from Latin *-phobus*, from Greek *-phobos*, fearing, from *phobos*, fear).]

RELATED WORDS:
> *noun*—**xen′o·pho′bi·a** (zĕn′ə-fō′bē-ə
> *or* zē′nə-fō′bē-ə)
> *adjective*—**xen′o·pho′bic** (zĕn′ə-fō′bĭk
> *or* zē′nə-fō′bĭk)

yeo·man (yō′mən)

noun
Plural: **yeo·men**

1a. An attendant, servant, or lesser official in a royal or noble household. **b.** A yeoman of the guard. **2.** A petty officer performing chiefly clerical duties in the US Navy. **3.** An assistant or other subordinate, as of a sheriff. **4.** A diligent, dependable worker. **5.** A farmer who cultivates his own land, especially a member of a former class of small freeholders in England.

[From Middle English *yoman,* possibly alteration of *yong man,* young man, or possibly from Old English **gēaman* (compare Old Frisian *gāman,* villager) : **gēa-, *geā-,* region, district (akin to Old Frisian *gā,* region, district; German *Gau,* province) + *man,* man.]

RELATED WORD:
noun — **yeo′man·ry**

zig·gu·rat (zĭg′ə-răt′)

noun

A temple tower of the ancient Assyrians and Babylonians, having the form of a terraced pyramid with successively receding stories.

[Akkadian *ziqqurratu,* temple tower, from *zaqāru,* to build high.]

Exercises to
Further Improve and
Enrich Your Vocabulary

Knowing and being able to use the *100 Words Every High School Graduate Should Know* is just one step that you can take to actively expand your vocabulary. Along with a good dictionary, such as *The American Heritage College Dictionary* or *The American Heritage High School Dictionary*, you can use these 100 words as a starting point to discover new words. The exercises shown below are among the many ways you can become more familiar with your dictionary and improve your vocabulary.

Building your vocabulary is an ongoing process that you can continue throughout your life. If you feel discouraged because you can't retain the definitions of all the words that you encounter, approach the task of expanding your vocabulary more slowly. If learning ten words a week is too difficult, aim for three, or five.

What is important is not the quantity of words you're learning. Rather, what is important is your process behind learning the words and the commitment you make to yourself to strengthen your vocabulary over time.

Choose ten words from the list of *100 Words Every High School Graduate Should Know*. Look these ten words up in your dictionary.

On each page that these ten words are listed, choose a new word whose meaning you do not know. Create a document on your computer and type in that word along with its definition, or write the word down on paper with its definition.

For example, the word **auspicious** appears on page 95 of the fourth edition of *The American Heritage College Dictionary* and *The American Heritage High School Dictionary*. Other words on that page that you might choose to learn include **austerity, australopithecine, Austronesia,** or **authenticate.**

Keep a record of the new words that you learn. Every so often, go back and refresh your memory by rereading the definitions to these words. Create sentences that use these words so that you can become comfortable using them.

EXERCISE II

Choose a magazine or newspaper that you like to read at least once a week. Create a document on your computer or start a journal in a notebook. Every time you read a word whose meaning you're unsure of, add that word to your computer file or journal.

Look up the word in your dictionary, and write or type out the definition. Does knowing the precise definition of the word help you better understand the article?

After you have acquired a list of ten words, memorize them until they are part of your active vocabulary.

EXERCISE III

Many of the words in the list of *100 Words Every High School Graduate Should Know* include terms from specific areas of study. For example, **parabola** and **hypotenuse** are both from the field of geometry. **Hemoglobin** and **photosynthesis** are from biology.

What fields of learning interest you? Create a list of ten words that you think people should know if they were to learn more about that topic. Think about how you would define those words, and compare your definitions with the definitions you find in your dictionary.

100

words almost

everyone

confuses

& misuses

Guide to the Entries

ENTRY WORD The 100 words that constitute this section are listed alphabetically. The entry words, along with inflected and derived forms, are divided into syllables by centered dots. These dots show you where you would break the word at the end of a line. The pronunciation of the word follows the entry word. Please see the key on page v for an explanation of the pronunciation system.

PART OF SPEECH At least one part of speech follows each entry word. The part of speech tells you the grammatical category that the word belongs to. Parts of speech include *noun, adjective, adverb, transitive verb,* and *intransitive verb.* (A transitive verb is a verb that needs an object to complete its meaning. *Wash* is a transitive verb in the sentence *I washed the car.* The direct object of *wash* is *the car.* An intransitive verb is one that does not take an object, as *sleep* in the sentence *I slept for seven hours.* Many verbs are both transitive and intransitive.)

INFLECTIONS A word's inflected forms differ from the main entry form by the addition of a suffix or by a change in the base form to indicate grammatical features such as number, person, or tense. They are set in boldface type, divided into syllables, and given pronunciations as necessary. The past tense, past participle, and the third person singular present tense inflections of all verbs are shown. The plurals of nouns are shown when they are spelled in a way other than by adding *s* to the base form.

LABELS The USAGE PROBLEM label warns of possible difficulties involving grammar, diction, or writing style. A word or definition with this label is discussed in a Usage Note, as at **flaunt.**

ORDER OF SENSES Entries having more than one sense are arranged with the central and often the most commonly sought meanings first. In an entry with more than one part of speech, the senses are numbered in separate sequences after each part of speech, as at **average.**

EXAMPLES OF USAGE Examples often follow the definitions and are set in italic type. These examples show the entry words in typical contexts. Sometimes the examples are quotations from authors of books. These quotations are shown within quotation marks, and the quotation's author and source are shown.

ETYMOLOGIES Etymologies appear in square brackets following the last definition. An etymology traces the history of a word as far back in time as can be determined with reasonable certainty. The stage most closely preceding Modern English is given first, with each earlier stage following in sequence. A language name, linguistic form (in italics), and brief definition of the form are given for each stage of the derivation. To avoid redundancy, a language, form, or definition is not repeated if it is identical to the corresponding item in the immediately preceding stage. Occasionally, a form will be given that is not actually preserved in written documents but which scholars are confident did exist—such a form will be marked by an asterisk (*). The word *from* is used to indicate origin of any kind: by inheritance, borrowing, or derivation. When an etymology splits a compound word into parts, a colon introduces the parts and each element is then traced back to its origin, with those elements enclosed in parentheses.

RELATED WORDS At the end of many entries, additional boldface words appear without definitions. These words are related in basic meaning to the entry word and are usually formed from the entry word by the addition of suffixes.

NOTES Some entries include Usage Notes that present important information and guidance on matters of grammar, diction, pronunciation, and nuances. Some refer to responses from our Usage Panel, a group of over 200 respected writers, scholars, and critics. The editors of the *American Heritage* dictionaries regularly survey these people on a broad range of usage questions.

Then a dog began to howl somewhere in a farm-house far down the road — a long, agonized wailing, as if from fear. . . . Then, far off in the distance, from the mountains on each side of us began a louder and a sharper howling — that of wolves — which **affected** both the horses and myself in the same way — for I was minded to jump from the caleche and run, whilst they reared again and plunged madly, so that the driver had to use all his great strength to keep them from bolting.

— Bram Stoker,
Dracula

ad·verse (ăd-vûrs′, ăd′vûrs′)

adjective

1. Acting or serving to oppose; antagonistic: *"And let thy blows, doubly redoubled, / Fall like amazing thunder on the casque / Of thy adverse pernicious enemy"* (William Shakespeare, *King Richard II*). **2.** Contrary to one's interests or welfare; harmful or unfavorable: *"[M]ost companies are fearful of adverse publicity and never report internal security breaches...to law enforcement agencies, security analysts contend"* (Peter H. Lewis, *New York Times*). **3.** Moving in an opposite direction: *As it ascended, the balloon was caught in an adverse current and drifted out to sea.*

[Middle English, from Old French *advers,* from Latin *adversus,* past participle of *advertere,* to turn toward : *ad-,* ad- + *vertere,* to turn.]

RELATED WORD:
   adverb —**ad·verse′ly**

SEE NOTE AT **averse** (ON PAGE 200).

af·fect¹ (ə-fĕkt′)

transitive verb
   Past participle and past tense: **af·fect·ed**
   Present participle: **af·fect·ing**
   Third person singular present tense: **af·fects**

---

1. To have an influence on or effect a change in: *Inflation affects the buying power of the dollar.* **2.** To act on the emotions of; touch or move: *"Then, far off in the distance, from the mountains on each side of us began a louder and a sharper howling—that of wolves—which affected both the horses and myself in the same way"* (Bram Stoker, *Dracula*). **3.** To attack or infect, as a disease: *Rheumatic fever is one of many afflictions that can affect the heart.*

noun (ăf′ĕkt′)

1. Feeling or emotion, especially as manifested by facial expression or body language: *"The soldiers seen on television had been carefully chosen for blandness of affect"* (Norman Mailer, *Vanity Fair*). **2.** *Obsolete* A disposition, feeling, or tendency.

[Middle English *affecten,* from Latin *afficere, affect-,* to do to, act on : *ad-,* ad- + *facere,* to do.]

SEE NOTE AT **effect** (ON PAGE 218).

3

af·fect² (ə-fĕkt′)

transitive verb

    Past participle and past tense: **af·fect·ed**
    Present participle: **af·fect·ing**
    Third person singular present tense: **af·fects**

1. To put on a false show of; simulate: *"He wheedled, bribed, ridiculed, threatened, and scolded; affected indifference, that he might surprise the truth from her"* (Louisa May Alcott, *Little Women*). **2.** To have or show a liking for: *affects dramatic clothes.* **3.** To tend to by nature; tend to assume: *In my chemistry class, we study substances that affect crystalline form.* **4.** To imitate; copy: *"Spenser, in affecting the ancients, writ no language"* (Ben Jonson, *Timber*).

[Middle English *affecten,* from Latin *affectāre,* to strive after, frequentative of *afficere, affect-,* to affect, influence; see AFFECT¹.]

RELATED WORD:
    noun — **af·fect′er**

SEE NOTE AT **effect** (ON PAGE 218).

ag·gra·vate (ăg′rə-vāt′)

transitive verb

> Past participle and past tense: **ag·gra·vat·ed**
> Present participle: **ag·gra·vat·ing**
> Third person singular present tense: **ag·gra·vates**

1. To make worse or more troublesome: *"Drinking alcohol (especially heavy drinking) or taking tranquilizers or sedating antihistamines shortly before bedtime can aggravate snoring by reducing muscle tone"* (Jane E. Brody, *New York Times*). **2.** To rouse to exasperation or anger; provoke.

[Latin *aggravāre, aggravāt-* : *ad-*, ad- + *gravāre*, to burden (from *gravis*, heavy).]

RELATED WORDS:

> *adverb*—**ag′gra·vat′ing·ly**
> *adjective*—**ag′gra·va′tive**
> *noun*—**ag′gra·va′tor**

☙ Some people claim that *aggravate* can only mean "to make worse," and not "to irritate," on the basis of the word's etymology. But in doing so, they ignore not only an English sense in use since the 17th century, but also one of the original Latin ones. *Aggravate* comes from the Latin verb *aggravāre,* which meant "to make heavier," that is, "to add to the weight of." The Latin word also had the extended senses "to annoy" and "to oppress." One-third of the Usage Panel does not approve of its use in the sentence *It's the endless wait for luggage that aggravates me the most about air travel.* When using *aggravate* in this sense, especially in formal writing, some of your readers may possibly view it as an error.

5

al·leged (ə-lĕjd′, ə-lĕj′ĭd)

adjective

Represented as existing or as being as described but not so proved; supposed: *"Cryptozoology is the study of unexplained and alleged sightings of strange creatures not documented by standard zoology"* (Chet Raymo, *Boston Globe*).

RELATED WORD:
adverb — al·leg′ed·ly

An *alleged* burglar is someone who has been accused of being a burglar but against whom no charges have been proved. An *alleged* incident is an event that is said to have taken place but has not yet been verified. In their zeal to protect the rights of the accused, newspapers and law enforcement officials sometimes misuse *alleged*. Someone arrested for murder may be only an *alleged* murderer, for example, but is a real, not an *alleged,* suspect in that his or her status as a suspect is not in doubt. Similarly, if the money from a safe is known to have been stolen and not merely mislaid, then we may safely speak of a theft without having to qualify our description with *alleged.*

all right (ôl rīt)

adjective

1. In good condition or working order; satisfactory: *The mechanic checked to see if the tires were all right.* **2.** Acceptable; agreeable: *"Men are all right for friends, but as soon as you marry them they turn into cranky old fathers, even the wild ones"* (Willa Cather, *My Ántonia*). **3.** Average; mediocre: *The performance was just all right, not remarkable.* **4.** Correct: *These figures are perfectly all right.* **5.** Uninjured; safe: *The passengers were shaken up but are all right.*

adverb

1. In a satisfactory way; adequately: *"Cobol was designed to be somewhat readable by nonprogrammers. The idea was that managers could read through a printed listing of Cobol code to determine if the programmer got it all right. This has rarely happened"* (Charles Petzold, *New York Times*). **2.** Very well; yes. Used as a reply to a question or to introduce a declaration: *All right, I'll go.* **3.** Without a doubt: *"They [Bonobos] are chimpanzees, all right, but almost the reverse of their more familiar cousins* (Phoebe-Lou Adams, *Atlantic Monthly*).

Despite the appearance of the form *alright* in works of such well-known writers as Langston Hughes and James Joyce, the single word spelling has never been accepted as standard. This is peculiar, since similar fusions such as *already* and *altogether* have never raised any objections. The difference may lie in the fact that *already* and *altogether* became single words back in the Middle Ages, whereas *alright* has only been around for a little more than a century and was called out by language critics as a misspelling. Consequently, if you use *alright,* especially in formal writing, you run the risk that readers may view it as an error or as the deliberate breaking of convention.

al·to·geth·er (ôl′tə-gĕth′ər)

adverb

1. Entirely; completely; utterly: *The three-year-old, then, is a grammatical genius—master of most constructions... avoiding many kinds of errors altogether"* (Steven Pinker, *The Language Instinct).* **2.** With all included or counted; all told: *"There were altogether eight official Crusades"* (*The Reader's Companion to Military History,* Robert Cowley). **3.** On the whole; with everything considered: *Altogether, I'm sorry it happened.*

noun

A state of nudity. Often used with *the: The artist's model posed in the altogether.*

[Middle English *al togeder.*]

🖎 *Altogether* and *all together* do not mean the same thing. *Altogether* is an adverb that indicates totality or entirety: *I rarely eat tomatoes, and I avoid peppers altogether. All together* is an adverb that indicates that the members of a group perform or undergo an action collectively: *The nations stood all together. The prisoners were herded all together. All together* is used only in sentences that can be rephrased so that *all* and *together* may be separated by other words: *The books lay all together in a heap. All the books lay together in a heap.*

The three-year-old, then, is a grammatical genius—master of most constructions, obeying rules far more often than flouting them, respecting language universals, erring in sensible, adultlike ways, and avoiding many kinds of errors **altogether**.

— Steven Pinker,
The Language Instinct

a·mong (ə-mŭng′)

also **a·mongst** (ə-mŭngst′)

preposition

1. In the midst of; surrounded by: *A tall oak tree grew among the pines.* **2.** In the group, number, or class of: *"Santería has a growing following among middle-class professionals, including white, black and Asian Americans"* (Lizette Alvarez, *New York Times*). **3.** In the company of; in association with: *I spent the summer in Europe traveling among a group of tourists.* **4.** By many or the entire number of; with many: *"It has long been a tradition among novel writers that a book must end by everybody getting just what they wanted, or if the conventional happy ending was impossible, then it must be a tragedy in which one or both should die"* (Molly Gloss, *Wild Life*). **5.** With portions to each of: *Distribute this among you.* **6.** With one another: *Don't fight among yourselves.*

[Middle English, from Old English *āmang* : *ā*, in + *gemang*, throng.]

SEE NOTE AT **between** (ON PAGE 202).

as·sure (ə-shŏor′)

transitive verb
    Past participle and past tense: **as·sured**
    Present participle: **as·sur·ing**
    Third person singular present tense: **as·sures**

1. To inform positively, as to remove doubt: *The ticket agent assured us that the train would be on time.* **2.** To cause to feel sure: *The candidate assured the electorate that he would keep his promises.* **3.** To give confidence to; reassure: *"Katharine assured her by nodding her head several times, but the manner in which she left the room was not calculated to inspire complete confidence in her diplomacy"* (Virginia Woolf, *Night and Day*). **4.** To make certain; ensure: *"Let every nation know, whether it wishes us well or ill, that we shall pay any price, bear any burden, meet any hardship, support any friend, oppose any foe, in order to assure the survival and the success of liberty"* (John F. Kennedy, Inaugural Address). **5.** *Chiefly British* To insure, as against loss.

[Middle English *assuren,* from Old French *assurer,* from Vulgar Latin **assēcūrāre,* to make sure : Latin *ad-,* ad- + Latin *sēcūrus,* secure.]

RELATED WORDS:
    adjective—**as·sur′a·ble**
    noun—**as·sur′er, as·sur′or**

SEE NOTE AT **insure** (ON PAGE 242).

au·ger (ô′gər)

noun

1a. Any of various hand tools, typically having a threaded shank and cross handle, used for boring holes in wood or ice: "[He] *can himself build a cabin with the three necessary implements: an ax, a broadax, and an auger*" (Michael Ennis, *Architectural Digest*). **b.** A drill bit. **2a.** A machine having a rotating helical shaft for boring into the earth. **b.** A rotating helical shaft used to convey material, as in a snow blower.

[Middle English, from *an auger,* alteration of *a nauger,* from Old English *nafogār,* auger.]

transitive verb
    Past participle and past tense: **au·gered**
    Present participle: **au·ger·ing**
    Third person singular present tense: **au·gers**

To bore by means of an auger: *The fishermen augered a hole in the ice.*

SEE NOTE AT **augur** (ON PAGE 197).

au·gur (ô′gər)

noun

1. One of a group of ancient Roman religious officials who foretold events by observing and interpreting signs and omens. **2.** A seer or prophet; a soothsayer.

verb
> Past participle and past tense: **au·gured**
> Present participle: **au·gur·ing**
> Third person singular present tense: **au·gurs**

transitive **1.** To predict, especially from signs or omens; foretell. **2.** To serve as an omen of; betoken: *Early returns augured victory for the young candidate.*

intransitive **1.** To make predictions from signs or omens. **2.** To be a sign or omen: *A smooth dress rehearsal augured well for the play.*

[Middle English, from Latin.]

RELATED WORD:
> *adjective*—**au′gu·ral** (ô′gyə-rəl)

An *auger* is a tool used for boring holes. An *augur* is a seer or soothsayer. The verb *augur* means "to foretell or betoken," as in *A good, well-grounded education augurs success. Augur* is also commonly used in phrases such as *augur well* or *augur ill*, as in *The quarterback's injury augurs ill for the game.*

av·er·age (ăv′ər-ĭj, ăv′rĭj)

noun

1. The value obtained by dividing the sum of a set of quantities by the number of quantities in the set. Also called *arithmetic mean*: *The average of 2, 5, 8, and 11 is 6.5.* **2.** A number that is derived from and considered typical or representative of a set of numbers. **3.** A typical kind or usual level or degree: *"My basic athletic skills—quickness, speed, coordination, all those things—were a little above average, but what I could do better than anybody my age was anticipate what a pitcher was going to throw and where he was going to throw it"* (David Huddle, *The Story of a Million Years*). **4.** The ratio of a team's or player's successful performances such as wins, hits, or goals, divided by total opportunities for successful performance, such as games, times at bat, or shots: *The team finished the season with a .500 average.*

adjective

1. Computed or determined as an average: *"By ten o'-clock average windspeed is forty knots out of the north-northeast, spiking to twice that and generating a huge sea"* (Sebastian Junger, *The Perfect Storm*). **2.** Being intermediate between extremes, as on a scale: *The teacher offered extra help for students with average grades.* **3.** Usual or ordinary in kind or character: *The firm conducted a poll of average people.*

---

average

verb

Past participle and past tense: **av·er·aged**
Present participle: **av·er·ag·ing**
Third person singular present tense: **av·er·ag·es**

transitive **1.** To calculate the average of: *The teacher explained how to average a set of numbers.* **2.** To do or have an average of: *The part-time employee averaged three hours of work a day.*

intransitive To be or amount to an average: *Our expenses averaged out to 45 dollars per day.*

[From Middle English *averay,* charge above the cost of freight, from Old French *avarie,* from Old Italian *avaria,* duty, from Arabic *'awārīya*, damaged goods, from *'awār*, blemish, from *'awira*, to be damaged.]

RELATED WORD:

noun — **av′er·age·ness**

SEE NOTE AT **median** (ON PAGE 258).

a·verse (ə-vûrs′)

adjective

Having a feeling of opposition, distaste, or aversion; strongly disinclined: *"Cheating on schoolwork has simmered on as long as there have been students averse to studying"* (Christina McCarroll, *Christian Science Monitor*).

[Latin *āversus,* past participle of *āvertere,* to turn away.]

RELATED WORDS:
>   *adverb* — **a·verse′ly**
>   *noun* — **a·verse′ness**

⚘ Who isn't *averse* to getting *adverse* reactions to their ideas? *Averse* normally refers to people and means "having a feeling of distaste or aversion," as in *As an investor I'm averse to risk-taking.* People sometimes mistakenly slip in *adverse* for *averse* in these constructions with *to.* However, *adverse* normally does not refer to people, but rather to things that are antagonistic or contrary to someone's interests. Thus we say *We're working under very adverse* (not *averse) circumstances* and *All the adverse* (not *averse) criticism frayed the new mayor's nerves.*

be·tween (bĭ-twēn′)

preposition

1a. In or through the position or interval separating: *"The shapes of the shoulder bones indicate that the animal may have swung by its arms between the branches of trees"* (Lisa Guernsey, *Chronicle of Higher Education*); *"Between 1970 and 1995, the average American's yearly sugar consumption increased from 120 pounds to 150 pounds"* (Richard A. Knox, *Boston Globe*). **b.** Intermediate to, as in quantity, amount, or degree: *It costs between 15 and 20 dollars.* **2.** Connecting over or through a space that is separating: *I walked down the long path between the cabin and the lake.* **3.** Usage Problem Associating or uniting in a reciprocal action or relationship: *The mediator hammered out an agreement between workers and management. The professor noted a certain resemblance between the two essays.* **4.** In confidence restricted to: *Between you and me, he is not qualified.* **5a.** By the combined effort or effect of: *"Sickly, it began to occur to him that between them, they might have killed the old man by mistake"* (Jane Stevenson, *London Bridges*). **b.** In the combined ownership of: *They had only a few dollars between them.* **6.** As measured or compared against: *"[She] went to the butcher's to choose between steak and pork chops"* (Sinclair Lewis, *Main Street).*

adverb

In an intermediate space, position, or time; in the interim.

IDIOM:

in between In an intermediate condition or situation: *"The methane, however, cannot exist in its normal* *gaseous form at such pressures and temperatures, but is transformed into a 'supercritical fluid'—neither a gas nor a liquid but something in between"* (Malcolm W. Browne, *New York Times*).

[Middle English *bitwene,* from Old English *betwēonum.*]

RELATED WORD:
    noun—**be·tween′ness**

🕮 According to a widely repeated but unjustified tradition, *between* is used for two, and *among* for more than two. It is true that *between* is the only choice when exactly two entities are specified: *the choice between* (not *among*) *good and evil, the rivalry between* (not *among*) *Great Britain and France.* When more than two entities are involved, however, or when the number of entities is unspecified, the choice of one or the other word depends on the intended sense. *Between* is used when the entities are considered as distinct individuals; *among,* when they are considered as a mass or collectivity. Thus in the sentence *The bomb landed between the houses,* the houses are seen as points that define the boundaries of the area of impact (so that we presume that none of the individual houses was hit). In *The bomb landed among the houses,* the area of impact is considered to be the general location of the houses, taken together (in which case it is left open whether any houses were hit). By the same token, we may speak of *a series of wars between the Greek cities,* which suggests that each city was an independent participant in the hostilities, or of *a series of wars among the Greek cities,* which allows for the possibility that the participants were shifting alliances of cities. To avoid this ambiguity, use *among* to indicate inclusion in a group: *She is among the best of our young sculptors. There is a spy among you.* Use *between* when the entities are seen as determining the limits or endpoints of a range: *They searched the area between the river, the farmhouse, and the woods. The truck driver had obviously been drinking between stops.*

15

bla·tant (blāt′nt)

adjective

1. Unpleasantly loud and noisy: *"There are those who find the trombones blatant and the triangle silly, but both add effective color"* (Musical Heritage Review). **2.** UsAGE PROBLEM Thoroughly or offensively conspicuous or obtrusive: *The child was caught telling a blatant lie.*

[From Latin *blatīre*, to blab (on the model of words such as *rampant*).]

RELATED WORDS:
> *noun* — **bla′tan·cy**
> *adverb* — **bla′tant·ly**

🖋 It is not surprising that *blatant* and *flagrant* are often confused, since the words have overlapping meanings. Both attribute conspicuousness and offensiveness to certain acts. *Blatant* emphasizes the failure to conceal the act. *Flagrant,* on the other hand, emphasizes the serious wrongdoing inherent in the offense. Certain contexts may admit either word depending on what is meant. Thus, a violation of human rights might be either *blatant* or *flagrant.* If the act was committed with contempt for public scrutiny, it is *blatant.* If its barbarity was monstrous, it is *flagrant.*

    Blatant is sometimes used to mean simply "obvious," as in *the blatant danger of such an approach,* but this use has not been established and is widely considered an error.

16

cap·i·tal (kăp′ĭ-tl)

noun

1a. A town or city that is the official seat of government in a political entity, such as a state or nation: *Trenton is the capital of New Jersey.* **b.** A city that is the center of a specific activity or industry: *Many consider Milan to be the fashion capital of the world.* **2a.** Wealth in the form of money or property that is used or accumulated in a business by a person, partnership, or corporation, and is often used to create more wealth. **b.** Human resources considered in terms of their contributions to an economy: *"Castro's swift unveiling of his communist plans provoked a flight of human capital"* (George F. Will, *Newsweek*). **3.** The remaining assets of a business after all liabilities have been deducted; net worth. **4a.** The total amount of stock authorized for issue by a corporation, including common and preferred stock. **b.** The total stated or par value of the permanently invested capital of a corporation. **5.** An asset or advantage: *"He has profited from political capital accumulated by others"* (Michael Mandelbaum, *Foreign Affairs*). **6.** A capital letter.

adjective

1. First and foremost; principal: *We were faced with a decision of capital importance.* **2.** First-rate; excellent: *Planning a kayaking trip is a capital idea!* **3.** Relating to or being a seat of government: *Albany, New York, is a capital city.* **4.** Punishable by or involving death: *Treason is a capital offense.* **5.** Of or involving wealth and its use in investment: *"A multi-billion-dollar capital improvement plan has produced construction, physical* *improvements, and repairs"* (Peter Edelman, *Searching for America's Heart*).

[From Middle English, principal, from Old French, from Latin *capitālis*, from *caput*, head, money laid out.]

🕮 *Capital* and *capitol* are terms that are often confused, mainly because they refer to things that are in some way related. The term for a town or city that serves as a seat of government is spelled *capital*. The term for the building in which a legislative assembly meets is spelled *capitol*.

17 **cap·i·tol** (kăp′ĭ-tl)

noun

1. A building or complex of buildings in which a state legislature meets. **2. Capitol** The building in Washington DC where the Congress of the United States meets.

[Middle English *Capitol*, Jupiter's temple in Rome, from Old French *capitole*, from Latin *Capitōlium*, after *Capitōlīnus*, Capitoline, the hill on which Jupiter's temple stood; perhaps akin to *caput*; see etymology at **capital** (#16).]

SEE NOTE AT **capital** (ABOVE).

The Pyncheon Elm, throughout its great circumference, was all alive, and full of the morning sun and a sweet-tempered little breeze, which lingered within this verdant sphere, and set a thousand leafy tongues a-whispering all at once. This aged tree appeared to have suffered nothing from the gale. It had kept its boughs unshattered, and its full **complement** of leaves; and the whole in perfect verdure, except a single branch, that, by the earlier change with which the elm-tree sometimes prophesies the autumn, had been transmuted to bright gold.

—Nathaniel Hawthorne,
The House of the Seven Gables

com·ple·ment (kŏm′plə-mənt)

noun

1a. Something that completes, makes up a whole, or brings to perfection. **b.** The quantity or number needed to make up a whole: "[The tree] *had kept its boughs unshattered, and its full complement of leaves* (Nathaniel Hawthorne, *The House of the Seven Gables*). **c.** Either of two parts that complete the whole or mutually complete each other. **2.** An angle related to another so that the sum of their measures is 90°. **3.** A word or words used after a verb to complete a predicate construction; for example, the phrase *to eat ice cream* is the complement of the predicate *We like to eat ice cream.* **4.** A complex system of proteins found in normal blood plasma that combines with antibodies to destroy pathogenic bacteria and other foreign cells.

transitive verb (kŏm′plə-mĕnt′)
> Past participle and past tense: **com·ple·ment·ed**
> Present participle: **com·ple·ment·ing**
> Third person singular present tense: **com·ple·ments**

To serve as a complement to: "*When chiles are dried, their flavor intensifies, and sometimes they take on a smoky, sweet flavor that complements the heat*" (Corby Kummer, *Atlantic Monthly*).

[Middle English, from Old French, from Latin *complēmentum*, from *complēre*, to fill out.]

> ✀ *Complement* and *compliment*, though quite distinct in meaning, are sometimes confused because they are pronounced the same. As a noun, *complement* means "something that completes or brings to perfection" *(The antique silver was a complement to the beautifully set table)*; used as a verb it means "to serve as a com-

plement to" (*The neutral color of the paint complements the warmth of the oak floors*). The noun *compliment* means "an expression or act of courtesy or praise" (*They gave us a compliment on our beautifully set table*), while the verb means "to pay a compliment to" (*We complimented our hosts for the lovely dinner party*).

19

com·pli·ment (kŏm′plə-mənt)

noun

1. An expression of praise, admiration, or congratulation: *I took their interest in my screenplay as a compliment.* **2.** A formal act of civility, courtesy, or respect: *"You must give me leave to judge for myself, and pay me the compliment of believing what I say"* (Jane Austen, *Pride and Prejudice*). **3. compliments** Good wishes; regards: *Extend my compliments to your parents.*

transitive verb

Past participle and past tense: **com·pli·ment·ed**
Present participle: **com·pli·ment·ing**
Third person singular present tense: **com·pli·ments**

To pay a compliment to: *The mayor complimented the volunteers who had cleaned up the park.*

[French, from Italian *complimento*, from Spanish *cumplimiento*, from *cumplir*, to complete, from Latin *complēre*, to fill out.]

SEE NOTE AT **complement** (ON PAGE 207).

20 com·prise (kəm-prīz′)

transitive verb
   Past participle and past tense: **com·prised**
   Present participle: **com·pris·ing**
   Third person singular present tense: **com·pris·es**

1. To consist of; be composed of: *"The French got what became known as French Equatorial Africa, comprising several territories"* (Alex Shoumatoff, *Vanity Fair*). **2.** To include; contain: *"The word 'politics' . . . comprises, in itself, a difficult study of no inconsiderable magnitude"* (Charles Dickens, *The Pickwick Papers*). **3.** USAGE PROBLEM To compose; constitute.

[Middle English *comprisen,* from Old French *compris,* past participle of *comprendre,* to include, from Latin *comprehendere, comprēndere.*]

🖉 The traditional rule states that the whole *comprises* the parts and the parts *compose* the whole. In strict usage: *The Union comprises 50 states. Fifty states compose* (or *constitute* or *make up*) *the Union.* Even though careful writers often maintain this distinction, *comprise* is increasingly used in place of *compose,* especially in the passive: *The Union is comprised of 50 states.* Our surveys show that opposition to this usage is abating. In the 1960s, 53 percent of the Usage Panel found this usage unacceptable; in 1996, only 35 percent objected.

con·sul (kŏn′səl)

noun

1. An official appointed by a government to reside in a foreign country and represent his or her government's commercial interests and assist its citizens there. **2.** Either of the two chief magistrates of the Roman Republic, elected for a term of one year. **3.** Any of the three chief magistrates of the French Republic from 1799 to 1804.

[Middle English *consul,* Roman consul, from Latin *cōnsul*; possibly akin to *cōnsulere,* to take counsel.]

RELATED WORDS:
> *adjective*—**con′su·lar** (kŏn′sə-lər)
> *noun*—**con′sul·ship′**

SEE NOTE AT **council** (ON PAGE 212).

con·vince (kən-vĭns′)

transitive verb
> Past participle and past tense: **con·vinced**
> Present participle: **con·vinc·ing**
> Third person singular present tense: **con·vinc·es**

To bring by the use of argument or evidence to firm belief or a course of action: *"I was now quite convinced that she had made a fresh will, and had called the two gardeners in to witness her signature. Events proved that I was right in my supposition"* (Agatha Christie, *The Mysterious Affair at Styles*).

[Latin *convincere,* to prove wrong : *com-,* intensive prefix + *vincere,* to conquer.]

RELATED WORDS:
> *noun* — **con·vinc′er**
> *adjective* — **con·vinc′a·ble**

🖘 According to a traditional rule, one *persuades* someone to act but *convinces* someone of the truth of a statement or proposition: *By convincing me that no good could come of staying, he persuaded me to leave.* If the distinction is accepted, then *convince* should not be used with an infinitive: He *persuaded* (not *convinced*) me to go. In a 1981 Usage Panel survey, 61 percent rejected the use of *convince* with an infinitive. But the tide of sentiment against the construction appears to be turning. In a 1996 survey, 74 percent accepted it in the sentence *I tried to convince him to chip in a few dollars, but he refused.* Even in passive constructions, a majority of the Usage Panel accepted *convince* with an infinitive. Fifty-two percent accepted the sentence *After listening to the teacher's report, the committee was convinced to go ahead with the new reading program. Persuade,* on the other hand, is perfectly acceptable when used with an infinitive or a *that* clause in both active and passive constructions. An overwhelming majority of Panelists in the 1996 survey accepted the following sentences: *After a long discussion with her lawyer, she was persuaded to drop the lawsuit. The President persuaded his advisors that military action was necessary.* You can observe the traditional distinction between these words, but it is not very likely that readers will appreciate the effort.

coun·cil (koun′səl)

noun

1a. An assembly of persons called together for consultation, deliberation, or discussion. **b.** A body of people elected or appointed to serve as administrators, legislators, or advisors. **c.** An assembly of church officials and theologians convened for regulating matters of doctrine and discipline. **2.** The discussion or deliberation that takes place in such an assembly or body.

[Middle English *counceil,* from Old French *concile,* from Latin.]

✍ *Council, counsel,* and *consul* have similar pronunciations but are never interchangeable, although their meanings are related. *Council* refers principally to a deliberative assembly (such as a city council or student council), its work, and its membership. *Counsel* pertains chiefly to advice and guidance in general and to a person (such as a lawyer or camp counselor) who provides it. *Consul* denotes an officer in the foreign service of a country.

coun·sel (koun′səl)

noun

1. The act of exchanging opinions and ideas; consultation: *Frequent counsel among the members kept the committee informed.* **2.** Advice or guidance, especially as solicited from a knowledgeable person: *"I wish to engage your keener faculties, your logic and reason, so that you are able to discern a greater truth than I can. In short, I seek counsel and instruction"* (*Audubon's Watch,* John Gregory Brown). **3.** Private, guarded thoughts or opinions: *The quiet loner always kept his own counsel.* **4.** A

lawyer or group of lawyers giving legal advice and especially conducting a case in court.

verb

Past participle and past tense: **coun·seled** *or*
coun·selled
Present participle: **coun·sel·ing** *or* **coun·sel·ling**
Third person singular present tense: **coun·sels**

transitive **1.** To give counsel to; advise: *"An Owl, in her
wisdom, counseled the Birds that when the acorn first began to sprout, to pull it all up out of the ground and not
allow it to grow"* (Aesop, *Fables: The Owl and the Birds*).
2. To recommend: *counseled care in the forthcoming ne-
gotiations.*

intransitive To give or take advice.

[Middle English *counseil*, from Old French *conseil*, from
Latin *cōnsilium*; akin to *cōnsulere*, to take counsel, consult.]

RELATED WORDS:
noun—**coun'sel·or, coun'sel·lor**
noun—**coun'sel·or·ship'**

SEE NOTE AT **council** (ON PAGE 212).

25

dis·creet (dĭ-skrēt′)

adjective

Marked by, exercising, or showing prudence and wise self-restraint in speech and behavior; circumspect: *"After-hours clubs are proliferating and are still the city's best-kept secrets. One need only make discreet inquiries as to the whereabouts of such places"* (Doris Pike, *Boston Magazine*).

[Middle English, from Old French *discret,* from Medieval Latin *discrētus,* from Latin, past participle of *discernere,* to separate, discern.]

RELATED WORDS:
> *adverb*—**dis·creet′ly**
> *noun*—**dis·creet′ness**

SEE NOTE AT **discrete** (ON PAGE 215).

dis·crete (dĭ-skrēt′)

adjective

Constituting a separate thing: *"Although hypertext may well turn out to be no more than an amusing detour in the history of the written word, its most ardent fans foresee a future in which traditional narratives would become obsolete, and discrete, self-contained books would also give way to vast interlinked electronic networks"* (Michiko Kakutani, *New York Times Magazine*).

[Middle English, from Old French, from Latin *discrētus*, past participle of *discernere*, to separate.]

RELATED WORDS:
    adverb—**dis·crete′ly**
    noun—**dis·crete′ness**

ℰ Because they are pronounced the same way, *discreet* and *discrete* are sometimes confused in print. *Discreet* means "prudent in speech and behavior": *He told me the news but asked me to be discreet about it.* The related word *discrete* means "separate, distinct": *The summer science program consists of four discrete units.*

dis·in·ter·est·ed (dĭs-ĭn′trĭ-stĭd, dĭs-ĭn′tə-rĕs′tĭd)

adjective

1. Free of bias and self-interest; impartial: *"Debates on the fluoridation issue are passionate and polemical. For this reason disinterested scientific opinion on fluorides in the water supply, which is itself hard to come by, is not always the basis for public policy"* (Ellen R. Shell, *Atlantic Monthly*). **2.** Usage Problem Not interested or having lost interest; indifferent.

RELATED WORDS:

> *adverb*— **dis·in′ter·est·ed·ly**
> *noun*— **dis·in′ter·est·ed·ness**

᠙᠊ In traditional usage, *disinterested* can only mean "having no stake in an outcome," as in *Since the judge stands to profit from the sale of the company, she cannot be considered a disinterested party in the dispute.* But despite critical disapproval, *disinterested* has come to be widely used by many educated writers to mean "uninterested" or "having lost interest," as in *After she discovered skiing, she grew disinterested in her schoolwork.* Oddly enough, "not interested" is the oldest sense of the word, going back to the 17th century. This sense became outmoded in the 18th century but underwent a revival in the first quarter of the 20th. Despite its resuscitation, this usage is often considered an error. In a 1988 survey, 89 percent of the Usage Panel rejected the sentence *His unwillingness to give five minutes of his time proves that he is disinterested in finding a solution to the problem.* In a 2001 survey, 88 percent rejected a similar sentence, indicating continued strong resistance to this usage.

ef·fect (ĭ-fĕkt′)

noun

1. Something brought about by a cause or agent; a result: *"Every cause produces more than one effect"* (Herbert Spencer, *Essays on Education*). **2.** The power to produce an outcome or achieve a result; influence: *The drug had an immediate effect on the pain. The government's action had no effect on the trade imbalance.* **3.** A scientific law, hypothesis, or phenomenon: *the photovoltaic effect.* **4.** Advantage; avail: *The lawyer used the words of the witness to great effect in influencing the jury.* **5.** The condition of being in full force or execution: *This new regulation that goes into effect on January 1.* **6a.** Something that produces a specific impression or supports a general design or intention: *The strange lighting effects emphasized the harsh atmosphere of the drama.* **b.** A particular impression: *These large windows give an effect of spaciousness.* **c.** Production of a desired impression: *spent lavishly on dinner just for effect.* **7.** The basic or general meaning; import: *He said he was greatly worried, or words to that effect.* **8. effects** Movable belongings; goods.

transitive verb
> Past participle and past tense: **ef·fect·ed**
> Present participle: **ef·fect·ing**
> Third person singular present tense: **ef·fects**

To produce as a result; cause to occur: *"It is known that the English pointer has been greatly changed within the last century, and in this case the change has, it is believed, been chiefly effected by crosses with the fox*" (Charles Darwin, *On the Origin of Species*).

IDIOM:

in effect In essence; to all purposes: *testimony that in effect contradicted her earlier statement.*

[Middle English, from Old French, from Latin *effectus,* from past participle of *efficere,* to accomplish : *ex-,* ex- + *facere,* to make.]

RELATED WORDS:
> noun—**ef·fect′er**
> adjective—**ef·fect′i·ble**

🖉 The words *affect* and *effect* are often confused, in no small part because they often sound the same. What's worse, two different words are spelled *affect.* One is solely a verb and means "to put on a false show of," as in *The actor affected a British accent.* The other can be both a noun and a verb. The noun meaning "emotion" is a technical term from psychology that sometimes shows up in general writing, as in the quote *"The soldiers seen on television had been carefully chosen for blandness of affect"* written by Norman Mailer in a piece about the Gulf War. In its far more common role as a verb, *affect* usually means "to influence," as in *The Surgeon General's report outlined how much smoking affects health.*

    Effect can also serve as a noun or a verb. The noun means "a result." Thus, if you *affect* something, you are likely to see an *effect* of some kind, and from this may arise further the confusion. As a verb, *effect* means "to bring about or execute." Thus, using *effect* in the sentence *These measures may effect savings* implies that the measures will cause new savings to come about. But using *affect* in the very similar sentence *These measures may affect savings* could just as easily imply that the measures may reduce savings that have already been realized.

29

en·er·vate (ĕn′ər-vāt′)

transitive verb
    Past participle and past tense: **en·er·vat·ed**
    Present participle: **en·er·vat·ing**
    Third person singular present tense: **en·er·vates**

1. To weaken or destroy the strength or vitality of: *"What is the nature of the luxury which enervates and destroys nations?"* (Henry David Thoreau, *Walden*). **2.** In medicine, to remove a nerve or part of a nerve.

[Latin *ēnervāre, ēnervāt-* : *ē-, ex-,* ex- + *nervus,* sinew.]

RELATED WORDS:
    noun—**en′er·va′tion**
    adjective—**en′er·va′tive**
    noun—**en′er·va′tor**

By mistakenly assuming that *enervate* is a close cousin of the verb *energize,* people sometimes use *enervate* incorrectly to mean "to invigorate" or "to excite" (as in *I was sleepy, so I took a cold shower hoping it would enervate me*). In fact, *enervate* does not come from the same source as *energize* (Greek *energos,* "active"). It comes from Latin *nervus,* "sinew." Thus *enervate* means "to cause to become 'out of muscle'," that is, "to weaken or deplete of strength."

e·nor·mi·ty (ĭ-nôr′mĭ-tē)

noun
> Plural: **e·nor·mi·ties**

1. The quality of passing all moral bounds; excessive wickedness or outrageousness. **2.** A monstrous offense or evil; an outrage. **3.** Usage Problem Great size; immensity: *The enormity of the hot-air balloon amazed all the onlookers.*

[French *énormité,* from Old French, from Latin *ēnormitās,* from *ēnormis,* unusual, enormous.]

Enormity is frequently used to refer simply to the property of being great in size or extent, but many would prefer that *enormousness* (or a synonym such as *immensity*) be used for this general sense and that *enormity* be limited to situations that demand a negative moral judgment, as in *Not until the war ended and journalists were able to enter Cambodia did the world really become aware of the enormity of Pol Pot's oppression.* According to this rule, the sentence *At that point, the engineers sat down to design an entirely new viaduct, apparently undaunted by the enormity of their task* would be considered incorrect. This distinction between *enormity* and *enormousness* has not always existed historically, but nowadays many observe it. You may want to avoid using *enormity* in phrases such as *the enormity of the support the mayor received in the election* as *enormity*'s sense of monstrousness may leave your audience misinterpreting what it is you are trying to say.

31

e·nor·mous·ness (ĭ-nôr′məs-nəs)

noun

The state or condition of being very great in size, extent, number, or degree: "[The whale] *seemed hardly to budge at all…good evidence was hereby furnished of the enormousness of the mass we moved*" (Herman Melville, *Moby-Dick*).

[enormous (from Latin *ēnormis*, unusual, huge, monstrous : *ē-, ex-*, ex- + *norma*, norm) + -ness (from Middle English *-nes*, from Old English).]

RELATED WORDS:
  adjective—**e·nor′mous**
  adverb—**e·nor′mous·ly**

SEE NOTE AT **enormity** (ON PAGE 220).

32

en·sure (ĕn-shŏŏr′)

transitive verb

   Past participle and past tense: **en·sured**
   Present participle: **en·sur·ing**
   Third person singular present tense: **en·sures**

To make sure or certain; insure: *"The world is still engaged in a massive armaments race designed to ensure
continuing equivalent strength among potential adversaries"* (Jimmy Carter, Inaugural Address).

[Middle English *ensuren,* from Anglo-Norman *enseurer* : Old
French *en-*, causative prefix + Old French *seur,* secure, variant of *sur.*]

SEE NOTE AT **insure** (ON PAGE 242).

The world is still engaged in a massive armaments race designed to **ensure** continuing equivalent strength among potential adversaries. We pledge perseverance and wisdom in our efforts to limit the world's armaments to those necessary for each nation's own domestic safety. And we will move this year a step toward ultimate goal—the elimination of all nuclear weapons from this Earth. We urge all other people to join us, for success can mean life instead of death.

— Jimmy Carter,
Inaugural Address

fac·toid (făk′toid)

noun

1. A piece of unverified or inaccurate information that is presented in the press as factual, often as part of a publicity effort, and that is then accepted as true because of frequent repetition: *"What one misses finally is what might have emerged beyond both facts and factoids—a profound definition of the Marilyn Monroe phenomenon"* (Christopher Lehmann-Haupt, *New York Times*). **2.** USAGE PROBLEM A brief, somewhat interesting fact.

RELATED WORD:
 adjective—**fac·toi′dal**

❧ The *–oid* suffix normally imparts the meaning "resembling, having the appearance of" to the words it attaches to. Thus the *anthropoid apes* are the apes that are most like humans (from Greek *anthrōpos*, "human being"). In some words *–oid* has a slightly extended meaning—"having characteristics of, but not the same as," as in *humanoid*, a being that has human characteristics but is not really human. Similarly, *factoid* originally referred to a piece of information that appears to be reliable or accurate, as from being repeated so often that people assume it is true.

 Factoid has since developed a second meaning, that of a brief, somewhat interesting fact, that might better have been called a *factette*, as in *Each day the newspaper prints a list of factoids such as what kinds of condiments people prefer on ham sandwiches.* If you wish to avoid this usage, you can instead choose *statistics, trivia, useless facts,* and just plain *facts.*

few·er (fyōō′ər)

adjective

The comparative form of **few.** Amounting to or con-sisting of a smaller number: *The catcher played fewer in-nings than the shortstop did.*

pronoun

A smaller number of persons or things: *Chris ate six slices of pizza, and Lee had fewer.*

[Middle English, from Old English *fēawe* + Middle English *-er,* comparative suffix.]

The traditional rule holds that *fewer* should be used for things that can be counted (*fewer than four players*), while *less* should be used with mass terms for things of measurable extent (*less paper; less than a gallon of paint*). However, *less* is used in some constructions where *fewer* would occur if the traditional rule were being followed. *Less than* can be used before a plural noun that denotes a measure of time, amount, or distance: *less than three weeks; less than $400; less than 50 miles. Less* is sometimes used with plural nouns in the expressions *no less than* (as in *No less than 30 of his colleagues signed the letter*) and *or less* (as in *Give your reasons in 25 words or less*).

fla·grant (flā′grənt)

adjective

Conspicuously bad, offensive, or reprehensible: *"[S]ome-times the very presence of received wisdom keeps blinders on us all, even when evidence of abuse of power or sloppy procedures is flagrant"* (Patricia Holt, *San Francisco Chronicle*).

[Latin *flagrāns, flagrant-*, present participle of *flagrāre*, to burn.]

RELATED WORDS:
> *noun*—**fla′grance**
> *adverb*—**fla′grant·ly**

SEE NOTE AT **blatant** (ON PAGE 203).

flam·ma·ble (flăm′ə-bəl)

adjective

Easily ignited and capable of burning rapidly; in-flammable: *"Until the early 1980's, many renderers had used flammable solvents to dissolve fats, and the solvents may have deactivated the agent that causes mad cow disease and scrapie"* (Sandra Blakeslee, *New York Times*).

[From Latin *flammāre*, to set fire to, from *flamma*, flame.]

RELATED WORDS:
> *noun*—**flam′ma·bil′i·ty**
> *noun*—**flam′ma·ble**
> *adverb*—**flam′ma·bly**

SEE NOTE AT **inflammable** (ON PAGE 241).

flaunt (flônt)

verb

    Past participle and past tense: **flaunt·ed**

    Present participle: **flaunt·ing**

    Third person singular present tense: **flaunts**

transitive **1.** To exhibit ostentatiously or shamelessly: *"In everything a prudent man acts with knowledge, but a fool flaunts his folly"* (Proverbs 13:16). **2.** USAGE PROBLEM To show contempt for; scorn.

intransitive **1.** To parade oneself ostentatiously; show oneself off. **2.** To wave grandly: *"Flaunt away, flags of all nations!"* (Walt Whitman, *Leaves of Grass*).

[Origin unknown.]

RELATED WORDS:

    noun — **flaunt′er**

    adverb — **flaunt′ing·ly**

☞ *Flaunt* as a transitive verb means "to exhibit ostentatiously": *They flaunted their wealth by wearing expensive clothing and jewelry.* To *flout* is "to show contempt for": *They flouted old civic traditions.* For some time now *flaunt* has been used in the sense "to show contempt for," even by educated users of English, but many people regard this usage as erroneous.

flout (flout)

verb

> Past participle and past tense: **flout·ed**
> Present participle: **flout·ing**
> Third person singular present tense: **flouts**

transitive To show contempt for; scorn: *"Considered on its face, suicide flouts the laws of nature, slashing through the sturdy instinct that wills all beings to fight for their lives until they can fight no longer"* (Natalie Angier, *The Beauty of the Beastly*).

intransitive To be scornful.

noun

A contemptuous action or remark; an insult: *"Bruise me with scorn, confound me with a flout; Thrust thy sharp wit quite through my ignorance; Cut me to pieces with thy keen conceit"* (William Shakespeare, *Love's Labours Lost*).

RELATED WORDS:
> *noun*—**flout′er**
> *adverb*—**flout′ing·ly**

[Perhaps from Middle English *flouten,* to play the flute, from Old French *flauter,* from *flaute,* flute.]

SEE NOTE AT **flaunt** (ON PAGE 227).

39

for·te (fôr′tā′, fôrt)

noun

1. Something in which a person excels: *"[O]ur senator had the misfortune to be a man who had a particularly humane and accessible nature, and turning away anybody that was in trouble never had been his forte"* (Harriet Beecher Stowe, *Uncle Tom's Cabin*). **2.** The strong part of a sword blade, between the middle and the hilt.

[French *fort*, from Old French, strong, from Latin *fortis*.]

⚘ Many claim that the word *forte,* coming from French *fort,* should properly be pronounced with one syllable, like the English word *fort.* Common usage, however, prefers the two-syllable pronunciation, (fôr′tā′), which has been influenced possibly by the music term *forte,* borrowed from Italian. Speakers can continue to pronounce it as one syllable knowing that the origin of the word supports this pronunciation, but they do so at an increasing risk of puzzling their listeners.

gen·der (jĕn′dər)

noun

1a. A grammatical category used in the classification of nouns, pronouns, adjectives, and, in some languages, verbs that may be arbitrary or based on characteristics such as sex or animacy and that determines agreement with or selection of modifiers, referents, or grammatical forms. **b.** The distinguishing form or forms used. **2.** Sexual identity, especially in relation to society or culture. **3a.** The condition of being female or male; sex. **b.** Females or males considered as a group: *The linguist studied expressions predominantly used by one gender.*

[Middle English *gendre,* from Old French, kind, gender, from Latin *genus, gener-.*]

 ❧ Traditionally, *gender* has been used primarily to refer to the grammatical categories of "masculine," "feminine," and "neuter," but in recent years the word has become well established in its use to refer to sex-based categories, as in phrases such as *gender gap* and *the politics of gender.* This usage is supported by the practice of many anthropologists and others concerned with the behaviors and attitudes of men and women. This distinction is sometimes summed up by the expression "Sex is who we are; gender is what we do." Accordingly, one would say *The effectiveness of the medication appears to depend on the sex* (not *gender*) *of the patient,* but *In peasant societies, gender* (not *sex*) *roles are likely to be more clearly defined.* This distinction is useful in principle, but it is by no means widely observed, and considerable variation in usage occurs at all levels.

41

hope·ful·ly (hōp′fə-lē)

adverb

1. In a hopeful manner. **2.** USAGE PROBLEM It is to be hoped: *Hopefully, it will stop raining before the game starts.*

୫୭ If you use *hopefully* as a sentence adverb, as in *Hopefully the measures will be adopted,* be aware that the usage is unacceptable to many critics, including a large majority of the Usage Panel. It is not easy to explain why critics dislike this use of *hopefully.* The use is justified by analogy to similar uses of many other adverbs, as in *Mercifully, the lecture was brief* or *Frankly, I have no use for your suggestions.* And though this use of *hopefully* may have been a vogue word when it first gained currency back in the early 1960s, it has long since lost any hint of jargon or pretentiousness. The wide acceptance of the usage reflects popular recognition of its handiness; there is no precise substitute. Someone who says *Hopefully, the treaty will be ratified* makes a hopeful prediction about the fate of the treaty, whereas someone who says *I hope* (or *We hope* or *It is hoped*) *the treaty will be ratified* expresses a bald statement about what is desired. Only the latter could be continued with a clause such as *but it isn't likely.*

It might have been expected, then, that the initial flurry of objections to *hopefully* would have subsided once the usage became well established. Instead, critics appear to have become more adamant in their opposition. In the 1969 Usage Panel survey, 44 percent of the Panel approved the usage, but this dropped to 27 percent in our 1986 survey. (By contrast, 60 percent in the latter survey accepted the comparable use of *mercifully* in the sentence *Mercifully, the game ended before the opponents could add another touchdown to the lopsided score.*) Perhaps it is not the use of sentence adverbs per se that bothers critics; rather, it seems that the specific use of *hopefully* in this way has become a shibboleth, a marker of poor education or a lack of refinement.

im·pact (ĭm′păkt′)

noun

1. The striking of one body against another; collision: *The impact of the meteorite left a large crater.* **2.** The effect or impression of one thing on another: *The report gauges the impact of automation on the lives of factory workers.* **3.** The power of making a strong, immediate impression: *Unfortunately, the candidate gave a speech that lacked impact.*

verb (ĭm-păkt′)

    Past participle and past tense: **im·pact·ed**
    Present participle: **im·pact·ing**
    Third person singular present tense: **im·pacts**

transitive **1.** To pack firmly together. **2.** To strike forcefully: *The astronomers observed meteorites impacting the lunar surface.* **3.** USAGE PROBLEM To have an effect or impact on: *The manufacturing industry has been impacted by recent trade agreements.*

intransitive USAGE PROBLEM To have an effect or impact.

[From Latin *impāctus*, past participle of *impingere*, to push against.]

RELATED WORD:
    noun — **im·pac′tion**

꿍 The use of impact as a verb meaning "to have an effect" often has a big impact on readers. Most language critics disapprove of the construction *to impact on*, as in *These policies are impacting on our ability to achieve success*, a sentence 85 percent of the Usage Panel found unacceptable in 2001. The use of *impact* as a transitive verb, as in the sentence *The court ruling will impact the education of minority students*, was unacceptable to 80 percent of the Panel.

It is unclear why this usage provokes such a strong response, but it cannot be because of novelty. *Impact* has been used as a verb since 1601, when it meant "to fix or pack in," and its modern, figurative use dates from 1935. It may be that its frequent appearance in the jargon-riddled remarks of politicians, military officials, and financial analysts continues to make people suspicious. Nevertheless, the verbal use of *impact* has become so common in the working language of corporations and institutions that many speakers have begun to regard it as standard.

im·peach (ĭm-pēch′)

transitive verb

> Past participle and past tense: **im·peached**
> Present participle: **im·peach·ing**
> Third person singular present tense: **im·peach·es**

1. To charge (a public official) with improper conduct in office before a proper tribunal: *The House of Representatives impeached Andrew Johnson in 1868 and Bill Clinton in 1998; neither was convicted.* **2.** To challenge the validity of; try to discredit: *The lawyer impeached the witness's credibility with a string of damaging questions.*

[Middle English *empechen*, to impede, accuse, from Anglo-Norman *empecher*, from Late Latin *impedicāre*, to entangle : Latin *in-*, in + Latin *pedica*, fetter.]

RELATED WORDS:

> *adjective*— **im·peach′a·ble**
> *noun*— **im·peach′er**
> *noun*— **im·peach′ment**

🐾 When an irate citizen demands that a disfavored public official be impeached, the citizen clearly intends for the official to be removed from office. This popular use of *impeach* as a synonym of "throw out" (even if by due process) does not accord with the legal meaning of the word. As recent history has shown, when a public official is impeached, that is, formally accused of wrongdoing, this is only the start of what can be a lengthy process that may or may not lead to the official's removal from office. In strict usage, an official is impeached (accused), tried, and then convicted or acquitted. The vaguer use of *impeach* reflects disgruntled citizens' indifference to whether the official is forced from office by legal means or chooses to resign to avoid further disgrace.

44
im·ply (ĭm-plī′)

transitive verb

    Past participle and past tense: **im·plied**

    Present participle: **im·ply·ing**

    Third person singular present tense: **im·plies**

1. To involve by logical necessity; entail: "*[S]chool would be a complete change: it implied a long journey, an entire separation from Gateshead, an entrance into a new life*" (Charlotte Brontë, *Jane Eyre*). **2.** To express or indicate indirectly: "*'Oh, shut up!' murmured his brother Dan. The manner of his words implied that this fraternal voice near him was an indescribable bore*" (Stephen Crane, *The Little Regiment*).

[Middle English *implien,* from Old French *emplier,* to enfold, from Latin *implicāre.*]

SEE NOTE AT **infer** (ON PAGE 240).

45

in·cred·i·ble (ĭn-krĕd′ə-bəl)

adjective

1. So implausible as to elicit disbelief: "*The next instant we were flying headlong through the air toward the surface of the lake a hundred feet below. Men have told me since that I never made that dive, or that I greatly overestimated the distance, and I admit that as I look back at it now it appears incredible*" (Rex Stout, *Under The Andes*).
2. Extraordinary: "*My father…became a busker and then a singing waiter and then a songwriter, and he felt incredible gratitude to this country for giving him the chance to become who he became*" (Mary Ellin Barrett, *Newsweek*).

[Middle English, from Latin *incrēdibilis* : *in-*, not + *crēdibilis*, believable.]

RELATED WORDS:

    noun — **in·cred′i·bil′i·ty**
    noun — **in·cred′i·ble·ness**
    adverb — **in·cred′i·bly**

❦ *Incredible* means "hard to believe, unbelievable": *His explanation of the cause of the accident was simply incredible.* It is often used more loosely to mean "extraordinary" or "astonishing," as in *The new pitcher has an incredible fastball. Incredulous* usually means "skeptical, disbelieving," as in *The incredulous reporters laughed at the manager's explanation of how the funds disappeared.* It is sometimes extended to mean "showing disbelief," as in *an incredulous stare.* You may occasionally see *incredulous* used where you would expect *incredible*, as in *an incredulous display of rudeness.* This usage is not well established, however, and is widely considered an error.

in·cred·u·lous (ĭn-krĕj′ə-ləs)

adjective

1. Disbelieving or doubtful; skeptical: *"[B]efore me the ice parted to reveal the cold, muddy swirl twisting below. . . . That's when common sense and terror hit and I headed for shore. . . . When I reached land, I looked back, incredulous that I'd thought I could actually make it across"* (William Least Heat-Moon, *River-Horse*). **2.** Expressive of or showing disbelief: *an incredulous stare.* **3.** Usage Problem Hard or impossible to believe.

[From Latin *incrēdulus* : *in-*, not + *crēdulus*, believing.]

RELATED WORDS:
    adverb—**in·cred′u·lous·ly**
    noun—**in·cred′u·lous·ness**

SEE NOTE AT **incredible** (ON PAGE 237).

I felt the floe I stood on begin to shake, then wobble, and before me the ice parted to reveal the cold, muddy swirl twisting below—a more fearsome thing I'd never seen. The frozen river wasn't locked in place as I'd supposed but was being forced slowly downstream, buckling, snapping, opening, closing, ready to swallow whatever came onto it. That's when common sense and terror hit and I headed for shore, unsure whether to go gently and slowly or hard and fast....When I reached land, I looked back, **incredulous** that I'd thought I could actually make it across.

—William Least Heat-Moon,
River-Horse

in·fer (ĭn-fûr′)

transitive verb

    Past participle and past tense: **in·ferred**

    Present participle: **in·fer·ring**

    Third person singular present tense: **in·fers**

1. To conclude from evidence or reasoning: *"Unlike many other functions, reading cannot be studied in animals; indeed, for many years the cerebral localization of all higher cognitive processes could be inferred only from the effects of brain injuries on the people who survived them"* (Sally E. Shaywitz, *Scientific American*). **2.** To hint; imply.

[Latin *īnferre*, to bring in, adduce : *in-*, in + *ferre*, to bear.]

RELATED WORDS:

    adjective—**in·fer′a·ble**

    adverb—**in·fer′a·bly**

    noun—**in′fer·ence**

℘ *Infer* is sometimes confused with *imply*, but it makes good sense to keep these verbs distinct. Inference is the activity performed by a reader or interpreter in drawing conclusions that are not explicit in what is said: *When the mayor said that she would not rule out a tax increase, we inferred that she had been consulting with some new financial advisers, since her old advisers were in favor of tax reductions.* On the other hand, when we say that a speaker or sentence implies something, we mean that it is conveyed or suggested without being stated outright: *When the mayor said that she would not rule out a business tax increase, she implied* (not *inferred*) *that some taxes might be raised.*

---

48   **in·flam·ma·ble** (ĭn-flăm′ə-bəl)

adjective

Easily ignited and capable of burning rapidly; flammable: *"Slurry decomposes in storage and produces a mixture of gases.... All are unpleasant, some can be inflammable, and one in particular, hydrogen sulphide, is extremely poisonous to humans and animals alike"* (Edna O'Brien, *Wild Decembers*).

[Middle English, liable to inflammation, from Medieval Latin *īnflammābilis*, from Latin *īnflammāre*.]

RELATED WORDS:
> *noun* — **in·flam′ma·bil′i·ty**
> *noun* — **in·flam′ma·ble**
> *adverb* — **in·flam′ma·bly**

Historically, *flammable* and *inflammable* mean the same thing. However, the presence of the prefix *in–* has misled many people into assuming that *inflammable* means "not flammable" or "noncombustible." The prefix *in–* in *inflammable* is not, however, the Latin negative prefix *in–*, which is related to the English *un–* and appears in such words as *indecent* and *inglorious*. Rather, this *in–* is an intensive prefix derived from the Latin preposition *in*. This prefix also appears in the word *inflame*. But many people are not aware of this derivation, and for clarity's sake it is advisable to use only *flammable* if you want to give a warning. If you wish to refer to the inability to catch on fire, use *nonflammable*, which is unambiguous.

in·sure (ĭn-shŏŏr′)

transitive verb

Past participle and past tense: **in·sured**
Present participle: **in·sur·ing**
Third person singular present tense: **in·sures**

1a. To provide or arrange insurance for: *"In the past two years, the number of patients [who are] insured by managed care plans has grown by about one-third"* (Lisa Belkin, *New York Times Magazine*). **b.** To acquire or have insurance for: *"More than 300,000 laptops were stolen last year alone, and so the company insures each bag with a computer compartment for up to $1,500 if it's stolen in the first year"* (Stephanie Cook, *Christian Science Monitor*). **2.** To make sure, certain, or secure: *"By relying primarily on voluntary cooperation and private enterprise…we can insure that the private sector is a check on the powers of the governmental sector and an effective protection of freedom of speech, of religion, and of thought"* (Milton Friedman, *Capitalism and Freedom*).

[Middle English *ensuren,* to assure, from Old French *enseurer,* possibly variant of *assurer.*]

RELATED WORDS:

noun — **in·sur′a·bil′i·ty**
adjective — **in·sur′a·ble**

௸ *Assure, ensure,* and *insure* all mean "to make secure or certain." Only *assure* is used with reference to a person in the sense of "to set the mind at rest": *The ambassador assured the Prime Minister of his loyalty.* Although *ensure* and *insure* are generally interchangeable, only *insure* is now widely used in American English in the commercial sense of "to guarantee persons or property against risk."

i·ro·ny (ī′rə-nē, ī′ər-nē)

noun
> Plural: **i·ro·nies**

1a. The use of words to express something different from and often opposite to their literal meaning. **b.** An expression or utterance marked by a deliberate contrast between apparent and intended meaning. **c.** A literary style employing such contrasts for humorous or rhetorical effect. **2a.** Incongruity between what might be expected and what actually occurs. **b.** An occurrence, result, or circumstance notable for such incongruity. **3.** The dramatic effect achieved by leading an audience to understand an incongruity between a situation in a play and its accompanying speeches, while the characters remain unaware of the incongruity; dramatic irony.

[French *ironie*, from Old French, from Latin *īrōnīa*, from Greek *eirōneia*, feigned ignorance, from *eirōn*, dissembler, probably from *eirein*, to say.]

RELATED WORDS:
> *adjective* — **i·ron′ic**
> *adverb* — **i·ron′i·cal·ly**

The words *ironic, irony,* and *ironically* are sometimes used of events and circumstances that might better be described as simply "coincidental" or "improbable," in that they suggest no particular lessons about human vanity or folly. The Usage Panel dislikes the looser use of these words; 78 percent rejected the use of *ironically* in the sentence *In 1969 Susie moved from Ithaca to California where she met her husband-to-be, who, ironically, also came from upstate New York.* Some Panelists noted that this particular usage might be acceptable if Susie had in fact moved to California in order to find a husband, in which case the story could be taken as exemplifying the folly of supposing that we can know what fate has in store for us. By contrast, 73 percent accepted the sentence *Ironically, even as the government was fulminating against American policy, American jeans and videocassettes were the hottest items in the stalls of the market,* where the incongruity of the government's statements and the practices it tolerates as necessary can be seen as an example of human inconsistency.

---

51 ir·re·gard·less (ĭr'ĭ-gärd'lĭs)

adverb

NONSTANDARD Regardless.

[Probably blend of *irrespective* and *regardless.*]

✍ *Irregardless* is a word that many mistakenly believe to be correct usage in formal style, when in fact it is used chiefly in nonstandard speech or casual writing. Coined in the United States in the early 20th century, it has met with a blizzard of condemnation for being an improper yoking of *irrespective* and *regardless* and for the logical absurdity of combining the negative *ir–* prefix and *–less* suffix in a single term. Although one might reasonably argue that it is no different from words with redundant affixes like *debone* and *unravel,* it has been considered a blunder for decades and will probably continue to be so.

---

52 its (ĭts)

adjective

The possessive form of **it.** Used as a modifier before a noun: *The airline canceled its early flight to New York.*

[Alteration of *it's* : it + 's.]

SEE NOTE AT **it's** (ON PAGE 245).

---

irregardless / kudos

it's (ĭts)

1. Contraction of *it is.* **2.** Contraction of *it has.*

✍ *Its* is the possessive form of the pronoun *it* and is correctly written without an apostrophe: *The kitten licked its paws.* It should not be confused with the contraction *it's* (for *it is* or *it has*), which should always have an apostrophe: *It's snowing outside. It's been years since I've visited Chicago.*

ku·dos (kōō′dōz′, kōō′dōs′, kōō′dŏs′, kyōō′dōz′, kyōō′dōs′, kyōō′dŏs′)

noun

Acclaim or praise for exceptional achievement.

[Greek *kūdos*, magical glory.]

✍ *Kudos* is one of those words like *congeries* that look like plurals but are etymologically singular. Acknowledging the Greek history of the term requires *Kudos is* (not *are*) *due her for her brilliant work on the score.* But *kudos* has often been treated as a plural, especially in the popular press, as in *She received many kudos for her work.* This plural use has given rise to the singular form *kudo.* These innovations follow the pattern whereby the English words *pea* and *cherry* were shortened from nouns ending in an (s) sound (English *pease* and French *cerise*), that were mistakenly thought to be plural. The singular *kudo* remains far less common than the plural use; both are often viewed as incorrect in more formal contexts.

It is worth noting that even people who are careful to treat *kudos* only as a singular often pronounce it as if it were a plural. Etymology would require that the final consonant be pronounced as a voiceless (s), as we do in *pathos,* another word derived from Greek, rather than as a voiced (z).

lay (lā)

verb

> Past participle and past tense: **laid**
> Present participle: **lay·ing**
> Third person singular present tense: **lays**

transitive **1a.** To place or put, especially on a flat surface or in a horizontal position: *I laid the baby in the crib.* **b.** To put or place in a certain position or condition: *The remark laid him open to criticism.* **2.** To put in place; set down: *The workers are laying tiles down in the kitchen.* **3.** To produce (an egg or eggs). **4.** To cause to subside or become calm: *". . . chas'd the clouds, and laid the winds"* (John Milton, *Paradise Regained*). **5.** To put in order; prepare: *"He did not look at her but busied himself with his breakfast. . . He prepared coffee and laid the table"* (Carson McCullers, *The Heart Is a Lonely Hunter*). **6.** To spread over a surface: *The artist lays paint on the canvas.* **7.** To impose as a burden or punishment: *The police officer laid a fine on the offender.* **8.** To put forth; present for examination: *The lawyer laid the case before the court.* **9.** To place or give (importance, for example): *The teacher lays great value on correct grammar.* **10.** To assign; charge: *They laid the blame on us.* **11.** To place (a bet); wager: *At the race track, the gambler laid $100 on his favorite horse.*

intransitive To produce an egg or eggs: *The hens stopped laying suddenly.*

---

noun

The way in which something is situated or organized: *"Duane peered through the branches and studied the lay of the land"* (Zane Grey, *The Lone Star Ranger*).

[Middle English *leien,* from Old English *lecgan.*]

⚘ *Lay* ("to put, place, or prepare") and *lie* ("to recline or be situated") have been confused for centuries; evidence exists that *lay* has been used to mean "lie" since the 1300s. Why? First, there are two *lay*s. One is the base form of the verb *lay,* and the other is the past tense of *lie.* Second, *lay* was once used with a reflexive pronoun to mean "lie" and survives in the familiar line from the child's prayer *Now I lay me down to sleep; lay me down* is easily shortened to *lay down.* Third, *lay down,* as in *She lay down on the sofa* sounds the same as *laid down,* as in *I laid down the law to the kids.* It's not surprising that all this similarity of sound has produced confusion of usage, but traditional grammar requires that the two words be kept distinct.

Lay and *lie* are most easily distinguished by the following guidelines: *Lay* is a transitive verb and takes a direct object. *Lay* and its principal parts (*laid, laying*) are correctly used in the following examples: *He laid* (not *lay*) *the newspaper on the table. The table was laid for four. Lie* is an intransitive verb and cannot take an object. *Lie* and its principal parts (*lay, lain, lying*) are correctly used in the following examples: *She often lies* (not *lays*) *down after lunch. When I lay* (not *laid*) *down, I fell asleep. The garbage had lain* (not *laid*) *there a week. I was lying* (not *laying*) *in bed when he called.*

leave (lēv)

verb

> Past participle and past tense: **left**
> Present participle: **leav·ing**
> Third person singular present tense: **leaves**

transitive

1. To go out of or go away from: *After she finished the report, she left the office.* **2.** To end one's association with; withdraw from: *After ten years in the service, he left the navy for civilian life.* **3.** To go without taking or removing; forget: *I left my book on the bus.* **4.** To allow to remain unused: *I left some milk in the glass.* **5.** To allow to remain in a certain condition or place: *He left the lights on all night.* **6.** To give to another to control, act on, or use; entrust: *Leave all the details to us.* **7.** To give by will; bequeath: *"Jonah argued that men liked to make a surprise of their wills, while Martha said that nobody need be surprised if he left the best part of his money to those who least expected it"* (George Eliot, *Middlemarch*). **8.** To have as a result, consequence, or remainder: *The car left a trail of exhaust fumes. Two from eight leaves six.* **9.** NONSTANDARD To allow or permit; let.

intransitive To set out or depart; go: *We left after lunch.*

leave alone *or* **let alone** To refrain from disturbing or interfering with: *"'Leave my books alone!' he said. 'You might have thrown them aside if you had liked, but as to soiling them like that, it is disgusting!'"* (Thomas Hardy, *Jude the Obscure*).

[Middle English *leaven*, from Old English *lǣfan*.]

༄ In formal writing, *leave* is not an acceptable substitute for *let* in the sense "to allow or permit." Thus in the following examples, only *let* can be used: *Let me be. Let him go. Let it lie.*

Leave alone is an acceptable substitute for *let alone* in the sense "to refrain from disturbing or interfering with," as in *Left alone, he was quite productive.* However, there are some who do not accept this usage and feel that *leave alone* should mean simply "to depart from someone who remains in solitude," as in *They were left alone in the wilderness.*

less (lĕs)

adjective

A comparative of **little. 1.** Not as great in amount or quantity: *I have less money than I did yesterday.* **2.** Lower in importance, esteem, or rank: *The speaker was no less a person than the ambassador.* **3.** Consisting of a smaller number.

preposition

With the deduction of; minus: *Five less two is three.*

adverb

The comparative of **little.** To a smaller extent, degree, or frequency: *"We replaced and screwed down the lid, and, having secured the door of iron, made our way, with toil, into the scarcely less gloomy apartments of the upper portion of the house"* (Edgar Allan Poe, *The Fall of the House of Usher*).

noun

1. A smaller amount: *She received less than she asked for.* **2.** Something not as important as something else: *People have been punished for less.*

IDIOMS:

less than Not at all: *He had a less than favorable view of the matter.*

much less *or* **still less** Certainly not: *I'm not blaming anyone, much less you.*

[Middle English *lesse,* from Old English *lǣssa* (*adjective*), and *lǣs* (*adverb*).]

SEE NOTE AT **fewer** (ON PAGE 225).

---

let (lĕt)

verb

> Past participle and past tense: **let**
> Present participle: **let·ting**
> Third person singular present tense: **lets**

1. To give permission or opportunity to; allow: *I let them borrow the car. The inheritance money let us finally buy a house.* **2.** To cause to; make: *Let me know what happens.* **3.** Used as an auxiliary verb to express a command, request, or warning: *Let's finish the job!* **4.** Used as an auxiliary verb to express a proposal or assumption: *Let x equal 3.* **5.** To permit to enter, proceed, or depart: "*When we returned home, we let the dogs out, as we always did, to run around before they were shut in for the night*" (Lydia Davis, *St. Martin*). **6.** To permit escape; release: *Who let the air out of the balloon?* **7.** To rent or lease: *The landlord lets rooms to students.*

intransitive To become rented or leased: *The apartment lets for $900 a month.*

IDIOMS:

let alone 1. Not to mention; much less: "*Their ancestors had been dirt poor and never saw royalty, let alone hung around with them*" (Garrison Keillor, *Lake Wobegon Days*). **2.** *or* **leave alone** To refrain from disturbing or interfering: "'*Let me alone! let me alone!' sobbed Catherine. 'If I've done wrong, I'm dying for it. It is enough!'*" (Emily Brontë, *Wuthering Heights*).

let go To cease to employ; dismiss: *The factory let 20 workers go.*

[Middle English *leten*, from Old English *lǣtan*.]

SEE NOTE AT **leave** (ON PAGE 248).

lie (lī)

intransitive verb
> Past tense: **lay**
> Past participle: **lain**
> Present participle: **ly·ing**
> Third person singular present tense: **lies**

1. To place oneself at rest in a flat, horizontal, or resting position; recline: *He lay under a tree to sleep.* **2.** To be in a flat, horizontal, or resting position: *"I collected the instruments of life around me, that I might infuse a spark of being into the lifeless thing that lay at my feet"* (Mary Wollstonecraft Shelley, *Frankenstein*). **3.** To be or rest on a surface: *Dirty dishes lay on the table.* **4.** To be located: *The lake lies beyond this hill.* **5.** To remain in a certain position or condition: *The dust has lain undisturbed for years.* **6.** To consist or have as a basis: *"Eric was pleased, but he always reminded himself that his success lay in promoting the talent of others"* (Louis Auchincloss, *Her Infinite Variety*). **7.** To extend: *Our land lies between these trees and the river.* **8.** To be buried in a specified place: *His ancestors lie in the town cemetery.*

noun

The manner or position in which something is situated, as the surface or slope of a piece of land.

[Middle English *lien,* from Old English *licgan.*]

SEE NOTE AT **lay** (ON PAGE 247).

It was on a dreary night of November that I beheld the accomplishment of my toils. With an anxiety that almost amounted to agony, I collected the instruments of life around me, that I might infuse a spark of being into the lifeless thing that **lay** at my feet. It was already one in the morning; the rain pattered dismally against the panes, and my candle was nearly burnt out, when, by the glimmer of the half-extinguished light, I saw the dull yellow eye of the creature open; it breathed hard, and a convulsive motion agitated its limbs.

—Mary Wollstonecraft Shelley,
Frankenstein

60

lit·er·al·ly (lĭt′ər-ə-lē)

adverb

1. In a literal manner; word for word: *The scholar translated the Greek passage literally.* **2.** In a literal or strict sense: *Don't take my remarks literally.* **3.** USAGE PROBLEM Really; actually. Used as an intensive before a figurative expression: *He was laughing so hard his sides literally burst.*

🖉 For more than a hundred years, critics have remarked on the incoherency of using *literally* in a way that suggests the exact opposite of its primary sense of "in a manner that accords with the literal sense of the words." In 1926, for example, H.W. Fowler cited the example "*The 300,000 Unionists…will be literally thrown to the wolves.*" The practice does not stem from a change in the meaning of *literally* itself—if it did, the word would long since have come to mean "virtually" or "figuratively"—but from a natural tendency to use the word as a general intensive, as in *They had literally no help from the government on the project,* where no contrast with the figurative sense of the words is intended.

61

mass (măs)

noun

1. A measure of the amount of matter contained in or constituting a physical body: "*The Sun will swallow the planet Mercury and its outer rim will reach beyond the present orbit of Venus. Our sister planet will no longer be there, however, because as the Sun has lost mass, its gravitational pull on Venus (and Earth) has become less, and these planets have moved away from the encroaching fires*" (James Trefil, *Smithsonian*). **2.** A unified body of matter with no specific shape: *"Cooks throughout the many nations also use yams, cassavas, green bananas and plantains. These staples are tasty on their own or combined with other ingredients to make a starchy mass for scooping up savory dishes"* (Jonell Nash, *Essence*). **3.** A large but nonspecific amount or number: *A mass of people entered the stadium.* **4.** The principal part; the majority: *The mass of the continent was visible from the rocketship.* **5.** The physical bulk or size of a solid body: *The huge mass of the ocean liner crept into the harbor.* **6. masses** The body of common people or people of low socioeconomic status: *"Give me your tired, your poor, / Your huddled masses yearning to breathe free"* (Emma Lazarus, *The New Colossus*).

verb

> Past participle and past tense: **massed**
> Present participle: **mass·ing**
> Third person singular present tense: **mass·es**

transitive To gather into a mass: *"[T]he population massed itself and moved toward the river, met the children coming in an open carriage drawn by shouting citizens, thronged around it, joined its homeward march, and swept magnificently up the main street roaring huzzah after huzzah!"* (Mark Twain, *The Adventures of Tom Sawyer*).

intransitive To be gathered into a mass: *The hikers massed together to stay warm.*

adjective

1. Of, relating to, characteristic of, directed at, or attended by a large number of people: *mass communication.* **2.** Done or carried out on a large scale: *mass pro-*

duction. **3.** Total; complete: *The mass result is impressive.*

[Middle English *masse,* from Old French, from Latin *massa,*
from Greek *māza, maza.*]

✍ Although most hand-held calculators can translate pounds into
kilograms, an absolute conversion factor between these two
units is not technically sound. A pound is a unit of force, and a
kilogram is a unit of mass. When the unit pound is used to indicate the force that a gravitational field exerts on a mass, the
pound is a unit of weight. Mistaking weight for mass is tanta-
mount to confusing the electric charges on two objects with the
forces of attraction (or repulsion) between them. Like charge,
the mass of an object is an intrinsic property of that object: electrons have a unique mass, protons have a unique mass, and
some particles, such as photons, have no mass. Weight, on the
other hand, is a force due to the gravitational attraction between
two bodies. For example, one's weight on the Moon is $\frac{1}{6}$ of
one's weight on Earth. Nevertheless, one's mass on the Moon is
identical to one's mass on Earth. The reason that hand-held calculators can translate between units of weight and units of mass
is that the majority of us use calculators on the planet Earth at
or near sea level, where the conversion factor is constant for all
practical purposes.

62

mean (mēn)

noun

1. Something having a position, quality, or condition
midway between extremes; a medium. **2.** A number
that typifies a set of numbers, especially an arithmetic
mean or average. **3.** Either the second or third term of
a proportion of four terms. In the proportion $\frac{2}{3} = \frac{4}{6}$,
the means are 3 and 4. **4. means** *(used with a singular
or plural verb)* A method, a course of action, or an instrument by which an act can be accomplished or an

end achieved: *The solar panels provide a practical means of using the sun's energy to generate electricity.* **5. means** *(used with a plural verb)* Money, property, or other wealth: *The mayor was a person of means and bankrolled his election campaign.*

adjective

1. Occupying a middle or intermediate position between two extremes: *The school district analyzed the mean test scores of each class.* **2.** Intermediate in size, extent, quality, time, or degree; average.

IDIOMS:

by any means In any way possible: *We must fix this problem by any means.*
by no means In no sense; certainly not: *By no means should you go sailing in rough weather.*

[Middle English *mene*, middle, from Old French *meien*, from Latin *mediānus*, from *medius*.]

🖎 In the sense of "financial resources" *means* takes a plural verb: *His means are more than adequate.* In the sense of "a way to an end," *means* may be treated as either a singular or plural. It is singular when referring to a particular strategy or method: *The best means of securing the cooperation of the builders is to appeal to their self-interest.* It is plural when it refers to a group of strategies or methods: *The most effective means for dealing with the drug problem have generally been those suggested by the affected communities.*

Means is most often followed by *of*: *a means of noise reduction.* But *for*, *to*, and *toward* are also used: *a means for transmitting sound; a means to an end; a means toward achieving equality.*

me·di·an (mē′dē-ən)

noun

1. Something that lies halfway between two extremes; a medium. **2.** The middle number of a sequence having an odd number of values or the average of the two middle values if the sequence has an even number of values. For example, in the sequence 1, 2, 5, 10, 19, the median is 5; in the sequence 7, 8, 12, 16, the median is 10. **3a.** A line that joins a vertex of a triangle to the midpoint of the opposite side. **b.** The line that joins the midpoints of the nonparallel sides of a trapezoid.

adjective

1. Located in or extending toward the middle: *The lanes of traffic were separated by a median barrier.* **2.** Constituting the middle value in a set of numbers: *The statisticians analyzed the median score.*

[Latin *mediānus,* from *medius,* middle.]

☙ In statistics, the concepts of *average* and *median* are often confused. To calculate an average, you add up all the items under consideration, and then divide by the number of items. So, for example, if a real estate agent sells five houses worth $95,000, $115,000, $190,000, $260,000, and $800,000, the average sales price is $292,000. Determining the *median* involves looking at the middle value in a series of values (if the series contains an even number of values, you then take the average of the middle two values). Using the above prices, the median sales price of these homes was $190,000. Median prices are often reported because it tells you that the same number of items fall above that value as fall below it, whereas if one of the values is much greater or lower than the other values, reporting the average may seem skewed, as in the example above.

mis·chie·vous (mĭs′chə-vəs)

adjective

1. Causing mischief; naughty: *"I've left my young children to look after themselves, and a more mischievous and troublesome set of young imps doesn't exist, ma'am"* (Kenneth Grahame, *The Wind in the Willows*). **2.** Showing a tendency or intent to play pranks or tease: *The child cast a mischievous glance.* **3.** Causing injury or damage: *The hard drive was destroyed by a mischievous computer virus.*

[Middle English *mischevous,* from *mischef,* mischief, from Old French *meschief,* misfortune, from *meschever,* to end badly : *mes-,* badly + *chever,* to happen, come to an end (from Vulgar Latin **capāre,* to come to a head, from **capum,* head, from Latin *caput*).]

RELATED WORDS:
> *adverb* — **mis′chie·vous·ly**
> *noun* — **mis′chie·vous·ness**

The pronunciation (mĭs-chē′vē-əs) is considered nonstandard, and is an example of *intrusion,* a phonological process that involves the addition or insertion of an extra sound. *Mischievous* is properly pronounced with three syllables, with the accent on the first syllable. The word is often misspelled with the suffix *-ious,* which matches the mispronunciation.

nu·cle·ar (nōō′klē-ər, nyōō′klē-ər)

adjective

1. Of, relating to, or forming a nucleus: *The biologist studied the cell's nuclear membrane under a microscope.* **2.** Of or relating to atomic nuclei: *"December 2 [1942]: Scientists at the University of Chicago achieve the first sustained nuclear chain reaction in human history"* (Alan Brinkley & Davis Dyer, eds., *The Readers Companion to the American Presidency*). **3.** Using or derived from the energy of atomic nuclei: *"[A]n attack on a nuclear power plant would not automatically mean a disaster on the scale of Chernobyl"* (Sonya Yee, *Christian Science Monitor*). **4.** Relating to, having, or involving atomic or hydrogen bombs: *"In the early 1980s, the U.S. experienced a nuclear hysteria—a morbid, near panicked fear of nuclear apocalypse"* (Charles Krauthammer, *Time*).

[Adjectival form of *nucleus*, from Latin *nuculeus*, nucleus, kernel, from *nucula*, little nut, diminutive of *nux, nuc-*, nut.]

🌿 The pronunciation (nōō′kyə-lər), which is generally considered incorrect, is an example of how a familiar phonological pattern can influence an unfamiliar one. The usual pronunciation of the final two syllables of this word is (-klē-ər), but this sequence of sounds is rare in English. Much more common is the similar sequence (-kyə-lər), which occurs in words like *particular, circular, spectacular,* and in many scientific words like *molecular, ocular,* and *vascular.* Adjusted to fit into this familiar pattern, the (-kyə-lər) pronunciation is often heard in high places. It is not uncommon in the military, even among commanders, in association with nuclear weaponry, and it has been a notable characteristic of the speech of presidents Dwight Eisenhower, Jimmy Carter, and George W. Bush. The prominence of these speakers, however, has done little to brighten the appeal of (nōō′kyə-lər) for many others.

66
pa·ram·e·ter (pə-răm′ĭ-tər)

noun

1. A variable or an arbitrary constant appearing in a mathematical expression, each value of which restricts or determines the specific form of the expression. **2a.** One of a set of measurable factors, such as temperature and pressure, that define a system and determine its behavior and are varied in an experiment. **b.** USAGE PROBLEM A factor that restricts what is possible or what results. **c.** A factor that determines a range of variations; a boundary: *The principal of the experimental school made sure that the parameters of its curriculum continued to expand.* **3.** USAGE PROBLEM A distinguishing characteristic or feature.

[New Latin *parametrum*, a line through the focus and parallel to the directrix of a conic : Greek *para-*, beside + Greek *metron*, measure.]

RELATED WORDS:
> *verb* — **pa·ram′e·ter·ize′** (pə-răm′ə-tə-rīz′)
> *adjective* — **par′a·met′ric** (păr′ə-mĕt′rĭk)
> *adverb* — **par′a·met′ri·cal·ly**

℘ The term *parameter*, which originates in mathematics, has a number of specific meanings in fields such as astronomy, electricity, crystallography, and statistics. Perhaps because of its ring of technical authority, it has been used more generally in recent years to refer to any factor that determines a range of variations and especially to a factor that restricts what can result from a process or policy. In this use it often comes close to meaning "a limit or boundary." Some of these new uses have a clear connection to the technical senses of the word. For example, the provisions of a zoning ordinance that limit the height or density of new construction can be reasonably likened to mathematical parameters that establish the limits of other variables. Therefore one can say *The zoning commission announced new planning parameters for the historic district of the city.* But other uses go one step further and treat *parameter* as a high-toned synonym for *characteristic.* In 1988, 80 percent of the Usage Panel rejected this use of *parameter* in the example *The Judeo-Christian ethic is one of the important parameters of Western culture.*

Some of the difficulties with the nontechnical use of *parameter* appear to arise from its resemblance to the word *perimeter,* with which it shares the sense "limit," though the precise meanings of the two words differ. This confusion probably explains the use of *parameter* in a sentence such as *US forces report that the parameters of the mine area in the Gulf are fairly well established,* where the word *perimeter* would have expressed the intended sense more exactly. This example of a use of *parameter* was unacceptable to 61 percent of the Usage Panel.

67

pe·nul·ti·mate (pǐ-nŭl′tə-mǐt)

adjective

1. Next to last: *"His cause for beatification, the penulti-mate step before sainthood, is still on course"* (Alessandra Stanley, *New York Times*). **2.** Of or relating to the next-to-last syllable of a word: *The word* renewal *has penulti-mate stress.*

noun

The next to the last.

[From Latin *paenultimus,* next to last : *paene,* almost + *ul-timus,* last.]

RELATED WORD:
adverb —**pe·nul′ti·mate·ly**

🖉 *Penultimate* is sometimes mistakenly used where the word *ulti-mate* is called for, especially in the sense of "representing or ex-hibiting the greatest possible development or sophistication" as in the sentence *This car is the penultimate in engineering design.* This mistake is probably due to a misconception that *pen-* is a prefix that acts as an intensifier of the word *ultimate,* when it actually derives from the Latin word *paene,* meaning "almost." Thus, people who know the correct meaning of *penultimate* would reject its use as a synonym of *ultimate* and they may view the speaker or writer as not only pretentious, but ignorant as well.

per·suade (pər-swād′)

transitive verb

Past participle and past tense: **per·suad·ed**
Present participle: **per·suad·ing**
Third person singular present tense: **per·suades**

To cause (someone) to do or believe something by means of argument, reasoning, or entreaty: *"Lord cardinal, will your grace / Persuade the queen to send the Duke of York / Unto his princely brother presently?"* (William Shakespeare, *Richard III*).

[Latin *persuādēre* : *per-*, per- + *suādēre*, to urge.]

RELATED WORD:

adjective —**per·suad′a·ble**
noun —**per·suad′er**

SEE NOTE AT **convince** (ON PAGE 211).

Fie, what an indirect and peevish course
Is this of hers! Lord cardinal, will your grace
Persuade the queen to send the Duke of York
Unto his princely brother presently?
If she deny, Lord Hastings, go with him,
And from her jealous arms pluck him perforce.

—William Shakespeare,
Richard III

pe·ruse (pə-rōōz′)

transitive verb

Past participle and past tense: **pe·rused**
Present participle: **pe·rus·ing**
Third person singular present tense: **pe·rus·es**

To read or examine, typically with great care: *"He that shall peruse the political pamphlets of any past reign, will wonder why they were so eagerly read, or so loudly praised"* (Samuel Johnson, *The Rambler*).

[Middle English *perusen,* to use up : Latin *per-,* per- + Middle English *usen,* to use.]

RELATED WORDS:
adjective —**pe·rus′a·ble**
noun —**pe·rus′al**
noun —**pe·rus′er**

🖎 *Peruse* has long meant "to read thoroughly." Seventy-eight percent of the Usage Panel accepts *She perused the pages, carefully looking for errors.* But the word is sometimes used loosely as a highfalutin synonym for *read,* and some people even use it to mean "to glance over, skim" as in *I only had a moment to peruse the manual quickly.* This sentence was unacceptable to 58 percent of the Panel in a 1999 survey, down somewhat from 66 percent in 1988, suggesting that resistance is still quite strong to this usage.

phe·nom·e·non (fə-nŏm′ə-nŏn)

noun

1. (Plural: **phe·nom·e·na**) An occurrence, circumstance, or fact that is perceptible by the senses or with aid of instrumentation: *"Typical manifestations of T cells at work include such diverse phenomena as the rejection of a foreign skin graft and the killing of tumor cells"* (Gary W. Litman, *Scientific American*). **2.** (Plural: **phe·nom·e·nons**) A remarkable, significant, or outstanding person or thing: *"In an industry famous for cutthroat competition, this summer's reality TV shows have become a pop culture phenomenon and left a string of stunned TV executives scrambling to catch up"* (Lauren Hunter, *cnn.com*).

[Late Latin *phaenomenon,* from Greek *phainomenon,* from neuter present participle of *phainesthai,* to appear.]

᭣ The word *phenomenon* comes to us from Greek via Latin and usually keeps its Greek plural form *phenomena* when it means "an occurrence, circumstance, or fact that is perceptible by the senses." You may sometimes come across *phenomena* used as a singular noun, as in *This is a very strange phenomena,* but this usage is widely considered incorrect. The plural *phenomenons* is used frequently in nonscientific writing when the meaning is "extraordinary things, occurrences, or persons," as in *The Beatles were phenomenons in the history of rock 'n' roll.*

plus (plŭs)

conjunction

1. Added to: *Three plus two equals five.* **2.** Increased by; along with: *Their strength plus their spirit makes them formidable.* **3.** USAGE PROBLEM And: *I bought a dining table, plus four chairs and a mirror.*

adjective

1. Positive or on the positive part of a scale: *a temperature of plus five degrees.* **2.** Added or extra: *a plus benefit.* **3.** *Informal* Increased to a further degree or number: *"At 70 plus, [he] is old enough to be metaphysical"* (Anatole Broyard, *New York Times Book Review*). **4.** Ranking on the higher end of a designated scale: *I received a grade of B plus in chemistry.* **5.** Relating to or designating an electric charge of a sign opposite to that of an electron; positive.

noun

Plural **plus·es** *or* **plus·ses**

1. The plus sign (+). **2.** A positive quantity. **3.** A favorable condition or factor: *The clear weather was a plus for the golf tournament.*

[Latin *plūs*, more.]

---

plus   **268**

When mathematical equations are pronounced as English sentences, the verb is usually in the singular: *Two plus two is* (or *equals*) *four.* By the same token, subjects containing two noun phrases joined by *plus* are usually construed as singular: *The construction slowdown plus the bad weather has made for a weak market.* This observation has led some to argue that in these sentences, *plus* functions as a preposition meaning "in addition to." But if this were true, the *plus* phrase could be moved to the beginning of the sentence. Clearly, this is not the case—we do not say *Plus the bad weather, the construction slowdown has made for a weak market.* It makes more sense to view *plus* in these uses as a conjunction that joins two subjects into a single entity requiring a single verb by notional agreement, just as *and* does in the sentence *Chips and beans is her favorite appetizer.*

The usage *plus which*, as in: *The construction industry has been hurt by the rise in rates. Plus which, bad weather has affected housing starts* is not well established in formal writing; nor is *plus* accepted as correct in introducing an independent clause, as in *She has a great deal of talent, plus she is willing to work hard.*

pre·cip·i·tate (prĭ-sĭp′ĭ-tāt′)

verb

> Past participle and past tense: **pre·cip·i·tat·ed**
> Present participle: **pre·cip·i·tat·ing**
> Third person singular present tense: **pre·cip·i·tates**

transitive **1.** To throw from or as if from a great height; hurl downward: *"[T]he finest bridge in all Peru broke and precipitated five travelers into the gulf below"* (Thornton Wilder, *The Bridge of San Luis Rey*). **2.** To cause to happen, especially suddenly or prematurely: *The political scandal precipitated a torrent of legislative reforms.* **3.** To cause (water vapor) to condense and fall from the air as rain, snow, sleet, or hail. **4.** To cause (a solid substance) to be separated from a solution: *The chemist precipitated the minerals from the water by adding borax.*

intransitive **1.** To condense and fall from the air as rain, snow, sleet, or hail. **2.** To be separated from a solution as a solid. **3.** To send into a sudden state or condition: *The ailing economy precipitated into ruin despite foreign intervention.*

adjective (prĭ-sĭp′ĭ-tĭt)

1. Moving rapidly and heedlessly; speeding headlong: *The meteorologists tracked the tornado's precipitate course.* **2.** Acting with or marked by excessive haste and lack of due deliberation; reckless: *They soon came to regret the precipitate decisions.* **3.** Occurring suddenly or unexpectedly: *The pundits couldn't explain the precipitate rise in oil prices.*

noun (prĭ-sĭp′ĭ-tāt′, prĭ-sĭp′ĭ-tĭt)

A chemical solid or solid phase separated from a solution.

[Latin *praecipitāre, praecipitāt-*, to throw headlong, from *praeceps, praecipit-*, headlong : *prae-*, pre- + *caput, capit-*, head.]

RELATED WORDS:
    adverb —**pre·cip′i·tate·ly**
    adjective —**pre·cip′i·ta′tive**
    noun —**pre·cip′i·ta′tor**

SEE NOTE AT **precipitous** (ON PAGE 272).

pre·cip·i·tous (prĭ-sĭp′ĭ-təs)

adjective

1. Resembling a precipice; extremely steep. **2.** Having several precipices: *"The Duchy of Grand Fenwick lies in a precipitous fold of the northern Alps and embraces in its tumbling landscape portions of three valleys, a river, one complete mountain with an elevation of two thousand feet and a castle"* (Leonard Wibberley, *The Mouse That Roared*). **3.** Usage Problem Extremely rapid, hasty, or abrupt; precipitate.

[Probably from obsolete *precipitious,* from Latin *praecipitium,* precipice.]

RELATED WORDS:

    adverb —**pre·cip′i·tous·ly**
    noun —**pre·cip′i·tous·ness**

The adjective *precipitate* and the adverb *precipitately* were once applied to physical steepness but are now used primarily of rash, headlong actions: *Precipitous* currently means "steep" in both literal and figurative senses: *the precipitous rapids of the upper river; a precipitous drop in commodity prices.* But *precipitous* and *precipitously* are also frequently used to mean "abrupt, hasty," which takes them into territory that would ordinarily belong to *precipitate* and *precipitately: their precipitous decision to leave.* This usage is a natural extension of the use of *precipitous* to describe a rise or fall in a quantity over time: *a precipitous increase in reports of measles* is also an abrupt or sudden event. Although the extended use of *precipitous* is well attested in the work of reputable writers, it is still widely regarded as an error and was considered unacceptable to two-thirds of the Usage Panel in 2001.

pre·scribe (prĭ-skrīb′)

verb

   Past participle and past tense: **pre·scribed**
   Present participle: **pre·scrib·ing**
   Third person singular present tense: **pre·scribes**

transitive **1.** To set down as a rule or guide; impose or direct: *"In all well-governed states too, not only judges are appointed for determining the controversies of individuals, but rules are prescribed for regulating the decisions of those judges"* (Adam Smith, *The Theory of Moral Sentiments*). **2.** To order the use of (a medicine or other treatment): *The doctor prescribed antibiotics and plenty of bed rest.*

intransitive **1.** To establish rules, laws, or directions. **2.** To order a medicine or other treatment.

[Middle English *prescriben,* from Latin *praescrībere* : *prae-,* pre- + *scrībere,* to write.]

RELATED WORD:
   noun —**pre·scrib′er**

SEE NOTE AT **proscribe** (ON PAGE 278).

75

pres·ent·ly (prĕz'ənt-lē)

adverb

1. In a short time; soon: *"She thought she must have been mistaken at first, for none of the scarecrows in Kansas ever wink; but presently the figure nodded its head to her in a friendly way"* (L. Frank Baum, *The Wonderful Wizard of Oz*). **2.** USAGE PROBLEM At this time or period; now: *Springfield is presently the capital of Illinois.*

≈ An original meaning of *presently* was "at the present time; currently." That sense is said to have disappeared from the literary language in the 17th century, but it has survived in popular usage and is widely found nowadays in literate speech and writing. Still, there is a lingering prejudice against this use. The sentence *General Walters is…presently the United States Ambassador to the United Nations* was acceptable to only 48 percent of the Usage Panel in the 1999 survey.

While Dorothy was looking earnestly into the queer, painted face of the Scarecrow, she was surprised to see one of the eyes slowly wink at her. She thought she must have been mistaken at first, for none of the scarecrows in Kansas ever wink; but **presently** the figure nodded its head to her in a friendly way. Then she climbed down from the fence and walked up to it, while Toto ran around the pole and barked.

—L. Frank Baum,
The Wonderful Wizard of Oz

prin·ci·pal (prĭn′sə-pəl)

adjective

1. First, highest, or foremost in importance, rank, worth, or degree; chief: *The principal character in* Gone With the Wind *is Scarlett O'Hara.* **2.** Of, relating to, or being a financial principal, or a principal in a financial transaction.

noun

1. A person who holds a position of presiding rank, especially the head of an elementary school or high school: *The rowdy students were sent to the principal's office.* **2.** A main participant, as in a business deal. **3.** A person having a leading or starring role: *The director cast the chorus before casting the principals.* **4a.** A financial holding as distinguished from the interest or revenue from it. **b.** A sum of money owed as a debt, upon which interest is calculated.

[Middle English, from Old French, from Latin *prīncipālis,* from *prīnceps, prīncip-,* leader, emperor.]

RELATED WORDS:

> *adverb* —**prin′ci·pal·ly**
> *noun* —**prin′ci·pal·ship′**

🖉 *Principal* and *principle* are often confused but have no meanings in common. *Principle* is only a noun and usually refers to a rule or standard: *The class was assigned to read an essay about the principles of democracy. Principal* is both a noun and an adjective. As a noun, in general usage it refers to a person who holds a high position or plays an important role: *A meeting was held among all the principals in the transaction.* As an adjective it has the sense of "chief" or "leading": *The coach's principal concern is the quarterback's health.*

---

principal / principle   **276**

prin·ci·ple (prĭn′sə-pəl)

noun

1. A basic truth or statement, especially a system of beliefs or ideals: *The senator swore to uphold the principles of democracy.* **2a.** A rule or standard, especially of good behavior: *The sheriff was a man of principle.* **b.** The general set of moral or ethical standards: *"He chose principle over partisanship and is respected by liberals and conservatives alike"* (Brent Staples, *New York Times Book Review*). **3.** A statement or set of statements describing the functioning of natural phenomena or mechanical processes: *"Quantum teleportation makes use of a strange aspect of quantum physics called the Heisenberg Uncertainty Principle, which says it is impossible to measure both the speed and position of an object at the same time"* (Peter O'Connor, *Star Tribune* [Minneapolis]).

IDIOMS:

in principle With regard to the basics: *"Monitoring systems can in principle be programmed to look for certain keywords, like* bomb *or* target, *within messages they capture"* (Susan Stellin, *New York Times*).

on principle According to or because of principle: *Because I am an environmentalist, I objected to the airport's expansion into the marsh on principle.*

[Middle English, alteration of Old French *principe,* from Latin *prīncipium,* from *prīnceps, prīncip-,* leader, emperor.]

SEE NOTE AT **principal** (ON PAGE 276).

pro·scribe (prō-skrīb′)

transitive verb
> Past participle and past tense: **pro·scribed**
> Present participle: **pro·scrib·ing**
> Third person singular present tense: **pro·scribes**

1. To forbid; prohibit: *The government proscribes the importation of certain plants.* **2.** To denounce; condemn: *"In June 1580, Philip II had proscribed William as 'the chief disturber of our state of Christendom' and offered twenty-five thousand ecus to anyone who might venture to kill him"* (Simon Schama, *American Scholar*). **3.** To banish; outlaw: *After the coup, the monarch was proscribed and ordered to leave the country.*

[Middle English *proscriben,* from Latin *prōscrībere,* to put up someone's name as outlawed : *prō-,* in front + *scrībere,* to write.]

RELATED WORD:
> *noun* —**pro·scrib′er**

☙ Some senses of *prescribe* and *proscribe* are opposite in meaning. But because the two words sound similar, they're often confused. In its most common senses, *proscribe* means "to forbid" and "to denounce." *Prescribe,* on the other hand, means "to set down as a rule or guide," as in *The company handbook prescribes acceptable ways of reassigning an employee.* The medical sense, "to order the use of a medicine or treatment," as in *The doctor prescribed two aspirin,* is related to this sense.

re·nown (rĭ-noun′)

noun

The quality of being widely honored and acclaimed; fame.

[Middle English *renoun,* from Anglo-Norman, from *renomer,* to make famous : *re-,* repeatedly + *nomer,* to name (from Latin *nōmināre,* from *nōmen, nōmin-,* name).]

RELATED WORD:
     adjective —**re·nowned′**

Because *renown* means "fame," and to be famous is to be well-known, *renown* is often misspelled with a *k.* For the same reasons, *renown* is often mispronounced as though it rhymed with *own. Renown* is properly pronounced with the same vowel sound as *noun* or *town.* The same holds true for the adjectival form, *renowned.*

ret·i·cent (rĕt′ĭ-sənt)

adjective

1. Inclined to keep one's thoughts, feelings, and personal affairs to oneself: *"The cowboy was usually soft-spoken and reserved of manner with strangers, so much so that he gained the reputation of being taciturn and reticent by nature, a conclusion which was erroneous"* (Ramon F. Adams, *Cowboy Lingo*). **2.** Usage Problem Reluctant; unwilling.

[Latin *reticēns, reticent-* present participle of *reticēre,* to keep silent : *re-,* re- + *tacēre,* to be silent.]

RELATED WORD:

    adverb —**ret′i·cent·ly**

☺ *Reticent* is generally used to indicate a reluctance to speak. Many people criticize its extended use as an all-purpose synonym for *reluctant.* In a 2001 survey, 83 percent of the Usage Panel found unacceptable the sentence *A lot of out-of-towners are reticent to come to the Twin Cities for a ballgame if there's a chance the game will be rained out.*

---

reticent / seasonable　　　　　　　　　　**280**

sac·ri·le·gious (săk′rə-lĭj′əs, săk′rə-lē′jəs)

adjective

Grossly irreverent toward what is or is held to be sacred: *"Most sacrilegious murder hath broke ope / The Lord's anointed temple"* (William Shakespeare, *Macbeth*).

[From *sacrilege* (from Old French, from Latin *sacrilegium*, from *sacrilegus*, one who steals sacred things : *sacer*, sacred + *legere*, to gather) + *-ous*, adjectival suffix.]

RELATED WORDS:
> *noun* —sac′ri·lege (săk′rə-lĭj)
> *adverb* —sac′ri·le′gious·ly
> *noun* —sac′ri·le′gious·ness

🖎 *Sacrilegious*, the adjective form of *sacrilege*, is often misspelled with the first *i* and the *e* switched, through confusion with the word *religious*.

sea·son·a·ble (sē′zə-nə-bəl)

adjective

1. In keeping with the time or the season: *"The weather was fair and seasonable, but Mary wore flannel underclothes beneath her dress and a heavy cloak as well"* (Michael Crummey, *River Thieves*). **2.** Occurring or performed at the proper time; timely: *The pundits praised the government's seasonable intervention in the trade dispute.*

RELATED WORD:
> *adverb* —sea′son·a·bly

SEE NOTE AT **seasonal** (ON PAGE 282).

---

sea·son·al (sēʹzə-nəl)

adjective

Of or dependent on a particular season: *"Among the important soil properties are natural soil drainage, permeability, . . . load bearing capacity, depth to water table, seasonal wetness, shrink-swell capacity and soil structure"* (Bobbi McDermott, *Yuma Sun*).

RELATED WORD:
  adverb —**sea′son·al·ly**

❧ *Seasonal* and *seasonable,* though closely related, have different uses. *Seasonal* applies to what depends on or is controlled by the season of the year: *a seasonal increase in employment. Seasonable* applies to what is appropriate to the season (*seasonable clothing*) or timely (*seasonable intervention*). Rains are *seasonal* if they occur at a certain time of the year; they are *seasonable* at any time if they save the crops.

84

sen·su·al (sĕn′shŏŏ-əl)

adjective

1. Of, relating to, given to, or providing gratification of the physical and especially the sexual appetites: *"The modern geisha is the aristocrat of the huge industry that has evolved through the centuries to cater to Japanese men's sensual desires"* (Jodi Cobb, *National Geographic*). **2.** Relating to or affecting any of the senses or a sense organ; sensory.

RELATED WORDS:

> *adverb* —**sen′su·al·ly**
> *noun* —**sen′su·al·ness**

SEE NOTE AT **sensuous** (ON PAGE 284).

sen·su·ous (sĕn′shoō-əs)

adjective

1. Of, relating to, or derived from the senses: *"[T]hough he turned the pages with the sensuous joy of the book-lover, he did not know what he was reading, and one book after another dropped from his hand"* (Edith Wharton, *The Age of Innocence*). **2.** Appealing to or gratifying the senses: *The sculpture featured sensuous curves juxtaposed with sharp facial features.* **3.** Easily affected through the senses.

RELATED WORDS:
> *adverb* —**sen′su·ous·ly**
> *noun* —**sen′su·ous·ness**

Both *sensual* and *sensuous* mean "relating to or gratifying the senses." *Sensuous* can refer to any of the senses but usually applies to those involved in aesthetic enjoyment, as of art or music: *The critic lectured about the sensuous imagery in 19th century poems.* *Sensual* more often applies to the physical senses or appetites, particularly those associated with sexual pleasure.

[T]hough he turned the pages with the **sensuous** joy of the book-lover, he did not know what he was reading, and one book after another dropped from his hand. Suddenly, among them, he lit on a small volume of verse which he had ordered because the name had attracted him: "The House of Life." He took it up, and found himself plunged in an atmosphere unlike any he had ever breathed in books; so warm, so rich, and yet so ineffably tender, that it gave a new and haunting beauty to the most elementary of human passions.

—Edith Wharton,
The Age of Innocence

set (sĕt)

verb

> Past participle and past tense: **set**
> Present participle: **set·ting**
> Third person singular present tense: **sets**

transitive **1.** To put in a specified position; place: *I set the book on the shelf.* **2.** To put into a specified state: *With a push he set the wagon in motion.* **3.** To put into a stable position: *She set the fence post into a bed of concrete.* **4.** To restore to a proper and normal state when dislocated or broken: *The doctor set the broken bone.* **5.** To adjust for proper functioning: *We set the mouse traps to prevent infestation.* **6.** To adjust (an instrument, tool, or device) so that some desired condition of operation is established: *She set the alarm clock for 7:00.* **7.** To arrange tableware on or at in preparation for a meal: *"'Where's Papa going with that ax?' said Fern to her mother as they were setting the table for breakfast"* (E.B. White, *Charlotte's Web*). **8.** To arrange (hair) in a certain style, as by rolling it up with clips and curlers. **9a.** To arrange (type) into words and sentences in preparation for printing. **b.** To arrange (matter to be printed) into type. **10a.** To compose (music) to fit a given text. **b.** To write (words) to fit a melody. **11.** To represent the unfolding of (a drama or narrative, for instance) in a specific place: *The play* Romeo and Juliet *is set in Verona.* **12.** To make as a rule or guideline; establish: *You should set an example for your younger brother.* **13.** To decide on; appoint or designate: *They set June 6 as the day of the wedding.* **14.** To detail or assign (someone) to a particular duty, service, or station: *The guards were set around the perimeter.* **15a.** To put in a mounting; mount: *The jeweler set an emerald in a pendant.* **b.** To apply jewels to; stud: *The museum displayed a tiara* *that was set with diamonds.* **16.** To cause to sit: *The host set the woozy guest on the couch.* **17.** To position (oneself) in such a way as to be ready to start running a race. **18.** To pass (a volleyball), usually with the fingertips, in an arc close to the net so that a teammate can drive it over the net. **19.** To fix at a given amount: *The judge set bail for the defendant at $50,000.* **20.** To point to the location of (game) by holding a fixed attitude. Used of a hunting dog.

intransitive **1.** To disappear below the horizon: *The sun set at seven that evening.* **2.** To sit on eggs. Used of fowl: *The hens were setting.* **3.** To become fixed; harden: *It will take 12 hours for the cement to set.* **4.** To become permanent. Used of dye. **5.** To become whole; knit. Used of a broken bone. **6.** NONSTANDARD To sit.

[Middle English *setten,* from Old English *settan.*]

The verbs *set* and *sit* have been confused since the Middle Ages, so it is not surprising that they sometimes get mixed up today. Throughout its history *set* has been a transitive verb. It originally meant "to cause (someone) to sit" and also "to cause (something) to be in a certain position." This second sense survives as a basic meaning of the verb today: *She set the book on the table.* But since about 1300, *set* has been used without an object to mean "to be in a seated position, sit." *Set* is still common as a nonstandard or regional word meaning "sit," especially in rural speech: *Stop on by and set a spell.* The most familiar of *set*'s intransitive uses describes the motion of the sun at the end of the day. The sun only *sets;* it never *sits.*

This would seem a bit anomalous, since *sit* is mainly an intransitive verb. Its basic meaning is "to rest supported on the hindquarters," as in *He sits at the table.* It has a variety of other uses that entail occupying a location (*The house sits on a small lot*) or existing in a resting or unused state (*The skis sat gathering dust*). Nevertheless, *sit* has its transitive uses, some of which date back to the 14th century. It has taken over the meaning that originally belonged to *set*, "to cause (someone) to sit," so that we can now say *They sat the winning ticket holder back in his chair.* A more recent transitive use of *sit* is "to provide seats for," as in *The theater sits 2,000.*

Fortunately, you don't have to worry about chickens. A hen can *sit* or *set* on her eggs, so in this usage you can't go wrong.

87
sex (sĕks)

noun

1a. The property or quality by which organisms are classified as female or male on the basis of their reproductive organs and functions: *Through amniocentesis, the sex of a developing fetus can be determined.* **b.** Either of the two divisions, designated female and male, of this classification: *The college's policy is that no student is allowed to have visitors of the opposite sex after midnight.* **2.** Females or males considered as a group. **3.** The condition or character of being female or male; the physiological, functional, and psychological differences that distinguish the female and the male. **4.** Sexual intercourse.

[Middle English, from Latin *sexus.*]

SEE NOTE AT **gender** (ON PAGE 230).

88
sit (sĭt)

verb

>Past participle and past tense: **sat**
>Present participle: **sit·ting**
>Third person singular present tense: **sits**

intransitive **1a.** To rest with the torso vertical and the body supported on the buttocks: *"I was leaning against a bar in a speak-easy on Fifty-second Street, waiting for Nora to finish her Christmas shopping, when a girl got up from the table where she had been sitting with three other people and came over to me"* (Dashiell Hammett, *The Thin Man*). **b.** To rest with the hindquarters lowered onto a supporting surface. Used of animals: *The dog sat at the foot of my bed.* **c.** To perch. Used of birds. **d.** To cover eggs for hatching; brood: *The hen sat on her eggs.* **2.** To be situated or located: *The farmhouse sits on a hill.* **3.** To lie or rest: *The dishes are sitting on a shelf.* **4.** To pose for an artist or photographer. **5.** To occupy a seat as a member of a body of officials: *Gerald Ford sat in Congress before becoming president.* **6.** To be in session: *The Supreme Court does not normally sit in the summer.* **7.** To remain inactive or unused: *Your expensive skis are sitting gathering dust in the corner.* **8.** To affect one with or as if with a burden; weigh: *Official duties sat heavily upon the governor's mind.* **9.** To fit, fall, or drape in a specified manner: *That jacket sits perfectly on you.* **10.** To be agreeable to one; please: *The idea didn't sit well with any of us.* **11.** To keep watch or take care of a child; babysit: *On weekends, I make extra money by sitting for the neighbors.*

intransitive **1.** To cause to sit; seat: *The ushers sat the wedding guests in the pews.* **2.** To sit on (eggs) for the purpose of hatching. **3.** To provide seating accommodation for: *This concert hall sits 1,000 people.*

[Middle English *sitten*, from Old English *sittan*.]

SEE NOTE AT **set** (ON PAGE 287).

that (*thăt, thət*)

pronoun
> Plural **those** (*thōz*)

1. Used to refer to the one designated, implied, mentioned, or understood: *What kind of soup is that?* **2.** Used to indicate the farther or less immediate one: *That is for sale; this is not.* **3. those** Used to indicate an unspecified number of people: *The aide wrote down the names of those who refused to attend the meeting.* **4.** Used as a relative pronoun to introduce a clause, especially a restrictive clause: *They towed the car that had the flat tire.* **5.** In, on, by, or with which: *The director returns to New York City each summer that the concerts are performed.*

adjective
> *Plural* **those** (*thōz*)

1. Being the one singled out, implied, or understood: *Those mountains are seventy miles away.* **2.** Being the one further removed or less obvious: *That route is shorter than this one.*

adverb

1. To such an extent or degree: *Is your problem that complicated?* **2.** To a high degree; very: *No one took what he said that seriously.*

conjunction

1. Used to introduce a subordinate clause stating a result, wish, purpose, reason, or cause: *She hoped that he would arrive on time. He was saddened that she felt so little for him.* **2a.** Used to introduce an anticipated subordinate clause following the expletive *it* occurring as subject of the verb: *It is true that dental work is expensive.* **b.** Used to introduce a subordinate clause modifying an adverb or adverbial expression: *They will go anywhere that they are welcome.* **c.** Used to introduce a subordinate clause that is joined to an adjective or noun as a complement: *She was sure that she was right. It is his belief that rates will rise soon.* **3.** Used to introduce a noun clause that is usually the subject or object of a verb or a predicate nominative: *"That America is richer today* [as compared to 100 years ago] *almost goes without saying"* (Peter Grier, *Christian Science Monitor*).

IDIOM

that is To explain more clearly; in other words: *The bakery is on the first floor, that is, the floor at street level.*

[Middle English, from Old English *thæt.*]

📙 The standard rule requires that *that* should be used only to introduce a restrictive (or defining) relative clause, which identifies the entity being talked about; in this use it should never be preceded by a comma. Thus, in the sentence *The house that Jack built has been torn down,* the clause *that Jack built* is a restrictive clause identifying the specific house that was torn down. Similarly, in *I am looking for a book that is easy to read,* the restrictive clause *that is easy to read* tells what kind of book is desired. A related rule stipulates that *which* should be used with nonrestrictive (or nondefining) clauses, which give additional information about an entity that has already been identified in the context; in this use, *which* is always preceded by a comma. Thus, we say *The students in Chemistry 101 have been complaining about the textbook, which* (not *that*) *is hard to follow.* The clause *which is hard to follow* is nonrestrictive in that it does not indicate which text is being complained about; even if the clause were omitted, we would know that the phrase *the textbook* refers to the text in Chemistry 101.

Some grammarians extend the rule and insist that, just as *that* should be used only in restrictive clauses, *which* should be used only in nonrestrictive clauses. Thus, they suggest that we should avoid sentences such as *I need a book which will tell me all about city gardening,* where the restrictive clause *which will tell me all about city gardening* indicates which sort of book is needed. But this extension of the rule is far from universally accepted, and the use of *which* with restrictive clauses is common. Furthermore, since *that* cannot be used with clauses introduced by a preposition (whether or not restrictive), *which* is used with both clauses when such a clause is joined by *and* or *or* to another that does not begin with a preposition, as in *It is a philosophy in which the common man may find solace and which many have found reason to praise.* Such constructions are often considered cumbersome, however, and it may be best to recast the sentence completely to avoid the problem.

That is often omitted in a relative clause when the subject of the clause is different from the word that the clause refers to. Thus, we may say either *the book that I was reading* or *the book I was reading.* In addition, *that* is commonly omitted before other kinds of subordinate clauses, as in *I think we should try again* where *that* would precede *we.* These constructions omitting *that* are entirely idiomatic, even in more formal contexts.

90
un·ex·cep·tion·a·ble (ŭn′ĭk-sĕp′shə-nə-bəl)

adjective

Beyond any reasonable objection; irreproachable: *Our accounting firm holds itself to the highest standards; therefore, any of its findings I believe to be unexceptionable.*

RELATED WORD:
> *adverb* —un′ex·cep′tion·a·bly

The confusion between *unexceptionable* and *unexceptional* is understandable, since both derive from the noun *exception*. *Unexceptionable* takes its meaning from *exception* in the sense "objection," as in the idiom *take exception to* ("find fault with, object to"). Thus *unexceptionable* is commendatory, meaning "not open to any objection or criticism," as in *A judge's ethical standards should be unexceptionable. Unexceptional,* by contrast, is related to the adjective *exceptional* ("outstanding, above average"), which takes its meaning from *exception* in the sense "an unusual case"; thus *unexceptional* generally has a somewhat negative meaning, "not superior, run-of-the-mill" as in *Some judges' ethical standards, sadly, have been unexceptional.*

91

un·ex·cep·tion·al (ŭn′ĭk-sĕp′shə-nəl)

adjective

Not varying from a norm; usual: *The professor gave the unexceptional paper a C.*

RELATED WORD:
adverb —**un′ex·cep′tion·al·ly**

SEE NOTE AT **unexceptionable** (ABOVE).

un·in·ter·est·ed

(ŭn-ĭn′trĭ-stĭd, ŭn-ĭn′tər-ĭ-stĭd, ŭn-ĭn′tə-rĕs′tĭd)

adjective

1. Marked by or exhibiting a lack of interest: *Uninterested voters led to a low turnout on Election Day.* **2.** Having no stake or interest; impartial: *Both sides requested a mediator who was uninterested in the dispute.*

RELATED WORDS:
   adverb —**un·in′ter·est·ed·ly**
   noun — **un·in′ter·est·ed·ness**

SEE NOTE AT **disinterested** (ON PAGE 216).

u·nique (yōo-nēk′)

adjective

1. Being the only one of its kind: *The scholar studied the unique existing example of the eighteenth-century author's handwriting.* **2.** Without an equal or equivalent; unparalleled: *The one-time offer presented them with a unique opportunity to buy a house.* **3.** Characteristic of a particular category, condition, or locality: *The marine biologist examined weather patterns unique to coastal areas.*

[French, from Old French, from Latin *ūnicus.*]

RELATED WORDS:
   adverb —**u·nique′ly**
   noun —**u·nique′ness**

For many grammarians, *unique* is the paradigmatic absolute term, a shibboleth that distinguishes between those who understand that such a term cannot be modified by an adverb of degree or a comparative adverb and those who do not. These grammarians would say that a thing is either unique or not unique and that it is therefore incorrect to say that something is *very unique* or *more unique* than something else. Most of the Usage Panel supports this traditional view. Eighty percent disapprove of the sentence *Her designs are quite unique in today's fashions.* But as the language of advertising in particular attests, *unique* is widely used as a synonym for "worthy of being considered in a class by itself, extraordinary," and if so construed it may arguably be modified. In fact, *unique* appears as a modified adjective in the work of many reputable writers. A travel writer states that *"Chicago is no less unique an American city than New York or San Francisco,"* for example, and the critic Fredric Jameson writes *"The great modern writers have all been defined by the invention or production of rather unique styles."* Although these examples of the qualification of *unique* are defensible, writers should be aware that such constructions are liable to incur the censure of some readers.

u·til·ize (yōōt′l-īz′)

transitive verb

> Past participle and past tense: **u·til·ized**
> Present participle: **u·til·iz·ing**
> Third person singular present tense: **u·til·iz·es**

To put to use, especially for a practical purpose: *"The… group has genetically engineered the bacterium so that more glucose is diverted toward the other main chemical pathway within the organism that utilizes the sugar"* (Gary Stix, *Scientific American*).

[French *utiliser,* from Italian *utilizzare,* from *utile,* useful, from Latin *ūtilis,* from *ūtī,* to use.]

RELATED WORDS:

> *noun* —**u′til·i·za′tion**
> *noun* —**u′til·iz′er**

🖋 A number of critics have remarked that *utilize* is an unnecessary substitute for *use.* It is true that many occurrences of *utilize* could be replaced by *use* with no loss to anything but pretentiousness, for example, in sentences such as *They utilized questionable methods in their analysis* or *We hope that many commuters will continue to utilize mass transit after the bridge has reopened.* But *utilize* can mean "to find a profitable or practical use for." Thus the sentence *The teachers were unable to use the new computers* might mean only that the teachers were unable to operate the computers, whereas *The teachers were unable to utilize the new computers* suggests that the teachers could not find ways to employ the computers in instruction.

weight (wāt)

noun

1. A measure of the heaviness of an object: *The weight of the car is 3,000 pounds.* **2.** The force with which a body is attracted to Earth or another celestial body, equal to the product of the object's mass and the acceleration of gravity. **3a.** A unit measure of gravitational force: *Comprehensive reference works contain a table of weights and measures.* **b.** A system of such measures: *Gemstones are measured using a system of measurement called "troy weight."* **4.** An object used principally to exert a force by virtue of its gravitational attraction to Earth, such as a paperweight or a dumbbell. **5.** A load or burden; oppressiveness: *"Adding features to run complex software adds weight and bogs down portability"* (Eric C. Evarts, *Christian Science Monitor*). **6.** Influence, importance, or authority: *Her opinion carries great weight in the medical community.*

transitive verb

Past participle and past tense: **weight·ed**
Present participle: **weight·ing**
Third person singular present tense: **weights**

1. To make heavy or heavier with a weight or weights: *"Marine mud [is] a blue-gray mud that settled 15,000 years ago while much of Maine was weighted down with glacial ice and Boston was underwater"* (Jamie Kageleiry & Christine Schultz, *Yankee Magazine*). **2.** To load down, burden, or oppress: *Until an extra associate was hired, I was weighted with heavy responsibilities at work.*

[Middle English *wight,* from Old English *wiht.*]

SEE NOTE AT **mass** (ON PAGE 256).

---

where·fore (hwâr′fôr′, wâr′fôr′)

adverb

For what purpose or reason; why: *"O Romeo, Romeo! wherefore art thou Romeo?"* (William Shakespeare, *Romeo and Juliet*).

noun

 A purpose or cause: *The editorial explained all the whys and wherefores of the tax proposal.*

৯ Many people mistakenly assume that *wherefore* is a synonym of *where* based on a misreading of one of Shakespeare's most well-known lines. Many mistakenly interpret Juliet's balcony speech as questioning Romeo's location (who as it turns out happens to be just below the balcony). However, Juliet is not asking *where* Romeo is. She is asking *why* Romeo is Romeo—that is, she wants to know why her love is who he is: a member of the family with whom her family has been feuding.

O Romeo, Romeo! **wherefore** art thou Romeo?

Deny thy father and refuse thy name;

Or, if thou wilt not, be but sworn my love,

And I'll no longer be a Capulet.

— William Shakespeare,
Romeo and Juliet

which (hwĭch, wĭch)

pronoun

1. What particular one or ones: *Which of these books is yours?* **2.** The one or ones previously mentioned or implied, specifically: **a.** Used as a relative pronoun in a clause that provides additional information about the antecedent: *I want to renovate my house, which is small and old.* **b.** Used as a relative pronoun preceded by *that* or a preposition in a clause that defines or restricts the antecedent: *The clerk provided him with that which he requested. I was fascinated by the subject on which she spoke.* **c.** Used instead of *that* as a relative pronoun in a clause that defines or restricts the antecedent: *The movie which was shown later was better.* **3.** Any of the things, events, or people designated or implied; whichever: *Choose which you like best.* **4.** A thing or circumstance that: *They left early, which was wise.*

adjective

1. What particular one or ones of a number of things or people: *Which part of town do you mean?* **2.** Any one or any number of; whichever: *Use which door you please.* **3.** Being the one or ones previously mentioned or implied: *It started to rain, at which point we ran.*

[Middle English, from Old English *hwilc*.]

🔊 The relative pronoun *which* is sometimes used to refer to an entire sentence or clause, rather than a noun or noun phrase, as in *They ignored me, which proved to be unwise. They swept the council elections, which could never have happened under the old rules.* While these examples are unexceptionable, using *which* in this way sometimes produces an ambiguous sentence. Thus *It emerged that Chris made the complaint, which surprised every-*

---

body leaves unclear whether it was surprising that a complaint was made or that Chris made it. The ambiguity can be avoided with paraphrases such as *It emerged that the complaint was made by Chris, a revelation that surprised everybody.*

ALSO SEE NOTE AT **that** (ON PAGE 291).

98 wreak (rēk)

transitive verb
> Past participle and past tense: **wreaked**
> Present participle: **wreak·ing**
> Third person singular present tense: **wreaks**

1. To inflict (vengeance or punishment) upon a person: "*I at last devised a desperate plan that would not only blow my wedding to pieces but would wreak a terrible revenge on my parents and my betrothed*" (Louis Auchincloss, *DeCicco v. Schweizer*). **2.** To express or gratify (anger, malevolence, or resentment); vent: "*In his little evil brain he sought for some excuse to wreak his hatred upon Tarzan*" (Edgar Rice Burroughs, *Tarzan of the Apes*). **3.** To bring about; cause: "*A harmful recessive gene doesn't wreak havoc unless it exists in two copies*" (Jennifer Ackerman, *Chance in the House of Fate*).

[Middle English *wreken,* from Old English *wrecan.*]

🖉 *Wreak* is sometimes confused with *wreck,* perhaps because the wreaking of damage may leave a wreck: *The storm wreaked* (not *wrecked*) *havoc along the coast.* The past tense and past participle of *wreak* is *wreaked,* not *wrought,* which is an alternative past tense and past participle of *work.*

In the morning, looking towards the sea side, the tide being low, I saw something lie on the shore bigger than ordinary, and it looked like a cask; when I came to it, I found a small barrel, and two or three pieces of the **wreck** of the ship, which were driven on shore by the late hurricane; and looking towards the wreck itself, I thought it seemed to lie higher out of the water than it used to do.

—Daniel Defoe,
Robinson Crusoe

wreck (rĕk)

noun

1. Accidental destruction of a ship; a shipwreck: *The wreck of the Titanic occurred in the Atlantic Ocean in April of 1912.* **2a.** The stranded hulk of a severely damaged ship: *"I found a small barrel, and two or three pieces of the wreck of the ship, which were driven on shore by the late hurricane"* (Daniel Defoe, *Robinson Crusoe*). **b.** Fragments of a ship or its cargo cast ashore by the sea after a shipwreck; wreckage. **3.** The remains of something that has been wrecked or ruined: *"Up went the axe again…four times the blow fell;…it was not until the fifth, that the lock burst and the wreck of the door fell inwards on the carpet"* (Robert Louis Stevenson, *The Strange Case of Dr. Jekyll and Mr. Hyde*). **4.** A person who is physically or mentally broken down or worn out.

verb

Past participle and past tense: **wrecked**
Present participle: **wreck·ing**
Third person singular present tense: **wrecks**

transitive **1.** To cause the destruction of (something) in or as if in a collision: *"The morning after the storm that has wrecked the ship and drowned his companions, Crusoe wakes on shore with only a pocket knife, a pipe, and a tin of tobacco"* (Hilary Masters, *Making It Up*). **2.** To dismantle or raze; tear down: *The contractor wrecked the old building to make way for the new apartment complex.* **3.** To cause to undergo ruin or disaster: *"I will not go along with a huge tax cut for the wealthy at the expense of everyone else and wreck our good economy in the process"* (Al Gore, speech to the Democratic National Convention).

intransitive To suffer destruction or ruin; become wrecked: *The ship wrecked in the shoals off the shore.*

[Middle English *wrek,* from Anglo-Norman *wrec,* of Scandinavian origin; akin to Old Norse *rec,* wreckage.]

SEE NOTE AT **wreak** (ON PAGE 301).

100 zo·ol·o·gy (zō-ŏl**′**ə-jē, zōō-ŏl**′**ə-jē)

noun

1. The branch of biology that deals with animals and animal life, including the study of the structure, physiology, development, and classification of animals. **2.** The animal life of a particular area or period: *The professor lectured on the zoology of the Pleistocene.* **3.** The characteristics of a particular animal group or category: *In biology class, we had a unit on the zoology of mammals.*

RELATED WORD:
noun —**zo·ol′o·gist**

🐾 Traditionally, the first syllable of *zoology* has been pronounced as (zō), rhyming with *toe.* However, most likely due to the familiarity of the word *zoo* (which is merely a shortened form of *zoological garden*), the pronunciation of the first syllable as (zōō) is also commonly heard. In 1999, 88 percent of the Usage Panel found the (zō) pronunciation acceptable, and 60 percent found the (zōō) pronunciation acceptable. In their own speech, 68 percent of the Panelists use the (zō) pronunciation, and 32 percent use the (zōō) pronunciation. Thus, while both pronunciations can be considered acceptable, the (zō) pronunciation may be perceived as more scientific.

100

words every

word lover

should know

Guide to the Entries

ENTRY WORD The 100 words that constitute this section are listed alphabetically. The entry words, along with inflected and derived forms, are divided into syllables by centered dots. These dots show you where you would break the word at the end of a line. The pronunciation of the word follows the entry word. Please see the key on page v for an explanation of the pronunciation system.

PART OF SPEECH At least one part of speech follows each entry word. The part of speech tells you the grammatical category that the word belongs to. Parts of speech include *noun, adjective, adverb, transitive verb,* and *intransitive verb.* (A transitive verb is a verb that needs an object to complete its meaning. *Wash* is a transitive verb in the sentence *I washed the car.* The direct object of *wash* is *the car.* An intransitive verb is one that does not take an object, as *sleep* in the sentence *I slept for seven hours.* Many verbs are both transitive and intransitive.)

INFLECTIONS A word's inflected forms differ from the main entry form by the addition of a suffix or by a change in the base form to indicate grammatical features such as number, person, or tense. They are set in boldface type, divided into syllables, and given pronunciations as necessary. The past tense, past participle, and the third person singular present tense inflections of all verbs are shown. The plurals of nouns are shown when they are spelled in a way other than by adding *s* to the base form.

ORDER OF SENSES Entries having more than one sense are arranged with the central and often the most commonly sought meanings first. In an entry with more than one part of speech, the senses are numbered in separate sequences after each part of speech, as at **halcyon.**

EXAMPLES OF USAGE Examples often follow the definitions and are set in italic type. These examples show the entry words in typical contexts. Sometimes the examples are quotations from authors of books. These quotations are shown within quotation marks, and the quotation's author and source are shown in parentheses.

ETYMOLOGIES Etymologies appear in square brackets following the last definition. An etymology traces the history of a word as far back in time as can be determined with reasonable certainty. The stage most closely preceding Modern English is given first, with each earlier stage following in sequence. A language name, linguistic form (in italics), and brief definition of the form are given for each stage of the derivation. To avoid redundancy, a language, form, or definition is not repeated if it is identical to the corresponding item in the immediately preceding stage. Occasionally, a form will be given that is not actually preserved in written documents but which scholars are confident did exist—such a form will be marked by an asterisk (*). The word *from* is used to indicate origin of any kind: by inheritance, borrowing, or derivation. When an etymology splits a compound word into parts, a colon introduces the parts and each element is then traced back to its origin, with those elements enclosed in parentheses.

NOTES Many entries include Notes that present interesting information regarding the history of the word, including the process by which it entered English from other languages.

To visit one's lover, with tears and reproaches, at his own residence, was an image so agreeable to Mrs. Penniman's mind that she felt a sort of **aesthetic** disappointment at its lacking, in this case, the harmonious accompaniments of darkness and storm. A quiet Sunday afternoon appeared an inadequate setting for it; and, indeed, Mrs. Penniman was quite out of humour with the conditions of the time, which passed very slowly as she sat in the front-parlour, in her bonnet and her cashmere shawl, awaiting Catherine's return.

— Henry James,
Washington Square

aes·thet·ic or es·thet·ic (ĕs-thĕt′ĭk)

adjective

1. Relating to beauty or the appreciation of beauty: *"To visit one's lover, with tears and reproaches, at his own residence, was an image so agreeable to Mrs. Penniman's mind that she felt a sort of aesthetic disappointment at its lacking, in this case, the harmonious accompaniments of darkness and storm"* (Henry James, *Washington Square*). **2.** Exhibiting beauty; pleasing in appearance: *The new website features a number of aesthetic enhancements.* **3.** Relating to the branch of philosophy that deals with the nature and expression of beauty, as in the fine arts.

noun

A conception of what is artistically valid or beautiful: *The aesthetics of Modernism can be seen as a reaction to the staid conventions of Victorian culture.*

[German *ästhetisch*, from New Latin *aesthēticus*, from Greek *aisthētikos*, of sense perception, from *aisthēta*, perceptible things, from *aisthanesthai*, to perceive.]

al·che·my (ăl′kə-mē)

noun

1. A medieval chemical philosophy having as its asserted aims the transmutation of base metals into gold, the discovery of the panacea, and the preparation of the elixir of longevity. **2.** A seemingly magical power or process of transmuting: *"He wondered by what alchemy it* [a killed deer] *was changed, so that what sickened him one hour, maddened him with hunger the next"* (Marjorie K. Rawlings, *The Yearling*).

[Middle English *alkamie,* from Old French *alquemie,* from Medieval Latin *alchymia,* from Arabic *al-kīmiyā'* : *al-,* the + *kīmiyā',* chemistry (from Late Greek *khēmeia, khumeia,* perhaps from Greek *Khēmia,* Egypt).]

al·le·go·ry (ăl′ĭ-gôr′ē)

noun
Plural: **al·le·go·ries**

1a. The representation of abstract ideas or principles by characters, figures, or events in narrative, dramatic, or pictorial form. **b.** A story, picture, or play employing such representation. John Bunyan's *Pilgrim's Progress* and Herman Melville's *Moby-Dick* are allegories. **2.** A symbolic representation: *The blindfolded figure with scales is an allegory of justice.*

[Middle English *allegorie,* from Latin *allēgoria,* from Greek, from *allēgorein,* to interpret allegorically : *allos,* other + *agoreuein,* to speak publicly (from *agorā,* marketplace).]

a·nach·ro·nism (ə-năk′rə-nĭz′əm)

noun

1. The representation of someone as existing or something as happening in other than chronological, proper, or historical order. **2.** One that is out of its proper or chronological order, especially a person or practice that belongs to an earlier time: *"A new age had plainly dawned, an age that made the institution of a segregated picnic seem an anachronism"* (Henry Louis Gates, Jr., *Colored People: A Memoir*). *"Cavalry regiments of cuirassiers with glistening metal breastplates and long black horsehair tails hanging down from their helmets were conscious of no anachronism. Following them came huge crates housing airplanes and wheeled platforms bearing the long narrow gray-painted field guns, the* soixante-quinzes *that were France's pride"* (Barbara W. Tuchman, *The Guns of August*).

[French *anachronisme*, from New Latin *anachronismus*, from Late Greek *anakhronismos*, from *anakhronizesthai*, to be an anachronism : Greek *ana-*, up, backward + Greek *khronizein*, to take time (from *khronos*, time).]

5

a·nath·e·ma (ə-năth′ə-mə)

noun
   Plural: **a·nath·e·mas**

1. An ecclesiastical ban, curse, or excommunication.
2. A vehement denunciation or curse: *"If the children gathered about her . . . Pearl would grow positively terrible in her puny wrath, snatching up stones to fling at them, with shrill, incoherent exclamations that made her mother tremble, because they had so much the sound of a witch's anathemas in some unknown tongue"* (Nathaniel Hawthorne, *The Scarlet Letter*). **3.** One that is cursed or damned. **4.** One that is greatly reviled, loathed, or shunned: *"Essentialism—a belief in natural, immutable sex differences—is anathema to postmodernists, for whom sexuality itself, along with gender, is a 'social construct'"*(Wendy Kaminer, *Atlantic Monthly*).

[Late Latin *anathema,* accursed thing, from Greek, something dedicated, something devoted (to evil), from *anatithenai, anathe-,* to dedicate : *ana-,* up, backward- + *tithenai,* to put.]

bail·i·wick (bāʹlə-wĭkʹ)

noun

1. A person's specific area of interest, skill, or authority: *"Tower liked people to be like himself: quick, sharp and to the point. A private school and a restricted cruise were his natural bailiwicks"* (Louis Auchincloss, "The Atonement"). **2.** The office or district of a bailiff: *"Another writ has been issued . . . and the defendant in that cause is the prey of the sheriff having legal jurisdiction in this bailiwick"* (Charles Dickens, *David Copperfield*).

[Middle English *bailliwik* : *baillif*, bailiff (ultimately from Latin *bāiulus*, carrier) + *wik*, town (from Old English *wīc*, from Latin *vīcus*).]

be·lea·guered (bĭ-lē′gərd)

adjective

1. Beset with troubles or problems: *"The beleaguered rider could do no better than cling to the horse's neck for dear life"* (Laura Hillenbrand, *Seabiscuit*). **2.** Surrounded with troops; besieged.

[Probably Dutch *belegeren* (*be-*, around + *leger,* camp) + *-ed,* past participle suffix.]

Seabiscuit didn't run, he rampaged. When the rider . . . tried to rein him in, the horse bolted, thrashing around like a hooked marlin. Asked to go left, he'd dodge right; tugged right, he'd dart left. The **beleaguered** rider could do no better than cling to the horse's neck for dear life.

—Laura Hillenbrand,
Seabiscuit

bro·mide (brō′mīd′)

noun

1a. A binary compound of bromine with another element, such as silver. **b.** Potassium bromide, a white crystalline solid or powder used as a sedative, in photographic emulsion, and in lithography. **2a.** A commonplace remark or notion; a platitude: *"The windows of buses and shops were adorned with bromides: 'The only magic to remove poverty—hard work, clear vision, iron will, strict discipline'"*(Katherine Frank, *Indira: The Life of Indira Nehru Gandhi*). **b.** A tiresome person; a bore.

[From *bromine* (from French *brome,* from Greek *brōmos,* stench + *-ine,* suffix used in names of chemical substances) + *-ide,* suffix in names of chemical compounds.]

Several bromine compounds, especially potassium bromide, have been used medicinally as sedatives. In 1906 Gelett Burgess (the coiner of the word *blurb*) wrote a book entitled *Are You a Bromide?* in which he used *bromide* to mean a tiresome person of unoriginal thoughts and trite conversation, the sort of person who might put you to sleep. *Bromide* was soon after extended to include the kind of commonplace remarks that could be expected from a bromide, such as "You're a sight for sore eyes."

cap·puc·ci·no (kăp′ə-chē′nō, kä′pə-chē′nō)

noun

Plural: **cap·puc·ci·nos**

Espresso coffee mixed or topped with steamed milk or cream.

[Italian, Capuchin, cappuccino (from the resemblance of its color to the color of the monk's habit).]

ℰ The history of the word *cappuccino* shows how words can develop new senses because of resemblances that the original coiners of the terms might not have dreamed possible. The Italian name of the Capuchin order of friars, established after 1525, came from the long pointed cowl, or *cappuccino,* that was worn as part of the order's habit. In Italian *cappuccino* went on to develop another sense, "espresso coffee mixed or topped with steamed milk or cream," probably because the color of the coffee resembled the color of the habit of a Capuchin friar.

ca·price (kə-prēs′)

noun

1a. An impulsive change of mind. **b.** An inclination to change one's mind impulsively. **c.** A sudden, unpredictable action, change, or series of actions or changes: *". . . six hours of alert immobility while the boat drove slowly or floated arrested, according to the caprice of the wind"* (Joseph Conrad, *Lord Jim*). **2.** *Music* An instrumental work with an improvisatory style and a free form; a capriccio.

[French, from Italian *capriccio,* from *caporiccio,* fright, sudden start : *capo,* head (from Latin *caput*) + *riccio,* curly (from Latin *ēricius,* hedgehog, from *ēr*).]

11
car·i·bou (kăr′ə-bōō′)

noun
    Plural: **caribou** *or* **car·i·bous**

Any of several large reindeer native to northern North America.

[Micmac *ĝalipu* (influenced by Canadian French *caribou,* also from Micmac), from Proto-Algonquin **mekālixpowa* : **mekāl-,* to scrape + **-ixpo-,* snow.]

12
chi·as·mus (kī-ăz′məs)

noun
    Plural: **chi·as·mi** (kī-ăz′mī′)

A rhetorical inversion of the second of two parallel structures, as in *"Each throat / Was parched, and glazed each eye"* (Samuel Taylor Coleridge, *The Rime of the Ancient Mariner*).

[New Latin *chīasmus,* from Greek *khīasmos,* syntactic inversion, from *khīazein,* to invert or mark with an X.]

chor·tle (chôr′tl)

noun

A snorting, joyful laugh or chuckle.

intransitive and transitive verb
Past participle and past tense: **chor·tled**
Present participle: **chor·tling**
Third person singular present tense: **chor·tles**

To utter a chortle or express with a chortle.

[Blend of *chuckle* and *snort.*]

🖎 "'O frabjous day! Callooh! Callay!' He chortled in his joy." Perhaps Lewis Carroll would chortle a bit himself to find that people are still using the word *chortle*, which he coined in *Through the Looking-Glass*, published in 1872. In any case, Carroll had constructed his word well, combining the words *chuckle* and *snort*. This type of word is called a *blend* or a *portmanteau word*. In *Through the Looking-Glass* Humpty Dumpty uses *portmanteau* ("a large leather suitcase that opens into two hinged compartments") to describe the word *slithy*, saying, "It's like a portmanteau—there are two meanings packed up into one word" (the meanings being "lithe" and "slimy").

coc·cyx (kŏk′sĭks)

noun

Plural: **coc·cy·ges** (kŏk-sī′jēz, kŏk′sĭ-jēz′)

A small triangular bone at the base of the spinal column in humans and tailless apes, consisting of several fused rudimentary vertebrae. Also called *tailbone.*

[New Latin *coccȳx,* from Greek *kokkūx,* cuckoo, coccyx (from its resemblance to a cuckoo's beak).]

cres·cen·do (krə-shĕn**′**dō)

noun

Plural: **cres·cen·dos** *or* **cres·cen·di** (krə-shĕn**′**dē)

1. *Music* **a.** A gradual increase, especially in the volume or intensity of sound in a passage. **b.** A passage played with a gradual increase in volume or intensity. **2.** A steady increase in intensity or force: "*Then the sound came, a long, deep, powerful rumble increasing in crescendo until the windows rattled, cups danced in their saucers, and the bar glasses rubbed rims and tinkled in terror. The sound slowly ebbed, then boomed to a fiercer climax, closer*" (Pat Frank, *Alas, Babylon*).

intransitive verb

Past participle and past tense: **cres·cen·doed**
Present participle: **cres·cen·do·ing**
Third person singular present tense: **cres·cen·does**

To build up to a point of great intensity, force, or volume.

[Italian, present participle of *crescere,* to increase, from Latin *crēscere.*]

16 **cru·ci·ver·bal·ist** (krōō′sə-vûr′bə-lĭst)

noun

1. A person who constructs crosswords. **2.** An enthusiast of word games, especially of crosswords.

[From Latin *crux, cruc-,* cross + Latin *verbum,* word (translation of English *crossword*).]

17 **des·ul·to·ry** (dĕs′əl-tôr′ē, dĕz′əl-tôr′ē)

adjective

1. Having no set plan; haphazard or random: *"[These] concert series, done mostly on a shoestring and involving many refugee musicians . . . were a beacon of enterprise on the desultory wartime musical scene"* (Meirion Bowen, *BBC Music Magazine*). **2.** Moving or jumping from one thing to another; disconnected: *"She had suddenly begun speaking, after sitting silently through several hours of desultory discussion with her husband about the Resistance"* (Adam Nossiter, *The Algeria Hotel*). *"Our conversation so far had been desultory, with lots of long silences and me staring fixedly out the window"* (Scott Anderson, *Men's Journal*).

[Latin *dēsultōrius,* leaping, from *dēsultor,* a leaper, from *dēsultus,* past participle of *dēsilīre,* to leap down : *dē-,* off + *salīre,* to jump.]

de·tri·tus (dǐ-trī′təs)

noun
 Plural: **detritus**

1. Loose fragments or grains that have been worn away from rock. **2.** Disintegrated or eroded matter; debris: *Archaeologists study the detritus of past civilizations.*

[French *détritus,* from Latin *dētrītus,* from past participle of *dēterere,* to lessen, wear away.]

didj·er·i·doo *or* **didg·er·i·doo**
(dǐj′ə-rē-dōō′, dǐj′ə-rē-dōō′)

noun
 Plural: **didj·er·i·doos** *or* **didg·er·i·doos**

A musical instrument of the Aboriginal peoples of Australia, consisting of a long hollow branch or stick that makes a deep drone when blown into while vibrating the lips.

[Imitative of its sound.]

e·bul·lient (ĭ-bŏŏl′yənt′)

adjective

1. Zestfully enthusiastic: *"She was one of those intensely ebullient people who are great at the right kind of party but wearing in a small space"* (Deirdre McNamer, *My Russian*). **2.** Boiling or seeming to boil; bubbling.

[Latin *ēbulliēns*, *ēbullient-*, present participle of *ēbullīre*, to bubble up : *ē-*, *ex-*, out, away + *bullīre*, to bubble, boil.]

ech·e·lon (ĕsh′ə-lŏn′)

noun

1a. A formation of troops in which each unit is positioned successively to the left or right of the rear unit to form an oblique or steplike line. **b.** A flight formation or arrangement of craft in this manner. **c.** A similar formation of groups, units, or individuals: *"By asking the right questions and choosing the right tests and drawing the right conclusions the mechanic works his way down the echelons of the motorcycle hierarchy until he has found the exact specific cause or causes of the engine failure, and then he changes them so that they no longer cause the failure"* (Robert Pirsig, *Zen and the Art of Motorcycle Maintenance*). **2.** A subdivision of a military or naval force. **3.** A level of responsibility or authority in a hierarchy; a rank: *The recent graduate took a job in the company's lower echelon.*

[French *échelon*, from Old French *eschelon*, rung of a ladder, from *eschiele*, ladder, from Late Latin *scāla*, back-formation from Latin *scālae*, steps, ladder.]

22

e·gre·gious (ĭ-grē′jəs, ĭ-grē′jē-əs)

adjective

Conspicuously bad or offensive: *"This is a difficult chapter for me to write — not because my own youthful mistakes were so egregious . . . but because I may be making a mistake now"* (Wendy Lesser, *Nothing Remains the Same: Rereading and Remembering*).

[From Latin *ēgregius*, outstanding : *ē-, ex-*, out, away + *grex, greg-*, herd.]

23

e·phem·er·al (ĭ-fĕm′ər-əl)

adjective

1. Lasting for a markedly brief time: *"There remain some truths too ephemeral to be captured in the cold pages of a court transcript"* (Irving R. Kaufman, *New York Times Magazine*). *"Despite his position, Shah Zaman smiled like the Genie through his pearly beard and declared that Scheherazade was right to think love ephemeral. But life itself was scarcely less so, and both were sweet for just that reason — sweeter yet when enjoyed as if they might endure"* (John Barth, *Chimera*). **2.** Living or lasting only for a day, as certain plants or insects do.

noun

Something that is markedly short-lived.

[From Greek *ephēmeros* : *ep-, epi-*, upon, during + *hēmerā*, day.]

24

ep·i·cure (ĕp′ĭ-kyŏor′)

noun

1. A person with refined taste, especially in food and wine. **2.** A person devoted to sensuous pleasure and luxurious living.

[Middle English, an Epicurean, from Medieval Latin *epicūrus,* from Latin *Epicūrus,* Latin form of the name of *Epikouros,* Greek philosopher (341–270 BC) who advocated the pursuit of pleasure enjoyed in moderation.]

er·satz (ĕr'zäts', ĕr-zäts')

adjective

Being an imitation or a substitute, usually an inferior one; artificial: *"Now when she flips through memories, they have an ersatz quality, the sort of tint applied to enhance photos"* (Carol Anshaw, *Seven Moves*).

[German, replacement, from *ersetzen,* to replace, from Old High German *irsezzan* : *ir-,* out + *sezzan,* to set.]

Chris is not sure anymore who it is she's searching for. Now that the person she loved turns out to have been in great part concocted for her approval, who she is missing and who she might find are quite different people. Now when she flips through memories, they have an **ersatz** quality, the sort of tint applied to enhance photos—rose on the cheeks of the sallow graduate, blue on the muddy lake of the dilapidated resort.

—Carol Anshaw,
Seven Moves

fa·ce·tious (fə-sē′shəs)

adjective

Playfully jocular; humorous: *"He pointed out—writing in a foolish, facetious tone—that the perfection of mechanical appliances must ultimately supersede limbs"* (H.G. Wells, *The War of the Worlds*). *"[A]unty gave George a nudge with her finger, designed to be immensely facetious, and turned again to her griddle with great briskness"* (Harriet Beecher Stowe, *Uncle Tom's Cabin*).

[French *facétieux*, from *facétie*, jest, from Latin *facētia*, from *facētus*, witty.]

℘ *Facetious* is one of a very small number of English words that contain all five vowels in alphabetical order. (Another is *abstemious*.) The adverb *facetiously* contains all the vowels and *y* in order.

27

fe·cun·di·ty (fĭ-kŭn′dĭ-tē)

noun

1. The quality or power of producing abundantly; fruitfulness or fertility: *"In the Permian and Triassic periods, what is now the continent of Europe was dominated by endless sandy wastes, blasted by hot dry winds. Lifelessness, aridity and blistering heat suddenly took the place of all that Carboniferous moisture and fecundity"* (Simon Winchester, The Map That Changed the World). **2.** Productive or creative power: *fecundity of the mind.*

[From *fecund* (from Middle English, from Old French *fecond*, from Latin *fēcundus*, fertile, fruitful) + *-ity*, noun-forming suffix.]

28

fo·cac·ci·a
(fə-kä′chē′ə, fō-kä′chē′ə, fō-kä′chə)

noun

A flat Italian bread traditionally flavored with olive oil and salt and often topped with herbs, onions, or other items.

[Italian, hearth-cake, from Late Latin *focācia*, of the hearth, feminine of *focācius*, from Latin *focus*, hearth.]

fus·ty (fŭsʹtē)

adjective
    Comparative: **fus·ti·er**
    Superlative: **fus·ti·est**

1. Smelling of mildew or decay; musty *"goggle-eyed headlines staring up at me on every street corner and at the fusty, peanut-smelling mouth of every subway"* (Sylvia Plath, *The Bell Jar*). **2.** Old-fashioned; antique.

[Middle English, from Old French *fust*, piece of wood, wine cask, from Latin *fūstis*, stick, club.]

It was a queer, sultry summer, the summer they electrocuted the Rosenbergs, and I didn't know what I was doing in New York. I'm stupid about executions. The idea of being electrocuted makes me sick, and that's all there was to read about in the papers — goggle-eyed headlines staring up at me on every street corner and at the **fusty,** peanut-smelling mouth of every subway. It had nothing to do with me, but I couldn't help wondering what it would be like, being burned alive all along your nerves.

—Sylvia Plath,
The Bell Jar

ge·müt·lich·keit

(gə-mo͞ot′lĭk-kīt′, gə-müt′lĭкн-kīt′)

noun

Warm friendliness; amicability.

[German *gemütlich,* congenial (from Middle High German *gemüetlich,* from *gemüete,* spirit, feelings, from Old High German *gimuoti,* from *muot,* mind, spirit, joy) + *-keit,* -ness.]

glos·so·la·li·a

(glô′sə-lā′lē-ə, glŏs′ə-lā′lē-ə)

noun

1. Fabricated and nonmeaningful speech, especially such speech associated with a trance state or certain schizophrenic syndromes. **2.** The ability or phenomenon to utter words or sounds of a language unknown to the speaker, especially as an expression of religious ecstasy. In this sense, also called *gift of tongues, speaking in tongues.*

[New Latin : Greek *glōssa,* tongue + Greek *lalein,* to babble.]

gos·sa·mer (gŏs′ə-mər)

adjective

1. Sheer, light, and delicate: *"[F]rom the looping cascades of communication and control emerge the particular parts of a body in perfect form, nearly every time: the needle nose of the narwhal, the gossamer wing of a butterfly, . . . the marvelous globe of the human eye somehow ready upon arrival out of a dark world instantly to receive light"* (Jennifer Ackerman, *Chance in the House of Fate*).
2. Tenuous; flimsy: *"He knew he was in trouble, but the trouble was glamorous, and he surrounded it with the gossamer lie of make-believe. He was living the storybook legend"* (Evan Hunter, "First Offense").

noun

1. A soft sheer gauzy fabric. **2.** Something delicate, light, or flimsy. **3.** A fine film of cobwebs often seen floating in the air or caught on bushes or grass.

[Middle English *gossomer* : *gos,* goose + *somer,* summer (probably from the abundance of gossamer during early autumn when geese are in season).]

gra·va·men (grə-vā**′**mən)

noun
    Plural **gra·va·mens** *or*
    gra·vam·i·na (grə-văm**′**ə-nə)

The part of a legal charge or an accusation that weighs most substantially against the accused.

[Medieval Latin *gravāmen,* injury, accusation, from Late Latin, encumbrance, obligation, from Latin *gravāre,* to burden, from *gravis,* heavy.]

hal·cy·on (hăl′sē-ən)

adjective

1. Calm and peaceful; tranquil: *"[I]t was the most halcyon summer I ever spent. We walked the river in the daytime, talking and watching and listening and holding hands, sitting in the dust, in the cool shade beneath the big oaks, and just listening to the mourning doves"* (Rick Bass, *The Sky, the Stars, the Wilderness*). **2.** Prosperous; golden: *"There is probably hardly a single American who does not yearn for a return to the halcyon years of the Eisenhower and Kennedy presidencies, when American manufacturers paid the highest wages in the world yet nonetheless almost effortlessly dominated world markets"* (Eammon Fingleton, *In Praise of Hard Industries*).

noun

1. A kingfisher, especially one of the genus *Halcyon*. **2.** A fabled bird, identified with the kingfisher, that was supposed to have had the power to calm the wind and the waves while it nested on the sea during the winter solstice.

[Middle English *alcioun*, from Latin *alcyōn, halcyōn*, from Greek *halkuōn*, a mythical bird, kingfisher, alteration (influenced by *hals*, salt, sea, and *kuōn*, conceiving, becoming pregnant) of *alkuōn*.]

They found a piglet caught in a curtain of creepers, throwing itself at the elastic traces in all the madness of extreme terror. . . . The three boys rushed forward and Jack drew his knife again with a flourish. He raised his arm in the air. There came a pause, a **hiatus,** the pig continued to scream and the creepers to jerk, and the blade continued to flash at the end of a bony arm. The pause was only long enough for them to understand what an enormity the downward stroke would be.

—William Golding,
Lord of the Flies

hi·a·tus (hī-ā′təs)

noun
    Plural: **hi·a·tus·es** *or* **hiatus**

1. A gap or interruption in space, time, or continuity; a break: *"There came a pause, a hiatus, the pig continued to scream and the creepers to jerk, and the blade continued to flash at the end of a bony arm"* (William Golding, *The Lord of the Flies*). **2.** A slight pause that occurs when two immediately adjacent vowels in consecutive syllables are pronounced, as in *reality* and *naïve*. **3.** A separation, aperture, fissure, or short passage in an organ or part of the body.

[Latin *hiātus,* from past participle of *hiāre,* to gape.]

hu·mu·hu·mu·nu·ku·nu·ku·a·pu·a·a

(hōō′mōō-hōō′mōō-nōō′kōō-nōō′kōō-ä′pōō-ä**′**ä′)

noun

Plural: **humuhumunukunukuapuaa** *or*
hu·mu·hu·mu·nu·ku·nu·ku·a·pu·a·as

Either of two triggerfishes, *Rhinecanthus aculeatus* or *R. rectangulus*, native to the outer reefs of Hawaii, the latter having a broad black band on the side and a black triangle at the beginning of the tail. The humuhumunukunukuapuaa is the state fish of Hawaii.

[Hawaiian *humuhumu-nukunuku-ā-pua'a*, trigger fish with a blunt snout like a pig's : *humuhumu*, small trigger fish (from reduplication of Proto-Polynesian **sumu*, trigger fish) + *nukunuku*, small snout, reduplication of *nuku*, snout + *ā*, like + *pua'a*, pig.]

i·con·o·clast (ī-kŏn′ə-klăst′)

noun

1. One who attacks and seeks to overthrow traditional or popular ideas or institutions: *"I think that nobody but a damned iconoclast could even conceive the atrocity you're proposing. I think you're one of those people who take pleasure in smashing apart anything that's stamped with tradition or stability"* (Stanley Ellin, "The Moment of Decision"). **2.** One who destroys sacred religious images.

[French *iconoclaste*, from Medieval Greek *eikonoklastēs*, smasher of religious images : *eikono-*, image + Greek *-klastēs*, breaker (from Greek *klān, klas-*, to break).]

Eikonoklastēs, the ancestor of our word *iconoclast*, was first formed in Medieval Greek from the elements *eikōn*, "image, likeness," and *-klastēs*, "breaker," from *klān*, "to break." The images referred to by the word are religious images, which were the subject of controversy among Christians of the Byzantine Empire in the eighth and ninth centuries, when iconoclasm was at its height. In addition to destroying many sculptures and paintings, those opposed to images attempted to have them barred from display and veneration. During the Protestant Reformation, images in churches were again felt to be idolatrous and were once more banned and destroyed. *Iconoclast*, the descendant of the Greek word, is first recorded in English (1641), with reference to the Byzantine iconoclasts.

38
in·sou·ci·ant (ĭn-sōō′sē-ənt)

adjective

Marked by blithe unconcern; nonchalant: *"No man, save the Texas Ranger, has ever carried it [the revolver] with the insouciant air and picturesque charm of the American cowboy"* (Ramon F. Adams, *Cowboy Lingo*).

[French : *in-*, not + *souciant*, present participle of *soucier*, to trouble (from Old French, from Vulgar Latin **sollicītāre*, alteration of Latin *sollicitāre*, to vex).]

in·ter·lop·er (ĭn′tər-lō′pər)

noun

1. One that interferes with the affairs of others, often for selfish reasons; a meddler: *"The Alexandria of my childhood was still a pure Southern culture, undiluted yet by suburban interlopers from up north"* (James Carroll, *An American Requiem*). **2.** One that intrudes in a place, situation, or activity. **3.** *Archaic* **a.** One that trespasses on a trade monopoly, as by conducting unauthorized trade in an area designated to a chartered company. **b.** A ship or other vessel used in such trade.

[From English *inter-* (from Latin, between) + probably Middle Dutch *lōper,* runner (from *lōpen,* to run).]

♟ The word *interloper* first appeared as England embarked on the course that led to the British Empire. First recorded around 1590 in connection with the Muscovy Company, the earliest major English trading company (chartered in 1555), *interloper* was soon used in connection with independent traders competing with the East India Company (chartered in 1600) as well. These monopolies held a dim view of independent traders, called *interlopers.* The term is probably partly derived from Dutch, the language of one of the great trade rivals of the English at that time. *Inter-* is simply the prefix *inter-,* meaning "between, among." The element *-loper* is probably related to the same element in *landloper,* "vagabond," a word adopted from Middle Dutch, where it is a compound of *land,* "land," and *lōper* (from *lōpen,* "to run, leap"). *Interloper* came to be used in the extended sense "busybody" in the 1600s.

in·ter·nec·ine

(ĭn′tər-nĕs′ēn′, ĭn′tər-nĕs′ĭn, ĭn′tər-nē′sīn′)

adjective

1. Of or relating to struggle within a nation, organization, or group: *"While he was becoming more and more closely drawn into the internecine politics of the Socialist party and its pro-Bolshevik and anti-Bolshevik offshoots, she was getting a broader sense of the country, of what the Russian experiment meant to various people"* (Mary V. Dearborn, *Queen of Bohemia*). **2.** Mutually destructive; ruinous or fatal to both sides. **3.** Characterized by bloodshed or carnage.

[Latin *internecīnus,* destructive, variant of *internecīvus,* from *internecāre,* to slaughter : *inter-,* intensive prefix + *nex, nec-,* death.]

꙳ Today, *internecine* usually means "relating to internal struggle," but in its first recorded use in English, in 1663, it meant "fought to the death," as did the Latin source of the word, derived from the verb *necāre,* "to kill." Here, the prefix *inter-* did not have the usual sense of "between, mutual" but rather that of an intensifier meaning "all the way, to the death." Samuel Johnson was unaware of this fact when he compiled his great dictionary in the 1700s. Misunderstanding the prefix, he defined *internecine* as "endeavoring mutual destruction." Johnson's dictionary was so popular and considered so authoritative that this error became widely adopted. It was further compounded when *internecine* acquired the sense "relating to internal struggle." Since the ultimate arbiter of language is how people use it, what was once a compounded error has long since become an acceptable usage.

in·vei·gle (ĭn-vā′gəl, ĭn-vē′gəl)

transitive verb

> Past participle and past tense: **in·vei·gled**
> Present participle: **in·vei·gling**
> Third person singular present tense: **in·vei·gles**

1. To win over by coaxing, flattery, or artful talk: *"Melmotte is, in short, a mighty con artist: we are on to him almost instantly. Our interest is not in finding out his scam, but in watching him inveigle and enmesh the gullible"* (Cynthia Ozick, *The New York Times Book Review*). **2.** To obtain by cajolery.

[Middle English *envegle,* alteration of Old French *aveugler,* to blind, from *aveugle,* blind, from Vulgar Latin **aboculus* : Latin *ab-,* away from + Latin *oculus,* eye (probably loan-translation of Gaulish *exsops* : *exs-,* from + *ops,* eye).]

jer·e·mi·ad (jĕr′ə-mī′əd)

noun

A literary work or speech expressing a bitter lament or a righteous prophecy of doom.

[French *jérémiade,* after *Jérémie,* Jeremiah, prophet to whom the biblical book of Lamentations is traditionally attributed, from Late Latin *Ieremiās,* from Hebrew *yirməyāhû,* Yahweh has established : *yirm,* he has established + *yāhû,* Yahweh.]

jux·ta·po·si·tion (jŭk′stə-pə-zĭsh′ən)

noun

The act or an instance of placing two items side by side, especially for comparison or contrast, or the state of being so placed: *"No human eye can isolate the unhappy coincidence of line and place which suggests evil in the face of a house, and yet somehow a maniac juxtaposition, a badly turned angle, some chance meeting of roof and sky, turned Hill House into a place of despair, more frightening because the face of Hill House seemed awake, with a watchfulness from the blank windows and a touch of glee in the eyebrow of a cornice"* (Shirley Jackson, *The Haunting of Hill House*).

[French *juxtaposition* : Latin *iūxtā*, close by + French *position*, position, from Latin *positiō, positiōn-*, placing, position, from *positus*, past participle of *pōnere*, to place.]

ko·an (kō′än′)

noun

A puzzling, often paradoxical statement or story, used in Zen Buddhism as an aid to meditation and a means of gaining spiritual awakening: *"Saskia will sit for an hour in the grass down by the shore, pondering a koan until she enters that space wherein silence and stillness press against her like solid walls"* (Brian Hall, *The Saskiad*).

[Japanese *kōan* : *kō*, public + *an*, matter for consideration, legal case.]

They were not welcomed home very cordially by their mother. Mrs. Bennet wondered at their coming, and thought them very wrong to give so much trouble, and was sure Jane would have caught cold again; but their father, though very **laconic** in his expressions of pleasure, was really glad to see them; he had felt their importance in the family circle.

—Jane Austen,
Pride and Prejudice

45 la·con·ic (lə-kŏn′ĭk)

adjective

Using few words; terse; concise: *"[T]heir father, though very laconic in his expressions of pleasure, was really glad to see them"* (Jane Austen, *Pride and Prejudice*).

[Latin *Lacōnicus,* Spartan, from Greek *Lakōnikos,* from *Lakōn,* a Spartan (from the reputation of the Spartans for brevity of speech).]

℘ The study of the classics allows us to understand the history of the term *laconic,* which comes to English via Latin from Greek *Lakōnikos.* The English word is first recorded in 1583 with the sense "of or relating to Laconia or its inhabitants." *Lakōnikos* is derived from *Lakōn,* "a Laconian, a person from Lacedaemon," the name for the region of Greece of which Sparta was the capital. The Spartans, noted for being warlike and disciplined, were also known for the brevity of their speech, and it is this quality that English writers still denote by the use of the adjective *laconic,* which is first found in this sense in 1589.

la·gniappe (lăn′yəp, lăn-yăp′)

noun

Chiefly southern Louisiana and Mississippi

1. A small gift presented by a storeowner to a customer with the customer's purchase. **2.** An extra or unexpected gift or benefit.

[Louisiana French, from American Spanish *la ñapa,* the gift : *la,* the + *ñapa* (variant of *yapa,* gift, from Quechua, from *yapay,* to give more).]

✧ *Lagniappe* derives from New World Spanish *la ñapa,* "the gift," and ultimately from Quechua *yapay,* "to give more." The word entered the rich Creole dialect mixture of New Orleans and there acquired a French spelling. It is still used in the Gulf states, especially southern Louisiana, to denote a little bonus that a friendly shopkeeper might add to a purchase. By extension, it may mean "an extra or unexpected gift or benefit."

lep·re·chaun (lĕp′rĭ-kŏn′, lĕp′rĭ-kôn′)

noun

One of a race of elves in Irish folklore who can reveal hidden treasure to those who catch them.

[Irish Gaelic *luprachán,* alteration of Middle Irish *luchrupán,* from Old Irish *luchorpán : luchorp* (*lú-,* small + *corp,* body, from *Latin* corpus) + *-án,* diminutive suffix.]

✧ Nothing seems more Irish than the leprechaun, yet hiding within the word *leprechaun* is a word from another language entirely. *Leprechaun* ultimately derives from Old Irish *luchorpán,* a compound of Old Irish *lú,* meaning "small," and the Old Irish word *corp,* "body." *Corp* is borrowed from Latin *corpus* (which can be seen in such words as *corporal,* "physical; relating to the body"). This fact is a piece of evidence attesting to the influence of Latin on the Irish language. Although *leprechaun* is old in Irish, it is fairly new in English, being first recorded in 1604.

48 li·to·tes (lī′tə-tēz′, lĭt′ə-tēz′, lī-tō′tēz)

noun
    Plural: **litotes**

A figure of speech consisting of an understatement in which an affirmative is expressed by negating its opposite, as in "*I showed him over the establishment, not omitting the pantry, with <u>no little</u> pride, and he commended it highly*" (Charles Dickens, *David Copperfield*).

[Greek *lītotēs*, from *lītos*, plain.]

49 lu·cu·brate (lōō′kyŏo-brāt′)

intransitive verb
    Past participle and past tense: **lu·cu·brat·ed**
    Present participle: **lu·cu·brat·ing**
    Third person singular present tense: **lu·cu·brates**

To write in a scholarly fashion; produce scholarship.

[Latin *lūcubrāre*, to work at night by lamplight.]

mag·nan·i·mous (măg-năn**′**ə-məs)

adjective

Noble in mind and heart; generous and unselfish: "*[S]ophisticated and intellectually wise as I like to think I am now, I have to admit I'm still inspired by a poetic phrase, a magnanimous gesture, a promise of a better tomorrow*" (Norma Sherry, *Baltimore Chronicle & Sentinel*).

[From Latin *magnanimus* : *magnus*, great + *animus*, soul, mind.]

ma·ha·ra·jah *or* **ma·ha·ra·ja**
(mä**′**hə-rä**′**jə, mä**′**hə-rä**′**zhə)

noun

1. A king or prince in India ranking above a rajah, especially the sovereign of one of the former native states. **2.** Used as a title for such a king or prince.

[Sanskrit *mahārājaḥ* : *mahā-*, great + *rājā, rājaḥ*, king.]

🐟 *Maharajah* comes from the Sanskrit word *mahārājaḥ*, meaning "great king." The element *mahā-* is related to Greek *mega-* and Latin *magnus*, both meaning the same thing as the Sanskrit term, "great." All three forms derive from an Indo-European root that also has descendants in Germanic, in particular, the Old English word *micel*, pronounced (mĭ**′**chəl). This survives today in *much* (shortened from Middle English *muchel*).

52 **mal·a·prop·ism** (măl′ə-prŏp-ĭz′əm)

noun

1. Ludicrous misuse of a word, especially by confusion with one of similar sound. **2.** An example of such misuse.

[After Mrs. Malaprop (from *malapropos*), a character in *The Rivals,* a play by Richard Brinsley Sheridan + *-ism*, nominal suffix.]

❧ "She's as headstrong as an allegory on the banks of the Nile" and "He is the very pineapple of politeness" are two of the absurd pronouncements from Mrs. Malaprop that explain why her name became synonymous with ludicrous misuse of language. A character in Richard Brinsley Sheridan's play *The Rivals* (1775), Mrs. Malaprop consistently uses language malapropos, that is, inappropriately. The word *malapropos* comes from the French phrase *mal à propos*, made up of *mal*, "badly," *à*, "to," and *propos*, "purpose, subject," and means "inappropriate." *The Rivals* was a popular play, and Mrs. Malaprop became enshrined in a common noun, first in the form *malaprop* and later in *malapropism*, which is first recorded in 1849. Perhaps that is what Mrs. Malaprop feared when she said, "If I reprehend any thing in this world, it is the use of my oracular tongue, and a nice derangement of epitaphs!"

mer·e·tri·cious (mĕr′ĭ-trĭsh′əs)

adjective

1a. Attracting attention in a vulgar manner: *"It was a platinum fob chain simple and chaste in design, properly proclaiming its value by substance alone and not by meretricious ornamentation—as all good things should do"* (O. Henry, "The Gift of the Magi"). **b.** Plausible but false or insincere; specious: *I saw through his meretricious arguments.* **2.** Of or relating to prostitutes or prostitution.

[Latin *meretrīcius,* of prostitutes, from *meretrīx, meretrīc-,* prostitute, from *merēre,* to earn money.]

54

mes·mer·ize (mĕz′mə-rīz′, mĕs′mə-rīz′)

transitive verb

Past participle and past tense: **mes·mer·ized**
Present participle: **mes·mer·iz·ing**
Third person singular present tense: **mes·mer·iz·es**

1. To spellbind; enthrall: *"He could mesmerize an audience by the sheer force of his presence"* (Justin Kaplan). *"The other morning I watched five game shows in a row on television. I wanted to turn them off, but I was too mesmerized by the contestants"* (Erma Bombeck, *If Life Is a Bowl of Cherries, What Am I Doing in the Pits?*). **2.** To hypnotize.

[After Franz Mesmer (1734–1815), Austrian physician.]

෴ Franz Anton Mesmer, a visionary eighteenth-century physician, believed cures could be effected by having patients do things such as sit with their feet in a fountain of magnetized water while holding cables attached to magnetized trees. He then came to believe that magnetic powers resided in himself, and during highly fashionable curative sessions in Paris he caused his patients to have reactions ranging from sleeping or dancing to convulsions. These reactions were actually brought about by hypnotic powers that Mesmer was unaware he possessed. One of his pupils, named Puységur, then used the term *mesmerism* (first recorded in English in 1802) for Mesmer's practices. The related word *mesmerize* (first recorded in English in 1829), having shed its reference to the hypnotic doctor, lives on in the sense "to enthrall."

me·tic·u·lous (mĭ-tĭk**′**yə-ləs)

adjective

1. Extremely careful and precise: *"[H]is wardrobe seemed to consist entirely of meticulous reconstructions of garments of the previous century"* (William Gibson, *Neuromancer*). **2.** Extremely or excessively concerned with details.

[From Latin *metīculōsus*, timid, from *metus*, fear.]

Case had never seen him wear the same suit twice, although his wardrobe seemed to consist entirely of **meticulous** reconstructions of garments of the previous century. He affected prescription lenses, framed in spidery gold, ground from pink slabs of synthetic quartz and beveled like the mirrors in a Victorian dollhouse.

—William Gibson,
Neuromancer

56 **mi·lieu** (mĭl-yōō′, mĭ-lyœ′)

noun
   Plural: **mi·lieus** *or* **mi·lieux** (mĭ-lyœ′)

An environment or a setting: *"I don't know that the arts have a milieu here, any of them; they're more like a very thinly settled outskirt"* (Edith Wharton, *The Age of Innocence*).

[French, from Old French, center : *mi,* middle (from Latin *medius*) + *lieu,* place (from Latin *locus*).]

57 **mi·to·chon·dri·on** (mī′tə-kŏn′drē-ən)

noun
   Plural **mi·to·chon·dri·a** (mī′tə-kŏn′drē-ə)

A structure that is found in the cytoplasm of all cells except bacteria; has an inner membrane enclosing a liquid that contains DNA (genetically different from nuclear DNA), RNA, small ribosomes, and solutes; and breaks down food molecules and converts them to usable energy in the presence of oxygen.

[New Latin : Greek *mitos,* warp thread + Greek *khondrion,* diminutive of *khondros,* grain, granule.]

58 nem·e·sis (něm′ĭ-sĭs)

noun
    Plural: **nem·e·ses** (něm′ĭ-sēz′)

1. A source of harm or ruin: *"The resolutions—calling for limitations on working hours, state support for education, nationalization of railways—were not very revolutionary. Reform was again showing itself to be the nemesis of revolution"* (John Kenneth Galbraith, *The Age of Uncertainty*). **2.** Retributive justice in its execution or outcome. **3.** An opponent that cannot be beaten or overcome. **4.** One that inflicts retribution or vengeance. **5. Nemesis** In Greek mythology, the goddess of retributive justice or vengeance.

[Greek, retribution, the goddess Nemesis, from *nemein,* to allot.]

59

nic·ti·tate (nĭk′tĭ-tāt′) *also* **nic·tate** (nĭk′tāt′)

intransitive verb
>Past participle and past tense: **nic·ti·tat·ed**
>Present participle: **nic·ti·tat·ing**
>Third person singular present tense: **nic·ti·tates**

To wink. Used especially in connection with the *nictitating membrane*, a transparent inner eyelid in birds, reptiles, and some mammals that closes to protect and moisten the eye.

[Medieval Latin *nictitāre*, frequentative of Latin *nictāre*, to wink.]

60 **nos·trum** (nŏs′trəm)

noun

1. A medicine whose effectiveness is unproved and whose ingredients are usually secret; a quack remedy: *"He was clearly a confirmed hypochondriac, and I was dreamily conscious that he was pouring forth interminable trains of symptoms, and imploring information as to the composition and action of innumerable quack nostrums, some of which he bore about in a leather case in his pocket"* (Arthur Conan Doyle, *The Sign of Four*). **2.** A favored but often questionable remedy: *"His economic nostrums of lowering taxes to feed the economy were the subject of furious debates"* (David Shribman, *Boston Globe*).

[From Latin *nostrum (remedium)*, our (remedy), neuter of *noster.*]

61 **nud·nik** *also* **nud·nick** (nŏŏd′nĭk)

noun

Slang An obtuse, boring, or bothersome person; a pest.

[Yiddish, from *nudne*, boring, from *nudyen*, to bore + *-nik*, -nik, nominal suffix.]

I find that all the fair and noble impulses of humanity, the dreams of poets and the agonies of martyrs, are shackled and bound in the service of organized and predatory Greed! And therefore I cannot rest, I cannot be silent; therefore I cast aside comfort and happiness, health and good repute — and go out into the world and cry out the pain of my spirit! Therefore I am not to be silenced by poverty and sickness, not by hatred and **obloquy,** by threats and ridicule — not by prison and persecution, if they should come — not by any power that is upon the earth or above the earth, that was, or is, or ever can be created.

— Upton Sinclair,
The Jungle

ob·lo·quy (ŏb′lə-kwē)

noun
    Plural: **ob·lo·quies**

1. Abusively detractive language or utterance; calumny: *"Therefore I am not to be silenced by poverty and sickness, not by hatred and obloquy, by threats and ridicule"* (Upton Sinclair, *The Jungle*). **2.** The condition of disgrace suffered as a result of abuse or vilification; ill repute.

[Middle English *obloqui,* from Late Latin *obloquium,* abusive contradiction, from Latin *obloquī,* to interrupt : *ob-,* against + *loquī,* to speak.]

ob·strep·er·ous (ŏb-strĕp′ər-əs)

adjective

Noisily unruly or defiant: *"Nurse Hopkins ran the day-care center on the top floor of the agency building, and if from time to time she used tranquilizers on the more obstreperous children, she was at least trained and qualified to do so, and she knew what side effects to look out for"* (Faye Weldon, *The Life and Loves of a She-Devil*).

[From Latin *obstreperus,* noisy, from *obstrepere,* to make a noise against : *ob-,* against + *strepere,* to make a noise (of imitative origin).]

ox·y·mo·ron (ŏk′sē-môr′ŏn′)

noun

Plural: **ox·y·mo·rons**
or **ox·y·mo·ra** (ŏk′sē-môr′ə)

A rhetorical figure in which incongruous or contradictory terms are combined, as in *deafening silence.*

[Greek *oxumōron,* from neuter of *oxumōros,* pointedly foolish : *oxus,* sharp, + *mōros,* foolish, dull.]

🐚 Interestingly, the word *oxymoron* is itself etymologically an oxymoron. Combined, the Greek words *oxus* and *mōros,* which mean respectively "sharp" and "dull," form the compound *oxumōros,* "pointedly foolish."

pa·lav·er (pə-lăv′ər, pə-lä′vər)

noun

1a. Idle chatter. **b.** Talk intended to charm or beguile: *"The girl glanced back at him over her shoulder and said with great bitterness: —The men that is now is only all palaver and what they can get out of you"* (James Joyce, "The Dead," *Dubliners*). **2.** A parley between two groups, especially European explorers and representatives of local populations.

[Portuguese *palavra,* speech, alteration of Late Latin *parabola,* speech, parable.]

—O, then, said Gabriel gaily, I suppose we'll be going to your wedding one of these fine days with your young man, eh?

The girl glanced back at him over her shoulder and said with great bitterness:

—The men that is now is only all **palaver** and what they can get out of you.

> — James Joyce,
> "The Dead," *Dubliners*

pe·jor·a·tive

(pĭ-jôr′ə-tĭv, pĕj′ə-rā′tĭv, pē′jə-rā′tĭv)

adjective

Disparaging; belittling: *"Unfortunately, the word 'diet' has come to have a pejorative meaning for many people because it suggests denial, restriction, or limitations"* (James E. Marti, *The Ultimate Consumer's Guide to Diets and Nutrition*).

noun

A disparaging or belittling word or expression.

[From *pejorate*, to make worse (from Late Latin *pēiōrātus*, past participle of *pēiōrāre*, to make worse, from Latin *pēior*, worse), + *-ive*, adjectival suffix (from Latin *-īvus*).]

pre·car·i·ous (prĭ-kâr′ē-əs)

adjective

1. Dangerously lacking in security or stability: *"And the recurring sight of hitch-hikers waiting against the sky gave him the flash of a sensation he had known as a child: standing still with nothing to touch him, feeling tall and having the world come all at once into its round shape underfoot and rush and turn through space and make his stand very precarious and lonely"* (Eudora Welty, "The Hitch-Hikers"). **2.** Subject to chance or uncertain conditions: *The people eked out a precarious existence in the mountains.* **3.** Based on uncertain, unwarranted, or unproved premises: *a precarious solution to a difficult problem.*

[From Latin *precārius*, obtained by entreaty, uncertain, from *precārī*, to entreat.]

68

pres·ti·dig·i·ta·tion (prĕs′tĭ-dĭj′ĭ-tā′shən)

noun

1. Performance of or skill in performing magic or conjuring tricks with the hands; sleight of hand. **2.** Skill or cleverness, especially in deceiving others.

[French (influenced by *prestigiateur,* juggler, conjurer, from *prestige,* illusion), from *prestidigitateur,* conjurer : *preste,* nimble (from Italian *presto*) + Latin *digitus,* finger.]

69

pre·ter·nat·u·ral
(prē′tər-năch′ər-əl, prē′tər-năch′rəl)

adjective

1. Differing from what is normal or natural; abnormal or extraordinary: *"Dickens, with preternatural apprehension of the language of manners, and the varieties of street life, with pathos and laughter, with patriotic and still enlarging generosity, writes London tracts"* (Ralph Waldo Emerson, *English Traits*). **2.** Transcending the natural or material order; supernatural.

[Medieval Latin *praeternātūrālis,* from Latin *praeter nātūrām,* beyond nature : *praeter,* beyond + *nātūra,* nature.]

quark (kwôrk, kwärk)

noun

Any of a group of elementary particles supposed to be the fundamental units that combine to make up the subatomic particles known as hadrons (baryons, such as neutrons and protons, and mesons). Quarks have fractional electric charges, such as one-third the charge of an electron.

[From "Three quarks for Muster Mark!," a line in *Finnegans Wake* by James Joyce.]

✿ "Three quarks for Muster Mark!/Sure he hasn't got much of a bark/And sure any he has it's all beside the mark." This passage from James Joyce's *Finnegans Wake,* part of a poem directed against King Mark, the cuckolded husband in the Tristan legend, has left its mark on modern physics. Packed with names of birds and words suggestive of birds, the poem and accompanying prose are a squawk against the king that suggests the cawing of a crow. The word *quark* comes from the standard English verb *quark,* meaning "to caw, croak," and also from the dialectal verb *quawk,* meaning "to caw, screech like a bird." But why should *quark* have become the name for a group of hypothetical subatomic particles proposed as the fundamental units of matter? Murray Gell-Mann, the physicist who proposed this name for these particles, said in a private letter of June 27, 1978, to the editor of the *Oxford English Dictionary* that he had been influenced by Joyce's words: "The allusion to three quarks seemed perfect" (originally there were only three subatomic quarks). Gell-Mann, however, wanted to pronounce the word with (ô), not (ä), as Joyce seemed to indicate by rhymes such as *Mark*. Gell-Mann got around that "by supposing that one ingredient of the line 'Three quarks for Muster Mark' was a cry of 'Three quarts for Mister . . .' heard in H.C. Earwicker's pub," a plausible suggestion given the complex punning in Joyce's novel. It seems appropriate that this perplexing and humorous novel should have supplied the term for particles that come in six "flavors" and three "colors."

71

quix·ot·ic (kwĭk-sŏt′ĭk)

adjective

Caught up in the pursuit of unreachable goals; foolishly idealistic and impractical: *"[W]hat I like best in you is this particular enthusiasm, which is not at all practical or sensible, which is downright Quixotic"* (Willa Cather, *The Song of the Lark*).

[After Don Quixote, hero of a novel by Miguel de Cervantes Saavedra (1547–1616).]

red·o·lent (rĕd′l-ənt)

adjective

1. Fragrant; aromatic. **2.** Suggestive; reminiscent: *"There was a ripe mystery about it, a hint . . . of romances that were not musty and laid away already in lavender, but fresh and breathing and redolent of this year's shining motor-cars and of dances whose flowers were scarcely withered"* (F. Scott Fitzgerald, *The Great Gatsby*).

[Middle English, from Old French, from Latin *redolēns, redolent-*, present participle of *redolēre,* to smell : *re-, red-,* re-, intensive prefix + *olēre,* to smell.]

It amazed him — he had never been in such a beautiful house before. But what gave it an air of breathless intensity was that Daisy lived there — it was as casual a thing to her as his tent out at camp was to him. There was a ripe mystery about it, a hint of bedrooms upstairs more beautiful and cool than other bedrooms, of gay and radiant activities taking place through its corridors, and of romances that were not musty and laid away already in lavender, but fresh and breathing and **redolent** of this year's shining motor-cars and of dances whose flowers were scarcely withered.

— F. Scott Fitzgerald,
The Great Gatsby

re·pug·nant (rĭ-pŭg′nənt)

adjective

Arousing disgust or aversion; offensive or repulsive: *"There was her milk, untouched, forgotten, barely tepid. She drank it down, without pleasure; all its whiteness, draining from the stringing wet whiteness of the empty cup, was singularly repugnant"* (James Agee, *A Death in the Family*).

[Middle English, antagonistic, from Old French, from Latin *repugnāns, repugnant-,* present participle of *repugnāre,* to fight against : *re-, red-,* against + *pugnāre,* to fight, from *pugnus,* fist.]

ru·bric (roō′brĭk)

noun

1. A class or category: *"This mission is sometimes discussed under the rubric of 'horizontal escalation' . . . from conventional to nuclear war"* (Jack Beatty, *Atlantic Monthly*). **2.** A part of a manuscript or book, such as a title, heading, or initial letter, that appears in decorative red lettering or is otherwise distinguished from the rest of the text. **3.** A title or heading in a code of law. **4.** A direction in a missal, hymnal, or other liturgical book: *"This kind of answer given in a measured official tone, as of a clergyman reading according to the rubric, did not help to . . . justify the glories of the Eternal City, or to give her the hope that if she knew more about them the world would be joyously illuminated for her"* (George Eliot, *Middlemarch*). **5.** An authoritative rule or direction: *"The creative ferment of the Internet . . . is frequently in-*

voked by the legislative legions in Washington who want to extend some version of electronic networking to every home, school, library and hospital in the country under the rubric of a National Information Infrastructure" (Gary Stix, *Scientific American*). **6.** A form of hematite used as a red pigment.

adjective

1. Red or reddish. **2.** Written in red.

[Middle English *rubrike*, heading, title, from Old French *rubrique*, from Latin *rubrīca*, red chalk, from *ruber, rubr-*, red.]

sang-froid *or* sang·froid (säN-frwä′)

noun

Coolness and composure, especially in trying circumstances: *"For a moment his face became a white mask of horror, but he soon recovered his sang-froid and, looking up at Lady Windermere, said with a forced smile, 'It is the hand of a charming young man'"* (Oscar Wilde, *Lord Arthur Savile's Crime*).

[French : *sang*, blood (from Old French, from Latin *sanguis*) + *froid*, cold (from Old French, from Vulgar Latin **frigidus*, alteration of Latin *frīgidus*).]

sar·coph·a·gus (sär-kŏf′ə-gəs)

noun

Plural: **sar·coph·a·gi** *or* **sar·coph·a·gus·es**
(sär-kŏf′ə-jī′)

A stone coffin, often inscribed or decorated with sculpture.

[Latin, from Greek *sarkophagos,* coffin, from *(lithos) sarkophagos,* limestone that consumed the flesh of corpses laid in it : *sarx, sark-,* flesh + *-phagos,* eating, feeding on.]

✥ The macabre word *sarcophagus* comes to us from Latin and Greek, having been derived in Greek from *sarx,* "flesh," and *phagein,* "to eat." The Greek word *sarkophagos* meant "eating flesh," and in the phrase *lithos* ("stone") *sarkophagos,* it denoted a limestone that was thought to decompose the flesh of corpses placed in it. Used by itself as a noun the Greek term came to mean "coffin." The term was carried over into Latin, where *sarcophagus* was used in the phrase *lapis* ("stone") *sarcophagus,* referring to the same stone as in Greek. *Sarcophagus* used as a noun in Latin meant "coffin of any material." This Latin word was borrowed into English, first being recorded in 1601 with reference to the flesh-consuming stone and then in 1705 with reference to a stone coffin.

schwa (shwä)

noun

1. A vowel that is articulated with the tongue in the middle of the oral cavity, typically occurring in unstressed syllables as the first vowel of *about* or the final vowel of *sofa.* **2.** The symbol (ə) used to represent this sound. In some phonetic systems it also represents the sounds of such vowels in stressed positions, as in *but*.

[German, from Hebrew, *šəwā*', probably from Syriac *(nuqzē)* *šwayyā*, even (points), plural passive participle of *šwā*, to be even.]

ser·en·dip·i·ty (sĕr′ən-dĭp′ĭ-tē)

noun
> Plural: **ser·en·dip·i·ties**

1. The faculty of making fortunate discoveries by accident. **2.** The fact or occurrence of such discoveries. **3.** An instance of making such a discovery.

[From the characters in the Persian fairy tale *The Three Princes of Serendip,* who made such discoveries, from Persian *Sarandīp,* Sri Lanka, from Arabic *Sarandīb.*]

ℱ We are indebted to the English author Horace Walpole for the word *serendipity,* which he coined in one of the 3,000 or more letters that make up an important part of his literary legacy. In a letter of January 28, 1754, Walpole says that "this discovery, indeed, is almost of that kind which I call Serendipity, a very expressive word." Walpole formed the word on an old name for Sri Lanka, *Serendip.* He explained that this name was part of the title of "a silly fairy tale, called *The Three Princes of Serendip:* as their highnesses traveled, they were always making discoveries, by accidents and sagacity, of things which they were not in quest of. . . ."

79

ses·qui·pe·da·lian (sĕs′kwĭ-pĭ-dāl′yən)

adjective

1. Given to or characterized by the use of long words.
2. Having many syllables; polysyllabic: *"[R]ecently a strange whimsy has started to creep in among the sesquipedalian prose of scientific journals"* (Stephen S. Hall, *The New York Times*).

noun

A long word.

[From Latin *sēsquipedālis*, of a foot and a half in length : *sēsqui-, sesqui-* + *pēs, ped-*, foot + *-ian*, nominal and adjectival suffix.]

80

sha·man (shä′mən, shā′mən)

noun
  Plural: **sha·mans**

A member of certain tribal societies who acts as a medium between the visible world and an invisible spirit world and practices magic or sorcery for healing, divination, and control over natural events.

[Russian, from Evenki *šaman*, Buddhist monk, shaman, from Tocharian B *ṣamāne*, monk, from Prakrit *ṣamana*, from Sanskrit *śramaṇaḥ*, from *śrámaḥ*, religious exercise.]

꯭ At first glance, *shaman* may seem to be a compound of *-man* and a mysterious prefix *sha-*. In fact, its far different and more remarkable history begins in India as the Sanskrit word *śramaṇaḥ*, "ascetic, Buddhist monk." In the Prakrit languages, which descended from Sanskrit, it developed into *ṣamana*, a term that spread with Buddhism over central Asia. It was borrowed into Tocharian B and probably from there into Evenki (a Tungusic language of Siberian reindeer herders), where the word referred to a healer or a person who communicated with the spirit world. The term was then borrowed into Russian and other European languages and then into English.

Shaman is probably the only English word that has come from or passed through a Tocharian language. The two closely related Tocharian languages, Tocharian A and Tocharian B, are now extinct. The Tocharians lived along the Silk Road in the eastern Turkistan (Xinjiang Uygur Autonomous Region in China). We know their languages from documents such as travelers' caravan passes and Buddhist sutras written around 600–800 AD. Together, Tocharian A and B constitute a separate branch of the family tree of the Indo-European languages, the family to which English also belongs.

81

si·ne·cure (sī′nĭ-kyŏŏr′, sĭn′ĭ-kyŏŏr′)

noun

1. A position or office that requires little or no work but provides a salary: *"Be it said, that in this vocation of whaling, sinecures are unknown; dignity and danger go hand in hand; till you get to be Captain, the higher you rise the harder you toil"* (Herman Melville, *Moby-Dick*). **2.** *Archaic* An ecclesiastical benefice not attached to the spiritual duties of a parish.

[From Medieval Latin *(beneficium) sine cūrā*, (benefice) without spiritual care (of souls).]

82

snake·bit (snāk′bĭt′)
  also **snake·bit·ten** (snāk′bĭt′n)

adjective

Experiencing a period of misfortune or inability to suc-
ceed; unlucky: *Having lost four games in a row by one
run, the pitcher was starting to feel a little snakebit.*

83

sop·o·rif·ic (sŏp′ə-rĭf′ĭk)

adjective

1. Inducing or tending to induce sleep: "*[T]he heavy
supper she had eaten produced a soporific effect: she was
already snoring before I had finished undressing*" (Charlotte Brontë, *Jane Eyre*). **2.** Drowsy.

noun

A drug or other substance that induces sleep; a hypnotic.

[From *sopor-*, sleep (from Latin *sopor*) + *-fic, -ific,* causing,
making (from Latin *-ficus,* from *facere,* to make, do).]

I had to sit with the girls during their hour of study; then it was my turn to read prayers; to see them to bed: afterwards I supped with the other teachers. Even when we finally retired for the night, the inevitable Miss Gryce was still my companion: we had only a short end of candle in our candlestick, and I dreaded lest she should talk till it was all burnt out; fortunately, however, the heavy supper she had eaten produced a **soporific** effect: she was already snoring before I had finished undressing.

— Charlotte Brontë,
Jane Eyre

84 **suc·co·tash** (sŭk′ə-tăsh′)

noun

A stew consisting of kernels of corn, lima beans, and tomatoes.

[Narragansett *msíckquatash,* boiled whole-kernel corn.]

85 **su·sur·ra·tion** (soō′sə-rā′shən)

noun

A soft whispering or rustling sound; a murmur: *"The rain was now falling more steadily, with a low, monotonous susurration, interrupted at long intervals by the sudden slashing of the boughs of the trees as the wind rose and failed"* (Ambrose Bierce, *Can Such Things Be?*).

[Middle English *susurracioun,* from Late Latin *susurrātiō, susurrātiōn-,* from Latin *susurrātus,* past participle of *susurrāre,* to whisper, from *susurrus,* whisper, ultimately of imitative origin.]

86 **syz·y·gy** (sĭz′ə-jē′)

noun
    Plural: **syz·y·gies**

An alignment of three celestial bodies, especially the sun, the moon, and Earth, in which all three bodies lie along a single straight line: *After a solar eclipse, it is likely that there will be another eclipse somewhere on Earth at the next syzygy.* **2.** The combining of two feet into a single metrical unit in classical prosody.

[Late Latin *sȳzygia*, from Greek *suzugiā*, union, from *suzugos*, paired : *sun-, su-*, with, together + *zugon*, yoke.]

tan·ta·lize (tăn′tə-līz′)

transitive verb

    Past participle and past tense: **tan·ta·lized**
    Present participle: **tan·ta·liz·ing**
    Third person singular present tense: **tan·ta·liz·es**

To excite (another) by exposing something desirable, especially while keeping it out of reach: *"Finer than human hair, lighter than cotton, and—ounce for ounce— stronger than steel, silk tantalizes materials researchers seeking to duplicate its properties or synthesize it for large-scale production"* (Richard Lipkin, *Science News*).

[From Latin *Tantalus*, Tantalus.]

♏ *Tantalize* comes from *Tantalus*, the name of a mythical king of Lydia, a territory on the Aegean Sea in the west of Asia Minor (now Turkey). Tantalus, originally one of the luckiest of mortals, enjoyed the privilege of feasting with the gods, but he subsequently violated their hospitality. Some say he stole the food of the gods, the *nectar* and *ambrosia* that bestow eternal life, and gave it to mortals. Others say that he killed his own son Pelops and served him to the gods to test whether they could recognize the forbidden meat. Accordingly, the gods condemned Tantalus to suffer everlasting hunger and thirst. He stands in a pool of water that recedes when he bends to drink, and the branches of the trees above him move out of reach when he tries to pluck their fruit, *tantalizing* him for all eternity.

the·o·ry (thē′ə-rē, thîr′ē)

noun

Plural: **the·o·ries**

1. A set of statements or principles devised to explain a group of facts or phenomena, especially one that has been repeatedly tested or is widely accepted and can be used to make predictions about natural phenomena. **2.** The branch of a science or art consisting of its explanatory statements, accepted principles, and methods of analysis, as opposed to practice: *He was a fine musician but had never studied theory.* **3.** A set of theorems that constitute a systematic view of a branch of mathematics. **4.** Abstract reasoning; speculation: *Her decision was based on experience rather than theory.* **5.** A belief or principle that guides action or assists comprehension or judgment: *The detectives staked out the house on the theory that criminals usually return to the scene of the crime.* **6.** An assumption based on limited information or knowledge; a conjecture.

[Late Latin *theōria,* from Greek *theōriā,* from *theōros,* spectator : probably *theā,* a viewing + *-oros,* seeing (from *horān,* to see).]

🙠 *Hypothesis, law,* and *theory* refer to different kinds of statements, or sets of statements, that scientists make about natural phenomena. A *hypothesis* is a proposition that attempts to explain a set of facts in a unified way. It generally forms the basis of experiments designed to establish its plausibility. Though a hypothesis can never be proven true (in fact, hypotheses generally leave some facts unexplained), it can sometimes be verified beyond reasonable doubt in the context of a particular theoretical approach. A scientific *law* is a hypothesis that is assumed to be universally true. A law has good predictive power, allowing a scientist to model a physical system and predict what will happen under various conditions. A *theory* is a set of statements, including laws and hypotheses, that explains a group of observations or phenomena in terms of those laws and hypotheses. A theory thus accounts for a wider variety of events than a law does. Broad acceptance of a theory comes when it has been tested repeatedly on new data and been used to make accurate predictions. Although a theory generally contains hypotheses that are still open to revision, sometimes it is hard to know where the hypothesis ends and the law or theory begins. Albert Einstein's theory of relativity, for example, consists of statements that were originally considered to be hypotheses (and daring at that). But all the hypotheses of relativity have now achieved the authority of scientific laws, and Einstein's theory has supplanted Newton's laws of motion. In some cases, such as the germ theory of infectious disease, a theory becomes so completely accepted, it stops being referred to as a theory.

tim·bre (tăm′bər, tĭm′bər)

noun

The combination of qualities of a sound that distinguishes it from other sounds of the same pitch and volume: *"John stared at Elisha all during the lesson, admiring the timbre of Elisha's voice, much deeper and manlier than his own"* (James Baldwin, *Go Tell It on the Mountain*).

[French, from Old French, drum, clapperless bell, probably from Medieval Greek *timbanon,* drum, from earlier Greek *tumpanon,* kettledrum.]

He was not much older than John, only seventeen, and he was already saved and was a preacher. John stared at Elisha all during the lesson, admiring the **timbre** of Elisha's voice, much deeper and manlier than his own, admiring the leanness, and grace, and strength, and darkness of Elisha in his Sunday suit, wondering if he would ever be holy as Elisha was holy.

— James Baldwin,
Go Tell It on the Mountain

trog·lo·dyte (trŏg′lə-dīt′)

noun

1a. A member of a fabulous or prehistoric race of people that lived in caves, dens, or holes: *"Awkward, red-faced, too big for his shrinking suit and towering over the room like some club-wielding troglodyte, O'Kane could only duck his head and mumble an apology"* (T. Coraghessan Boyle, *Riven Rock*). **b.** A person considered to be reclusive, reactionary, out of date, or brutish. **2a.** An anthropoid ape, such as a gorilla. **b.** An animal that lives underground.

[From Latin *Trōglodytae*, a people said to be cave dwellers, from Greek *Trōglodutai*, alteration (influenced by *trōglē*, hole, and *-dutai*, those who enter), of *Trōgodutai*.]

ul·lage (ŭl′ĭj)

noun

1. The amount of liquid within a container that is lost, as by leakage, during shipment or storage. **2.** The amount by which a container, such as a bottle, cask, or tank, falls short of being full: *The ullage allows wine to expand in response to the changes in temperature without pushing the cork out or bursting the bottle.*

[From Middle English *ulage*, from Old French *ouillage*, from *ouiller*, to fill up a cask, from *ouil*, eye, bunghole, from Latin *oculus*, eye.]

um·laut (o͞om′lout′)

noun

1a. A change in a vowel sound caused by partial assimilation especially to a vowel or semivowel in the following syllable. **b.** A vowel sound changed in this manner. **2.** The diacritic mark (¨) over a vowel, indicating an umlaut, especially in German.

[German : *um-*, around, alteration (from Middle High German *umb-*, from *umbe,* from Old High German *umbi*) + *Laut,* sound (from Middle High German *lūt,* from Old High German *hlūt*).]

℘ The symbol ¨ is called an *umlaut* when it refers to change in the quality of a vowel, as in the German pair *Mann/Männer* ("man/men"), where the *a* is pronounced like the *a* in *father,* and the *ä* is pronounced like the *e* in *bet.* The same symbol is called a *dieresis* when it is placed over the second of two consecutive vowels, where it indicates that the two sounds are to be pronounced separately instead of as a diphthong, as in *Zoë* or *naïve.*

vi·cis·si·tude (vĭ-sĭs′ĭ-to͞od′, vĭ-sĭs′ĭ-tyo͞od′)

noun

A sudden or unexpected change of fortune; a variation in one's life, activities or situation: "*The aspect of the venerable mansion has always affected me like a human countenance, bearing the traces not merely of outward storm and sunshine, but expressive, also, of the long lapse of mortal life, and accompanying vicissitudes that have passed within*" (Nathaniel Hawthorne, *The House of the Seven Gables*).

[Latin *vicissitūdō,* from *vicissim,* in turn, probably from *vicēs,* plural of **vix,* change.]

vis·cer·al (vĭs′ər-əl)

adjective

1. Immediate and emotional; not deliberate or thought out: "*People are wary of Dag when meeting him for the first time, in the same visceral way prairie folk are wary of the flavor of seawater when tasting it for the first time at an ocean beach*" (Douglas Coupland, *Generation X*). **2.** Relating to, situated in, or affecting the viscera.

[Medieval Latin *vīscerālis:* Latin *vīscus,* plural *vīscera,* internal organs, innards + *-ālis,* adjectival suffix.]

vo·lup·tu·ous (və-lŭp′chōo-əs)

adjective

1. Characterized by or arising from sensual pleasure: *"Once in my room, I spread my clothes on my bed. The cufflinks were beaten up and had someone else's initials on them, but they looked like real gold, glinting in the drowsy autumn sun which poured through the window and soaked in yellow pools on the oak floor — voluptuous, rich, intoxicating"* (Donna Tartt, *The Secret History*). **2.** Sexually attractive, especially from having a curvaceous figure. **3.** Devoted to or indulging in sensual pleasures.

[Middle English, from Old French *voluptueux,* from Latin *voluptuōsus,* full of pleasure, from *voluptās,* pleasure.]

was·sail (wŏs′əl, wŏ-sāl′)

noun

1a. A salutation or toast given in drinking someone's health or as an expression of goodwill. **b.** The drink used in such toasting, commonly ale or wine spiced with roasted apples and sugar: *"When Duncan is asleep / . . . his two chamberlains / Will I with wine and wassail so convince / That memory, the warder of the brain, / Shall be a fume, and the receipt of reason / A limbeck only"* (William Shakespeare, *Macbeth*). **2.** A festivity characterized by much drinking: *"[L]ong had I nursed, in secret, the unnatural hatred—it blazed forth in an hour of drunken wassail"* (Walter Scott, *Ivanhoe*).

verb

> Past participle and past tense: **was·sailed**
> Present participle: **was·sail·ing**
> Third person singular present tense: **was·sails**

transitive To drink to the health of; toast.
intransitive To engage in or drink a wassail.

[Middle English, contraction of *wæshæil*, be healthy, from Old Norse *ves heill* : *ves*, imperative singular of *vera*, to be + *heill*, healthy.]

xer·o·phyte (zîr′ə-fīt′)

noun

A plant adapted to living in an arid habitat; a desert plant.

[From *xero-*, dry (from Greek *xēro-*, from *xēros*) + *-phyte*, plant (from Greek *phuton*, from *phuein*, to make grow).]

yogh (yŏg)

noun

The Middle English letter ꝫ, used to represent the sound (y) and the voiced and voiceless velar fricatives.

[Middle English, possibly from Old English *īw, ēoh,* yew.]

ᵠᵃ In addition to the many grammatical differences and unfamiliar words, one of the things that modern readers find so difficult (or so charming) about Old and Middle English texts is the use of letters that have now become obsolete. These include yogh (ꝫ), wynn or wen (ρ), thorn (þ), edh (ð), and ash (æ). Yogh, originally the Old English form of the letter *g*, was used to represent several sounds, including the sound *ch* in Scottish *loch* that began to disappear from most varieties of English in the 1400s. The letters *y* or *gh* have replaced yogh in modern spelling. Wynn, which represented the sound (w), was borrowed by Old English scribes from the runes, the writing system of the early Germanic peoples. It was later superseded by the letter *w,* which was developed from two *u*'s or *v*'s written together. Both thorn (also a rune in origin) and edh were used indiscriminately to spell the two sounds (th) and *(th)*—the sounds in *breath* and *breathe,* respectively. The combination *th* now fills their role. Ash was used in Old English to represent the vowel (ă), as in the word *stæf,* meaning both "staff, stick of wood" and "letter (of the alphabet)." In this regard, it is interesting that several of the names for these old letters also relate to wood and trees, like *ash* and *thorn. Yogh* probably comes from Old English *īw* or *ēoh,* "yew tree."

Zeit·geist (tsīt′gīst′, zīt′gīst′)

noun

The spirit of the time; the taste and outlook character-istic of a period or generation: *"The prescription of psychoactive drugs for children has increased roughly threefold in the past decade, a particularly vivid demon-stration of the shift in the national Zeitgeist vis-à-vis psychological health"* (Arthur Allen, *Salon.com*).

[German : *Zeit*, time (from Middle High German *zīt*, from Old High German + *Geist*, spirit).]

ze·nith (zē′nĭth)

noun

1. The point on the celestial sphere that is directly above the observer: *"The sky stays clear, and when the sun reaches its zenith, I take a break and go down to the river"* (Sarah Pemberton Strong, *Burning the Sea*). **2.** The up-per region of the sky. **3.** The highest point above the observer's horizon attained by a celestial body. **4.** The point of culmination; the peak: *Her tenure as CEO was the zenith of her career.*

[Middle English *senith*, from Old French *cenith*, from Me-dieval Latin, from Arabic *samt* (*ar-ra's*), path (over the head), from Latin *sēmita*, path.]

The sky stays clear, and when the sun reaches its **zenith,** I take a break and go down to the river. The banks are always empty at noon. It's too hot to wash clothes, and all the cows are out grazing. In a few more hours, when the day will have cooled down, people will appear again to bathe, bringing pails to fill or leading their animals down to drink.

— Sarah Pemberton Strong,
Burning the Sea